# STRINGS
## FROM ABOVE
### HAVE FAITH IN GOD
-MARK 11:22

## KIRBY SMITH

authorHOUSE®

*AuthorHouse™*
*1663 Liberty Drive*
*Bloomington, IN 47403*
*www.authorhouse.com*
*Phone: 1 (800) 839-8640*

*Published by AuthorHouse 03/09/2015*

*ISBN: 978-1-4969-7443-3 (sc)*
*ISBN: 978-1-4969-7442-6 (e)*

*Library of Congress Control Number: 2015903557*

*Print information available on the last page.*

*This book is printed on acid-free paper.*

Scripture quotations marked NIV are taken from the *Holy Bible, New International Version*®. *NIV*®. Copyright © 1973, 1978, 1984 by International Bible Society. Used by permission of Zondervan. All rights reserved. [Biblica]

"Tell the Untold 'God Thing' Stories in Your Life" – Ken Williams and "Schmidt Sisters Make Their Mark" – Tosha Rae (Long) Heavican

# CONTENTS

# About the Author

Kirby Smith is a wife, mother of three, and full-time paralegal who, in May 2014, received a sign to share the untold "God thing" events occurring in her life. She started a blog to document her family's multiple spiritual experiences. The blog attracted such a great following she decided to continue to spread the news of God's great work by writing *Strings from Above*. During her mother's terminal illness and her sister's diagnosis of cancer, she developed a deeper relationship with God and learned there are no coincidences. She also found out she carries a genetic mutation that drastically increases her risk of breast cancer. Kirby underwent preventative surgery to significantly reduce her risk of breast cancer and to honor her mother, who died from the disease. She and her husband, Josh, and their three sons reside in Olathe, Kansas.

# Chapter 1

# Background and Inspiration

Our family has had so many unexplainable things happen to us in recent years that it made sense to start documenting them. I felt the desire to start writing, but I was not sure if I could fully capture and articulate all of the signs and blessings we have received from God. I contemplated keeping a private journal and wondered whether I should write anything at all.

One evening in April 2014 I opened a blank document on my computer and started reflecting. My goal was to give our children and future grandchildren a picture of what our family had experienced. I also wanted to give the children the opportunity to get to know my mom by seeing her positivity radiate, despite the hardships she endured along the way. I wanted them to know what an amazing woman their nana was during her time on this earth.

I had several bullet points with brief notes. I spent many hours reflecting on the events, but I could not find a way to bring all of my thoughts together. I abandoned the idea of writing and focused on being a mom of three young boys, a wife to an amazing man, and a dedicated paralegal.

May 5, 2014, started out like every other workday. I left home at six thirty in the morning and was ready to start my day at seven. When I arrived at the office, there was an article lying on my chair. The title caught my attention: "Tell the Untold 'God Thing' Stories in Your Life" by Ken Williams. My boss is an avid reader of religious media, and he occasionally puts articles on my chair so I can e-mail them to his contacts. Usually, I do not read the articles, but for some reason I could not put this one down.

Ken Williams is the executive director of Catholic Charities of Northeast Kansas. In the article, he states, "Here at Catholic Charities most of our best stories go untold." This is not due to a lack of stories, he writes, but perhaps a lack of time, and sometimes people overlook the story altogether.

I was really into the article, but when I read the last paragraph, I knew God was talking to me:

> ... A common phrase I hear used these days to describe stories like this is, "It was a God thing." It's amazing to watch God work through people. It's amazing to watch God's perfect timing unfold. It's amazing to see God work in seemingly desperate or hopeless situations. During this year of evangelization we are all challenged ... to share the story of God's best work: the story of our Lord and Savior, Jesus Christ. I suspect we can all do a better job of telling the untold stories in our lives.

I received the answer to my lingering question as soon as I read the title of the article. The answer could not be more obvious. It was as if God were grabbing me by my shoulders and shaking me, telling me I need to share all of His graces with others. I tracked down my boss and thanked him for the article. He looked at me, confused, because he did not know why I was thanking him. He told me the article had not been intended for me; in fact, he wanted me to e-mail the story on the other side to his friend. I never would have read "Tell the Untold 'God Thing' Stories in Your Life" had the article been face down on my chair. Coincidence? In my opinion, there is no such thing as coincidence. I was supposed to see that article, and I am supposed to share our awesome stories with the world.

After that, I could not get the idea of writing out of my head. All I could think about was how exciting it would be to share our family experiences with others.

On May 8, I was running out of the office in my typical fashion— late. As I pulled out of the parking lot, I heard on my car radio, "Go to our website at www.klove.com, and search for 'God thing.'" I could not believe what I'd just heard. I was intrigued; as soon as I got home, I greeted the boys, and then I went to the K-LOVE website and searched for "God thing." I learned about a book called *It's a God Thing: When Miracles Happen to Everyday People* cowritten by Don Jacobson. The book is a collection of real stories illustrating modern-day miracles. It encourages people to start looking for "God moments." The messages in the article and on the radio fueled my fire and desire to begin writing.

I used to think I had to give a disclaimer before I told our story to people. Before our experiences, I'd heard stories similar to ours, but admittedly, some of them were hard to believe. I now hear others' spiritual stories in a different light. After experiencing what we have, I know they are real. I promise you spiritual things are happening in your life too. You may not recognize them as signs, but I invite you to open your hearts and eyes to see the beauty of God's work. Some of the simplest moments in life can be God's greatest miracles.

We grew as individuals and as a family during trying times. You never realize how strong you are until you are put in a difficult situation and are forced to deal with it. People often tell us, "I don't know how you guys got through that." We did not get through it by ourselves. God gave us incredible strength when we needed it the most. We are also blessed to have amazing family and friends to lean on for support. Our wounds will never be healed, and our hearts will always be broken, but we face each new day and see it as an amazing gift.

As a family, we experienced the lowest of lows during my mom's illness and her eventual passing on October 13, 2012. We are all still healing from the loss, but we promised her we would continue to live and be happy. Some days are easier than others, but overall we feel extremely blessed as a family. It is human nature to sit back and say, "It is not fair," and "Why me?" Our family has learned to make the best out of the situations we are in, no matter how grim the circumstances. At the end of Mom's illness, we shed many tears, but we also laughed hard. We felt we had three options for handling the bleak situation: (1) be angry, (2) feel sorry for ourselves, or (3) enjoy the time we were given and make the most of it. We chose number three. We knew Mom's time on earth was limited, so we did the best we could by pulling together and continuing to make memories.

We are so thankful that Mom was able to meet four of her grandchildren. At the time of her passing, Bryson was four; Anisten, three; Holden, two; and Kardyn Grace, four months. Mom held Kardyn only a few times before she became too weak and ill. That was heartbreaking to experience, but we are so grateful we have pictures of Mom doing what she did best— loving and spoiling her grandchildren.

Signs from God are all around us. Mom continues to live through us, and we know she is present. Our family story illustrates the amazing gifts we have received from God by opening our hearts and our eyes.

Life is full of ups and downs, and things may not always turn out the way you planned. I never imagined Mom would depart this earth as a young, vibrant, fifty-five-year-old woman. I envisioned Mom and Dad living to a ripe old age, and when one passed away the other would follow right behind. I never imagined my sister would be diagnosed with cancer at a young age. Many other events in my life were not in *my* plans for how things were supposed to play out. I learned everything happens for a reason and every detail of our lives is already planned. We have to have faith in the good times and bad times. It is normal to want to know why things happen the way they do, especially in the darkest of days.

The song "Already There" by Casting Crowns spoke to me during Mom's terminal illness. It illustrates that our lives are well planned; while at times they seem chaotic, our lives are part of God's master plan. I found myself repeating lyrics from the song during Mom's final days: "One day I'll stand before You and look back on the life I've lived, I can't wait to enjoy the view and see how all the pieces fit." During times of uncertainty, we have to trust God and know that He will see us through the situation according to His will.

I learned so much about life from Mom's death. Her death was meaningful and part of God's beautiful master plan. I do not want to spoil all of the surprises, but Mom ultimately saved my sister's life and my life. Things happened along the way, and twenty-plus years later, we can see how *some* of the pieces fit together. As the song says, we will see how *all* of the pieces fit at the end of our lives. Now that the stage is set, I will do my best to illustrate that God's constant love is present and the beautiful reminders we receive along the way.

# CHAPTER 2

# TRIBUTE TO DAD

Rochelle and I were blessed to be born into a wonderful, loving family. Our parents were the perfect example of true love. (I remember thinking on my wedding day, *If Josh and I can have even half of what Mom and Dad have, we are going to be all right.*) They always supported our hopes and dreams. They showed us how to love and respect people and to work hard for what we want. I am sure we had our squabbles growing up, but honestly my childhood is filled with many wonderful memories. I loved growing up on a farm in a small, rural community. I would not trade growing up in a small town for anything. Now as adults, Rochelle and I often hear comments about our work ethic. Mom and Dad worked very hard and were amazing role models for us.

We lived in the small farmhouse where my grandpa Schmidt and his siblings had lived. The house was built in 1925. It took my great-grandpa Fred almost one year to dig out the basement by hand. The house was very small—two bedrooms, one bathroom. Our kitchen also served as our laundry room, and we eventually got a portable dishwasher. I also remember how hot the summers were, especially since the only air conditioner we had was a small window unit in our cozy living room. Dad and Mom decided to expand in the early 1990s; they finally got the master bedroom and bathroom they had been dreaming of. Rochelle and I were excited too, because we finally got our own rooms.

I will never forget the evening Mom, Rochelle, and I got home and found two blackbirds flying around the house. As soon as we walked through the front door, the birds dove toward our heads. Mom instructed Rochelle and me to go to into the bathroom and shut the door. We started running toward the bathroom, and Mom got a broom. She chased the birds with the broom until they flew out of the front door. It was scary at the time, but we still laugh about it today.

Rochelle and I spent many hours playing outside and building a fort. We found things in the farm dump and took them back to the fort to play make-believe. I cannot remember the names of all the areas in our fort, but one that comes to mind is "lookout mountain." We would climb up a tree and use binoculars made of paper-towel rolls to see if people were coming. We also made "hamburgers" out of dog food. We'd soak the dog food in water and then press it together to make patties and grill the hamburgers over a pretend campfire. We tried to make a tepee in the fort. We spent several hours piling up large branches to make the tepee. I asked Mom for a sheet so we could use our watercolors to paint it, like Native Americans used to do. Mom gave us one with a green-and-white pattern to use. We decorated our tepee and spent hours and hours playing in the fort.

Summertime was filled with many wonderful memories. We helped Dad on the farm. He took us irrigating, and we were responsible for shutting the gates on the pipes and dragging irrigation socks from one part of the field to the next. Occasionally, we found yellow-and-black salamanders in the pipe gates and in the ends of the socks. We rode from field to field in the back of the pickup until we were done irrigating for the day. We'd sing "God Bless America" as we held up the irrigation socks and the flags blew in the wind. We'd sit on the wheel well in the back of the truck and enjoy the breeze. We also spent time in the bean fields, pulling weeds. We each took several rows at a time, and we walked up and down the rows until the fields were spotless.

Wintertime was lots of fun for our family. We always looked forward to ski trips to Keystone, Colorado. When we were little, we stayed with Uncle Lloyd and Aunt Mary Ogorzolka for the weekend while the adults went skiing. We were so excited when we were old enough to go along. From being stuffed into our brown conversion van with nine people to braving the blizzards to falling of the ski lifts to losing our van keys on the side of the mountain, our annual ski trips were always an adventure.

Our childhood seemed carefree until 1993, when our lives were turned upside down. The year started similar to years past, except for a very large snowstorm that occurred night before our aunt's wedding. We received nearly twenty-four inches of snow in less than twenty-four hours. Grandpa Schmidt was diagnosed with lung cancer in 1993. Rochelle and I spent a lot of time at Grandma and Grandpa Schmidt's house, especially during his battle with lung cancer. Grandpa fought hard, but we lost him on June 23, 1993, when he was sixty-two.

The farming season did not go well in 1993. We had hail at least two times during the summer. Shortly after Grandpa passed away, Rochelle and I went to California with Grandma Schmidt. Mom and Dad called to tell us they'd gotten hail for the second time, and during one storm, the winds were so fierce our trampoline blew over the house. Little did we know, an even larger storm was brewing and getting ready to strike our family.

I never will forget the cold morning in December when Mom came to my room. I was getting ready for school. I was in fourth grade, and Rochelle was in sixth grade. We sat on the side of my new waterbed, and she told me she was going to go to the doctor because she'd found a lump in her left breast. I felt scared and started to cry. Mom reassured me by hugging me and telling me everything was going to be fine. I am not sure I was convinced, but I finished getting ready for school. I have always been a worrier, and I am confident I inherited that ability from my dad.

Our snow-covered Christmas tree was decorated with bubble lights and antique Christmas ornaments that Mom adored. Grandma Schmidt was at our house and greeted us as we got off the school bus. Mom and Dad were not home, and I did not ask where they were. We always had so much fun with Grandma. We had a good time, wrapping presents and listening to Christmas music. It was such a fun time of the year.

One detail I vividly remember is the look on Mom and Dad's faces as they walked into the living room. Their eyes were red as if they had been crying. They both tried so hard to be strong, as they delivered the dreaded news to my sister, Grandma, and me. Mom reminded us that she'd gone to the doctor, who looked at the lump in her breast. She said that she had been diagnosed with breast cancer; she was only thirty-seven. I was ten years old and had no idea what the news meant, but I could tell it was bad based on the way the adults were reacting. Mom continued to reassure us that everything was going to be okay. My parents did a great job of protecting my sister and me; they spared us the details.

Shortly after we learned about Mom's diagnosis, we decided to move in with Grandma across the canyon. I was excited. Mom and Dad sat us down to explain that they would be traveling back and forth between Omaha and our hometown of Indianola, Nebraska, so Mom could get better. They said Mom would be taking some medicine that might make her sick. Mom was all about normalcy. My parents decided to move in with Grandma, so she could take care of us when they traveled to Omaha for Mom's numerous appointments.

The only memory I have of the move is Uncle Brett coming over to take apart our new waterbeds, which he had put together just a few weeks before, so we could move them to Grandma's house. Rochelle and I took over the basement, and Mom and Dad moved into the guest bedroom upstairs. Rochelle's new room had brown paneling and a brown shag carpet, and my new room was pink and purple. The walls were pink-and-white panel, and the carpet was pink-and-purple shag. We were excited to have the whole basement to ourselves. We moved in right before Christmas 1993. Mom said she was sad because she wanted the holidays to be a happy time, and she did not want us to always associate Christmas with her diagnosis.

During Mom's illness, we obtained pathology reports, doctors' notes, and other records for insurance purposes. It is extremely difficult to read the reports because they shed light on how serious her situation was. I cannot imagine the heartache and fear my parents must have felt each time the doctors delivered the diagnosis. As an adult, I learned that Mom was diagnosed with stage 3, high-risk, triple-negative breast cancer, and thirteen out of seventeen lymph nodes were malignant. She had a left-side mastectomy and was treated with chemotherapy followed by a stem-cell transplant and radiation.

Martina McBride released the track "I'm Gonna Love You Through It" in 2011. The first time I heard the song, I immediately thought of my dad. The song talks about a thirty-eight-year-old woman who has just been diagnosed with breast cancer; her loving husband supports her through her journey. The following lyrics bring me to tears because I can hear Dad reassuring Mom during their battle. The lyrics are so fitting and describe my dad perfectly: "When this road gets too long, I'll be the rock you lean on. Just take my hand, together we can do it, I'm gonna love you through it." Several chapters in this book depict Mom's strength but Dad's strength matched hers. He was there every step of the way. Dad was forced to play several roles during Mom's illnesses. He is a wonderful man, and he continues to be the pillar of strength for our family.

# Chapter 3

# Faith, Grace, and Strength

It was tradition to go to Grandma and Grandpa Schmidt's on Christmas Eve. We would have supper, celebrate Rochelle's birthday, and open Christmas presents. Rochelle never liked having her birthday on Christmas Eve, but Mom and Dad always went out of their way to make her birthday special. Mom always wrapped her presents in birthday paper rather than Christmas paper. When we were little, Rochelle and I stayed at Grandma and Grandpa's while Mom and Dad attended midnight mass. I played Uncle Wiggly and Husker-doo with Grandma while we drank eggnog. Grandma loved to dance and sing. She had a large record player in her living room, and she always had music on while we played games.

I do not have very many memories from Christmas 1993. I know we got Nintendo Gameboys, and that may have been the year Rochelle got her brown leather jacket. Rochelle has never liked surprises. As a kid, she would sniff and shake her presents and guess at what was wrapped under the tree. That year was no exception. Leave it to Mom and Dad; they were so organized and had special gifts for us despite what they were going through. I remember the excitement the morning of Christmas but also the dark cloud hanging over us. Mom did her best to put on a brave face, but I could sense the sadness. After all of the presents had been opened and the paper cleaned up, I went downstairs and played my new Gameboy in front of the fireplace.

I have very little memory of Mom's initial treatment. She underwent a single mastectomy without reconstruction right before Christmas. She really wanted to have both breasts removed, but her doctor assured her that this was a "freak occurrence" and her chances of getting breast cancer on her right side were "nil." In 1993, the research was slim, and breast cancer was not very well understood. Mom was a woman who knew what she wanted, and she was adamant that both breasts be removed. She never wanted to find herself in this position again. She begged and pleaded to no avail. Mom told us she wanted to focus on getting better; then she would go back and have her other breast removed.

Mom's work ethic is worthy of praise. During her treatment plan, she took off only a couple of weeks to recover from surgery, and she missed a day here and there to travel to Omaha to see her doctors. Regardless of how bad she was feeling, she would make it to work. Again, that was Mom's way of keeping things normal as possible.

Just after the New Year in 1994, Rochelle came home from a basketball game. Small towns are wonderful for many reasons, but news definitely spreads like wildfire. Mom and Dad did their best to protect us and spare us from the graphic details. All we needed to hear was "things are going to be okay," and we were able to live our seemingly carefree lives. When Rochelle walked through the front door, she was crying. Some people at the game had said to her, "I hear your Mom is full of cancer." She was obviously devastated and frightened by this news. Mom and Dad reassured us that she was not full of cancer, but she had to continue to travel to Omaha so she could take the medicine and get better. I was angry at the people who had asked my sister questions about Mom. Little did we know that was one of life's lessons, and it paved the way for Rochelle to learn to react to the things that come out of people's mouths during trying times.

My sister and I were somewhat oblivious to the situation we faced. We knew Mom was sick, but we believed she would get better, and life would return to the way it was before her diagnosis. I saw lines connected to Mom's chest, and Dad pushed clear fluids through them to keep them clean. I saw a very large bruise on Mom's hip. I had never seen a bruise so big and black. I asked her what happened, and she told me the doctors had to make sure her bone marrow was healthy so they did a test to check her out. Not once did she complain about how bad it hurt or how big the needle was. Once again she reassured me that everything was on track, and she was doing well. It wasn't until years later that she shared with me just how painful the procedure and just how large the needle was.

The night before Mom had treatment, she and Dad would pack up and leave for Lincoln. They would stay with her brother Eldon, and his wife, Carol, the night before and then drive into Omaha early the following morning. Mom would get her treatment, and they would make the four-and-a-half-hour trek back to Indianola so Mom could return to work the following day. I do not remember her getting sick from the medicine, but I am sure she was.

One Saturday morning, Mom and Dad told us that it was time to shave her head. "Shave your head?" I asked. "Why would you shave your head?" Mom's hair had started to fall out because the medicine she received—through her lines in her chest—was killing all the bad cells in her body, and some of the good ones as well. She invited us into the kitchen as Grandma draped a blue bath towel around her and started shaving her head. Mom smiled from ear to ear, and not once did a tear roll down her face. I was somewhat confused but knew Mom had this and was in control. She had purchased a wig in anticipation of her hair falling out. Grandma finished shaving her head and placed the wig on her. I thought she was beautiful, and that her wig looked real, but even more that Mom was so brave.

The amount of courage she had is hard to comprehend. Mom continued to smile and was a warrior for her children. There is no way I could have handled that situation with her grace and confidence. Years later, Mom told us that she went to her room, put her face in a pillow, and cried and cried and cried. Losing her hair and seeing a bald reflection in the mirror made the fact she had cancer a reality. Her physical strength, emotional strength, and spiritual strength were just a few of the traits I admired. She was so brave and confident in the face of a very sad and real experience.

Mom would take naps, saying she was tired. I watched her gurgle with salt water because her mouth developed sores due to the treatment. Mom brushed off these inconveniences and continued to be very positive. We got used to our "new normal." Rochelle and I were busy with school, and farming season started to pick up. I cannot remember how many treatments Mom received, but they seemed to go by relatively fast.

She had to take about six weeks off from work because of the travel time associated with her radiation treatments. Dad drove Mom to Grand Island, Nebraska, five days a week for six weeks so she could receive radiation at Saint Francis Medical Center. At times Dad could not drive because he had to tend to the farm, so our wonderful family and friends stepped in and helped. Mom did not complain about her burned skin due to radiation. She saw it as reassurance: whatever the chemo did not get the radiation would. Her skin was very raw and red, comparable to a severe sunburn.

Mom and Dad obviously did an amazing job at keeping our lives as normal as possible. I really cannot remember much of anything during Mom's treatment. I cannot imagine the level of stress and anxiety they must have had. It had to be extremely difficult to always put on a brave face and reassure my sister and me that things were fine when, in fact, things really were not as good as they had hoped at that stage of her treatment. Many tears were shed and many prayers were said during their road trips to and from Omaha and during the nights when they could not sleep due to the fear and physical burden cancer brings.

# CHAPTER 4

# COVENANT AND MARK 11:22

Following chemo treatment and radiation, Mom was enrolled in a clinical trial. She was given the opportunity to receive a stem-cell transplant because the initial treatment was not as effective as they would have liked it to be. We learned later on down the road that the decision makers actually flipped a coin to determine who would be accepted and who would be denied. Plans had been in place to sell the farm in the 50 percent chance that Mom was not accepted into the program. Endless prayers were said in hopes of getting the call. Once again, God delivered!

The graphic details of the clinical trial were given to Mom and Dad during one of their many meetings with her doctors. Rochelle and I were told that Mom would be in the hospital in Omaha for a portion of the summer so she could continue to get well. We were invited to tour the Lied Transplant Center at the University of Nebraska Medical Center so we could better understand where Mom would be spending her time. I have faint memories meeting Mom's oncologist, Dr. Reed, and her staff. We sat around a table in a small conference room and were given a synopsis of what was in store. I did not fully understand what was going on, but I felt sad for my mom. Little did we know that Mom was going to experience "hell on earth" during her lengthy stay at the transplant center. She was scheduled to check in on July 5, 1994.

To maintain the impression of normalcy, we hosted a July 4 party. Despite the upcoming hospital stay, everything seemed very normal at the party. I dreaded the next day because I knew Mom and Dad were leaving for Omaha, but I also was excited about the party because our friends and family were gathering at our house for a cookout and fireworks. I am sure Mom and Dad had terrible pits in their stomach, knowing what was waiting for them in Omaha. To help us pass the time during the first part of Mom's high-dose chemotherapy, a trip to California was booked for Rochelle, Grandma Schmidt, and me. We spent seven to ten days in Redwood, visiting our aunt and uncle.

The protocol for the treatment was extremely intense. One of the doctors told Dad that Mom would knock on death's doorstep and then would be brought back again. From what I understand, that was a pretty accurate representation. She was hooked up to a continuous drip of high-dose chemo for four straight days, and then she had the stem-cell transplant. Thankfully the cancer was not in her bone marrow, but her immune system had bottomed out. The slightest cold or infection could have killed her, so Mom was kept in isolation for the duration of her stay.

She had very few memories of her month-long hospital stay. She said it was God's way of protecting her so she could move on and not be haunted by the memories of the (lifesaving) experience. One experience that Mom and Dad shared with us is a terrifying story, about when Mom thought she would never be able to speak again. She was violently ill from all of the toxic chemo medications. At one point, she vomited, and up with it came a large collection of tissue. Mom thought it was her voice box. She was horrified, afraid she would never be able to talk again. The doctors reassured her that it just the dead cells from her mouth, throat, and stomach, not her voice box.

Celine Dion's "Because You Loved Me" was a song Mom and Dad held close to their hearts. During Mom's one-month stay, she could not talk, she was very weak, and she slept a lot due to the multiple medications. This song symbolizes the strength and love Mom and Dad had for one another:

> You were my strength when I was weak,
> you were my voice when I couldn't speak,
> you were my eyes when I couldn't see.
> Because you loved me.

I am sure it was awful being the patient, but I cannot imagine what Dad went through—having to see it firsthand, knowing there was nothing he could do other than pray and remain by Mom's side.

Dad told us years later about a high-powered antibiotic the doctors referred to as "shake and bake." During her hospital stay, Mom exhibited signs of an infection. In an effort to save her life, the doctors administered the antibiotic. It did not take long for Dad to see why it was called "shake and bake." Mom started shaking hard once the drugs entered her system. Dad said it was as if she were having a seizure. The experience will forever be imprinted in his mind, but thankfully, Mom did not recall most of the traumatic events that accompanied her stem-cell transplant.

Dad spent most of his time by Mom's side. Our wonderful neighbors and friends helped with the farm back in Indianola so Dad could spend as much time in Omaha with Mom as possible. Our neighbors are some of the nicest, most compassionate people I have ever met. They look out for their neighbors, and they do not think twice about lending a helping hand. The farmers took care of the farm for the entire summer. They helped with wheat harvest, even though they had their own farms to tend to. They watered the irrigated fields and prayed for a speedy recovery for Mom.

Dad occasionally drove approximately four hours west to Indianola, checked on the farm, and drove back to Omaha, all in one day. He is such a dedicated man, father, husband, farmer, friend, etc. I am sure it was extremely difficult to leave Mom's side but he did what any father would do. He tried to maintain balance and normalcy for my sister and me.

One evening Dad was on his way back to Omaha. He was driving down I-80, and he was so angry. He was under so much stress, consumed with the thought of losing his wife, the mother of his children, the love of his life. He was thirty-seven years old, and the thought of walking through life without his young wife and raising two daughters by himself was more than he could handle. He prayed, asking God to show him He was there. The next thing Dad knew, there were some lights right behind him, riding his bumper. Dad hit his brakes to send a signal to the other driver: *quit tailgating me.* The vehicle passed Dad, and as he looked to his left, he saw "Covenant Transport" written on the side of the truck.

A covenant is a promise. In that moment of despair and weakness, God reminded Dad that He is always present. What an awesome message Dad received; God's timing was impeccable. God knew at that very moment that Dad needed reassurance that Mom would get through that very trying time. Signs are all around us. We just have to open ourselves up and be aware. That was a defining moment for Dad. He knew we still had a long road ahead of us, but that was God's way of reassuring Dad that He is in control.

Dad had a lot of down time at the hospital. Mom spent the days in a deep sleep due to all of her medications. Dad spent a lot of time with the other husbands whose wives were going through the clinical trial. One day when Dad was visiting with the group of husbands, he decided to pick up the Bible. He had never read the Bible before, so he randomly flipped to the book of Mark. He looked at chapter 11, verse 22 (because his birthday is November 22). He read, "Have faith in God." Once again, God knew Dad was struggling and reminded him to have faith because He is in control.

Rochelle and I decided to make a gift for Mom. We wrote the following poem:

> For all the things you've done for us
> You know we love you very much.
>
> The cooking, washing, and the sewing
> You also do the outside mowing.
>
> When you come home from McCook
> You help us with our spelling book
>
> Of all the good things God has done
> Saving you, Mom has been the best one!

We were so proud of our poem; however, looking back, I have to laugh. Mom did not sew, but we needed a word that rhymed with mowing. We wrote each verse in a different color, using our collection of colored pencils. We used a wallet-size photo from our school pictures and glued our pictures to the top right (Rochelle) and bottom left (me) of the paper. Rochelle wore a pink sweater, and I wore a blue-and-white sweater. I believe we both had turtle necks on underneath and we both sported huge,

1990s-style, permed bangs. We found a five-by-seven-inch wood frame and put our masterpiece inside it. Mom's brother Lloyd and his wife, Mary, and our good friends Dennis and Kem McConville took our gift to Mom, who was in the ICU. The poem is so simple but as a mother, I am sure it brought tears to her eyes. She cherished the poem, and it eventually became a permanent fixture on the dresser in her bedroom.

I will never forget when Mom and Dad surprised us by coming home early. Mom had been discharged a little early because she had recovered so well. I'd called Dad and asked what he was doing. He said, "Oh, just driving around Omaha." That should have been a red flag because Dad was not one to drive around an unfamiliar city by himself.

Shortly after I talked to Dad, I went to my room and pulled out my new trumpet. School would soon start; I was going into fifth grade, and Rochelle was getting ready for seventh grade. Fifth grade was the year I could join band. Grandma Schmidt took me to Hershberger's in McCook to pick out the perfect trumpet. I was looking at my new Holton trumpet when I heard the doorbell. I ran upstairs and was so excited to see Mom and Dad. It was so nice to have our family under one roof again.

# Chapter 5

# Remission

The summer of 1994 was miserable, but it is one we are thankful for as we feel it scientifically saved Mom's life. We know that it was God's plan all along to allow Mom an additional nineteen years on earth so she could help raise her children—watch my sister and me participate in sports, graduate from college, and marry our college sweethearts—meet four of her grandchildren, and live life to its fullest.

Mom really knew how to live. She was a dedicated wife, mother, friend, confidant, coworker, and employee, just to name a few. She truly was a cheerleader for many people. Many people turned to her because she had a gift of always finding the positive in any situation. Sure, she occasionally got angry, but she always kept her mind on the big picture. She was always thankful for the many blessings she'd received.

On top of her full-time job at Community Hospital, Mom was Dad's number-one helper on the farm. During harvest, Mom drove the combine. She went to work in the very early hours of the morning so she could get in a half to a full day of work before she headed out to the farm, where she worked until late evening and sometimes into the night. I would talk to Mom on the phone at four thirty or five in the morning as we both drove to work. She really enjoyed harvest and operating the combine.

Mom was employed at Community Hospital for thirty-three years. She knew the ins and outs of her job. She started at the hospital in 1979, shortly after she married Dad. In December 1981, Rochelle was born.

Mom took a short maternity leave and returned to work but only for one day. She could not stand being away from her newborn baby, so she decided to be a stay-at-home mom. Twenty-three months later, I was born and shortly thereafter, Mom received a call from her former boss offering her job back at the hospital. At that point, Mom knew she'd better accept, because if she turned down this opportunity, it could be gone forever.

Mom had quite the social network. It seemed like everywhere we went she knew somebody. She was a friend to everyone and a stranger to no one. Mom was a soundboard for her family and friends. She was great at giving advice and challenging others to stay positive. I talked to her on the phone daily about work, kids, family, and life in general. Rochelle talked to her every day as well. We could easily spend an hour or more, just catching up on the day. Mom also cheered Dad on during the very hot, dry summers. I always tried to be strong for Mom, but I remember her reassuring us as she was going through cancer treatments between 2010 and 2012. I was extremely angry when she was diagnosed again in March 2012. She told me it was okay to be mad but that we had to pray hard. I feel bad for imposing my negative feelings on her, but knowing Mom, she was happy to comfort me. She always knew what to say to make sure we did not worry about her.

During the seventeen years when Mom was in remission, we made some lifetime memories. We were busy with high-school sports. We had the most amazing support system. Mom and Dad never missed one game during our high-school careers. It was always so much fun to see our biggest fans in the stands on game day, wearing their purple-and-gold Republican Valley Mustangs gear.

Rochelle was very active in USA Track and Field. Her success in track took us on many adventures. We traveled to regional and national meets in Texas, Minnesota, and Wisconsin. We met actor Chris Farley at a small airport in Wisconsin. He was traveling back to California after a weekend visit with his mother. The movie *Beverly Hills Ninja* had just been released. We contemplated asking Farley for a picture. Dad had been drinking some coffee as we were waiting for our flight. Right before we saw Farley, Dad spilled the coffee on his lap but that didn't stop him from taking a picture of his daughters with the movie star. Dad picked up the small camera bag, slung it around his forearm, attempted to keep the bag over his stain, and took a picture of us. I laughed so hard because all Dad wanted was for us to get a picture, and not even a coffee stain on the crotch of his pants was going to stop him.

Our USA Track and Field days were before September 11. We got sunburned sitting outside during track meets. We purchased one of those large umbrellas so we could have some shelter from the sun. Grandma Nettie made a bag so we could travel with the umbrella. When we were in Texas, Mom had to go through extra security so they could check the large bag she had over her shoulder. It looked like she was traveling with a bazooka.

Rochelle graduated from high school in 2000. We were really sad to see her leave, but we were excited for her new adventures at Doane College in Crete, Nebraska. Having a daughter in college and a daughter in high school presented some scheduling issues. Mom and Dad did their best to continue to make it to all of my activities as well as to most of Rochelle's college volleyball games and indoor and outdoor track meets.

Rochelle's track career continued in college. We traveled to Johnson City, Tennessee; Vancouver, British Columbia; and Louisville, Kentucky. We met a lot of people along the way, and Dad has stayed in contact with some of them to this day. In March 2002, I stayed at home alone while Mom and Dad traveled to Tennessee for the indoor national track meet. They met a nice couple on the airplane and were invited to their home in the mountains for breakfast the following day. I was worried sick about my parents, thinking they would never been seen again. I'm a bit of a worry wart and a pessimist by nature. Needless to say, I was relieved when I heard from them after their adventures in the Smoky Mountains with Doug and Barb Harrel. I believe we cross paths with certain people for certain reasons. Mrs. Harrel is a breast cancer survivor, and she and Mom connected on many levels.

The following year, I traveled to Johnson City for the indoor national meet. We arranged another meeting with Doug and Barb and stayed one night with them in their quaint cottage in the mountains. It was an amazing experience, and I am forever grateful for Mom and Dad's ability to talk to others and trust their instincts. To this day, I can talk to anybody about anything, and I believe I have a very strong intuition.

Life got a little easier in terms of schedules when I graduated high school and joined the Doane College volleyball team. Mom and Dad made it to almost every game, wearing their black-and-orange Doane Tigers gear. They spent many long hours driving from Indianola to Doane and beyond. Mom arrived at work early so she could leave by noon to make our games. She and Dad would not get home until well after midnight. I got e-mails the next day that said, "Our heads hit the pillow at 2:30 a.m." Mom and Dad would go back to work the following day; they did not miss a beat! They went through at least two vehicles during our college years. At the height of the volleyball season, the suburban was in the shop every other week, getting oil changes due to the amount of miles they traveled.

I recently found an article that was published in the school newspaper, *The Doane Owl*, in fall 2004. It was titled "Schmidt Sisters Make Their Mark." I love this article because the author, Tosha Rae (Long) Heavican, did a great job interviewing our parents and captured quotes from them that I will hold onto forever. Here are some excerpts:

> "Game point! This one's for the championship!" the two girls yelled loudly from their backyard. She serves, she scores and the imaginary crowd goes wild. The girls trade high fives for a game well played.
>
> For senior Rochelle Schmidt and sophomore Kirby Schmidt, this scenario had been a dream since the 4th grade. The two girls began playing at this very young age, attending camps that the area high school hosted. It was at the junior high level the girls began to play competitively. This competitiveness has been the driving force ever since. "They always had ambition to play college ball," the girls' mother, Nancy Schmidt, said. "They have always been so focused and knew to set goals of what they wanted to do."
>
> The closeness in age between Rochelle and Kirby allowed the two girls to compete together for most of their sports careers. Their strength as a duo has been more than rewarding "When you are siblings you tend to compete," Nancy said. "But because of Rochelle being right-handed and Kirby being left-handed, they both have been able to

play. One never had to be in the shadow of the other. I think they complement each other."

Rochelle and Kirby left their mark in high school volleyball, winning two state championships together, followed by Kirby winning the next two consecutive years, accumulating four state championship titles. Despite this colorful volleyball record, the recruitment of Rochelle to Doane College surprisingly was not to play volleyball. Rochelle's first love, track, is what got Doane interested. She had triple jumped in the state track meet and was awarded a scholarship to jump at Doane. "Track is why I originally came to Doane," Rochelle said. "I was able to get two scholarships for playing both sports." Two years later, Kirby followed in her sister's footsteps. "I came to Doane mostly because of Rochelle," Kirby said. "I also like the program and the size of the school. I also like the atmosphere but mostly I thought it would be fun to play volleyball two more years with Rochelle."

Playing together for so many years the girls have come to learn each other's playing styles. "We have a lot of background together," said Rochelle. "We both know how to play to win. We know when to critique each other and we know what the other thinks." Both girls feel their parents have been the biggest impact on their careers. "They are our role models," Kirby said. "They have always been there. They didn't push us to play, just supported our decisions." Rochelle recalls one year alone their parents put over 18,000 miles on the car traveling to games. "You can probably count on one hand the number of games we've missed in the last four years," father Les Schmidt said. "It has been a great experience. A lot of late night driving but it has been worth it."

Coach Cindy Meyer has noticed the support Kirby and Rochelle have and feel it has added to the success these girls have had. "They are super athletes with great attitudes and very, very competitive." Meyer said. "They are also very family-oriented and come from an awesome background. They have very supportive parents."

... The girls have come a long way since the days of backyard ball and invisible crowds, but those days are what set the path to stardom.

## CHAPTER 6

# GRADUATIONS, WEDDINGS, AND GRANDCHILDREN

Doane College was an amazing place to go to school. I will be forever thankful for all of the experiences and friendships that developed at the family-friendly college in Crete, Nebraska. From the late nights to volleyball games, track meets, raising money for cancer in the annual Relay for Life, and the small town atmosphere, it was the perfect place for my sister and me to attend college.

Rochelle had been recruited by Ed Fye, one of the track coaches at Doane. He stopped by Republican Valley High School when she was in junior high and it happened to be spirit day. Rochelle was dressed in her junior-high cheerleading outfit, with pigtails and a face painted in purple and gold. We laugh about their first meeting to this day. Ed knew there was something special about Rochelle, as a person and as an athlete. She was breaking records left and right in the long jump and triple jump.

Ed invited Rochelle to attend a private lesson with him at the indoor facility at Doane College. Dad and Rochelle spent several hours learning the secrets of jumping from Ed. This experience was invaluable to my sister. She and Dad were so motivated that they made plans to put in a pit at home so Rochelle could continue to practice the long jump and triple jump. It did not take long for her to become one of the best jumpers in the state of Nebraska. During her freshman year of high school she jumped an astounding thirty-nine feet, three inches. Only one other girl in the state of Nebraska came close to those marks. Rochelle ended up winning the all-class gold medal for the triple jump at the Nebraska State Track Meet during her freshman year of high school.

During my senior year of high school, our team won a fourth consecutive state volleyball championship. I was offered a scholarship to play volleyball for Doane. I accepted and was so excited to play volleyball with Rochelle for another two years. Rochelle was given the nickname Ro at Doane. It took some getting used to, but now that is what we call her.

It was always exciting to have Mom and Dad attend the events at Doane. I always dreaded seeing them leave, but I knew it would be a matter of days before we saw them at the next event. When we parted ways, we always said "see you later" rather than "good-bye." Mom once said, "Good-bye is too permanent." That is something that stuck with us, and it has more meaning to me now than ever before.

Doane has a high marriage rate among its students. I do not know the actual statistic but I know several people who married their Doane College sweethearts. Ro met Scott at Doane. He was a member of the basketball team and the track team. Ro had described Scott to us, so at a Kearney indoor meet, Mom and I scoped out the place, looking for a tall, redheaded jumper. We thought we'd spotted him, but Ro later told us that Scott was not at that meet because he was finishing up basketball season. We met Scott's wonderful family at an indoor meet at Doane, and we spent more time getting to know them during an indoor national meet in Johnson City, Tennessee.

I met Josh in March 2003 during the second semester of my freshman year. I had just gotten back from cheering on Ro and Scott at nationals. My awesome roommate, Amanda, told me that she'd spent some time getting to know the people in one of the dorms, Hansen, room number 201. She invited me to meet them, and I am so glad I took her up on the offer. Josh was one of seven people who lived in Hansen 201. Strangely enough, Scott had lived there the year before. Josh had been introduced to Doane by family friends Rich and Dena Bartlett. He'd worked for the Bartlett family throughout high school. In May 2001, during Josh's senior year of high school, he had yet to decide where to go to college. Rich and Dena are both graduates of Doane, and they talked Josh into a campus visit; that is where he finally decided to attend college.

After he graduated from Doane, Scott moved back to Utica, Nebraska, to work on the family farm. Ro finished up her senior year at Doane and was accepted into the accelerated nursing program at the Creighton College of Nursing, specifically the Mary Lanning Campus in Hastings, Nebraska. She moved into a two-bedroom apartment in Hastings and charged forward with the program. She and Scott were engaged in June 2004 and married on September 3, 2005, at Saint Catherine's Catholic Church in Indianola. Scott went back to Doane and received his teaching degree, and Ro worked the night shift at Mary Lanning on the ortho-neuro floor.

Rochelle's graduation from Doane College (2004)

Ro and Scott bought their first home in Gretna, Nebraska, in June 2007. Gretna is a suburb of Omaha. Ro, Scott, Dad, and Mom spent several hours touring homes in Gretna, and after a long day, and thirteen houses later, they found the perfect home. The layout was nice and open, and it was exactly what Ro and Scott were looking for. Later that week, Mom informed us that she'd started spotting. She was shocked because she'd gone through menopause in 1994 after her high-dose chemotherapy. Mom had a biopsy, and the pathology report came back clean; however, her doctor recommended that she undergo a preventative total hysterectomy. Mom was proactive, and she opted for the surgery.

Josh graduated from Doane in 2005 and moved back to Olathe, Kansas. He lived with his parents for almost a year, and then he moved into an apartment in Shawnee, Kansas. He worked for two years at Biomune and then accepted a lab job at Merck Animal Health. I started the paralegal certificate program at the College of Saint Mary's (CSM) in the fall of 2005 while I was finishing my undergraduate studies. I decided to live off campus during my final year at Doane. I moved into a three-bedroom apartment with two other girls and commuted to Crete. I completed the thirty-six-hour program in one year and received my paralegal certificate on December 2, 2006. Josh and I were married on December 9, 2006, at Saint Catherine's Catholic Church in Indianola.

The Schmidt Family at Kirby's Graduation
from Doane College (2006)

The weather in 2006 was strange. Harvest was running behind, and I offered to help drive the tractor and grain cart. I was attending the weekend program at CSM, planning a wedding, and looking for a job.

I had interviewed at some placement agencies in Kansas City, but I was underwhelmed by the job offers. Rich Bartlett gave my résumé to an attorney in Overland Park, Kansas and I was told the attorney would call me to set up a time for an interview. One afternoon, Dad and I were in the field, trying to get the corn out. Before we'd started for the day, I told him that if the attorney called while we were working, I would need to stop and take the call. Of course, Dad agreed.

I waited impatiently for my phone to ring. Since we were harvesting irrigated corn, we unloaded on the go. Naturally, as we were unloading, an 816 area code showed up on my phone. I knew this was the mystery attorney calling, so I waved at Dad, signaling him to stop. He did not see me waving, and he continued to dump corn from the combine into my grain cart. He was so focused on unloading that he did not see me begging him to stop the combine. This was my one opportunity to take the call. Finally, I got Dad's attention, but unfortunately it was on the last ring. I quickly called the number back, and thankfully Mike Matteuzzi answered the phone. I was panicked but tried to be as calm as possible. I apologized for missing his call. I explained that I was in the tractor helping with harvest. He understood and asked when I would be available for an interview. I told him I could be at his office at eight o'clock the following morning. He questioned that, knowing I had a seven-hour drive ahead of me. Dad and I finished for the day, and I went home, packed my bags and headed for Kansas City.

The following day I showed up in my new suit and interviewed at Matteuzzi and Brooker, PC, for a paralegal position. After a three-hour interview with the paralegals and two partners, I was offered a full-time position. I had no idea what I was getting myself into, but I knew I would give it 100 percent and prove that I was the right person for the job. Rich and Mike are good friends, and Mike hired me as a favor to Rich. I do not think Mike thought it would work out, but he took a leap of faith anyway. Eight years later, I am still with the firm. Mike occasionally brings up the story of our first telephone call. God's master plan is amazing! The whole time I was stressed out about finding a job, He knew what the final outcome would be. I truly believe God places certain people in our lives as part of His plan.

God had a plan when he connected Josh's family with the Bartlett family, and ultimately with me.

After her journey with cancer in 1993, Mom told Dad she wanted to live long enough to see her girls graduate. I am sure she had strong feelings about wanting to see us get married and have kids as well as see her great-grandchildren. By the grace of God, Mom saw both of us graduate from high school and college. She also saw her daughters get married, and she met four of her grandchildren.

Papa and Nana with their grandchildren,
Bryson, Anisten, Kardyn and Holden

Josh and I bought our first home in Olathe in December 2007, just three weeks before our first baby was due. Mom and Dad were excited to help us get the house ready before the birth of our baby boy. Bryson Isaiah was the first grandson and first grandchild on both sides of the family. He was born on January 15, 2008, weighing ten pounds, four ounces. Anisten Noel was Nana and Papa's first granddaughter, and she was born on December 16, 2008, weighing in at a whopping ten pounds, ten ounces. I am not sure how Ro carried such a big baby with a small frame, but she said she was not that uncomfortable throughout her pregnancy.

My son Holden Elijah was born on May 14, 2010, weighing eight pounds, fifteen ounces, and Ro's daughter Kardyn Grace joined the family on June 22, 2012. Kardyn was awarded the "smallest baby" award among the Schmidt cousins, weighing in at eight pounds, thirteen ounces.

Mom loved her grandchildren with everything she had. They brought more joy to her life than she ever knew was possible. Mom often told me to make sure nothing happened to her grandkids as she could not live without any one of them. Mom was an amazing nana. She did anything to make her grandkids happy, and the kids really loved her. It is hard to not have Mom here in person so she can watch them grow, but we know she is walking with us each day. In fact, Kardyn has many of Mom's personality characteristics. Kardyn is a little spitfire just like she was. It is fun to see Mom living on through her kids and grandkids.

Before she became terminally ill in 2012, Mom expressed gratitude over and over again for having healthy grandchildren. Ro had a tubal ligation after Kardyn was born; she and Scott decided they wanted to be a family of four. Mom knew that Josh and I were thinking about having another child, but she asked me not to do so, given her history with cancer. She was so fearful that her history of cancer would be passed to her children and grandchildren.

# CHAPTER 7

# CURVEBALL

I always enjoy getting away from city life and visiting home. Indianola always will be home to me. In 2009, Josh and I decided to go home for harvest. Bryson was just shy of two years old. Surprisingly, he could sit in the combine with Dad and Josh for hours and hours. He sat on Papa's lap and drove the combine. Thankfully, we have several video clips Josh captured during Bryson's first harvest.

In October 2010 we took part in the harvest. Bryson was almost three, and Holden was five months old. Once again Bryson spent hours in the combine. Holden was too little, so he only got to sit on Papa's lap for a photo opportunity. Mom and Dad had a field they called "the grandkids' field." They worked hard to get out the corn, but they saved a patch for the kids to pick. The weather was not ideal that weekend. It rained on and off, so it took some time to get out the corn. Dad said a quick prayer, asking God to get the corn out and then to let it rain. Shortly thereafter, a rainbow appeared. The boys got the corn out that Saturday afternoon. In the evening, we went to the Rocket Inn for pizza to celebrate. We almost had dinner by candlelight that night because the restaurant was having problems with the electricity. The lights eventually came back on, and we enjoyed our pizza with some good friends.

Papa and Nana along with Holden and Bryson by
the grandkids' field" during harvest (2010)

Visits home are never long enough. We hugged and said "see you later"
as we got into our vehicle. We were sad to leave but knew we would see
each other the following weekend at Mahoney State Park; Ro and Scott
had planned a weekend camping trip. Everything seemed normal as we
pulled out of the circle drive and headed toward Olathe. We arrived home
approximately seven hours later and got ready for another workweek.

I had been called for jury duty that Monday in the Johnson County
(Kansas) District Court. I went to the office early that morning to make
up some of the time I'd lose on jury duty. I sent an e-mail to remind Mom
I would be out of the office that morning and possibly the entire day. She
did not respond right away but that was not out of the ordinary. I figured
she was busy at work and did not see my e-mail.

I arrived at the courthouse, got checked in, and filed into the holding
room with the other potential jurors. We were seated and informed that
the case had been settled that morning; therefore, the trial was cancelled.
I walked back to my car and reached for my cell phone to call Mom. I

accidentally called her cell phone rather than her work phone. As the phone was ringing I looked at my phone and realized I had misdialed. When Mom answered, I instantly was sick to my stomach. I could tell by the sound of her voice something was not right. Mom said I am like a bloodhound because I have a way of sniffing out problems.

Mom said she and Kem were at the house, waiting for her doctor from Omaha to call back. I broke down and started crying. I knew exactly what she meant. Mom told me she'd found a lump in her right breast. She tried to reassure me but said flat out she was certain she had breast cancer. I felt as if I were in the middle of a nightmare and could not wake up. Mom said she found the lump in early September, but she had not though it could possibly be cancer again. During the seventeen years she was in remission, there was always the thought "what if the cancer comes back," but honestly, I never thought it would. Back in 1993, Mom had asked for a double mastectomy so she would never have to face this again, but her request was denied. In fact, Mom was told that the cancer typically skips a generation so she would not have to worry about my sister and me. Naturally, this upset her, but she needed to focus on the situation at hand rather than on years down the road.

I had flashbacks to the day Mom had sat on the side of my bed and said she was going to the doctor to get a lump in her breast checked. All of those feelings came rushing back tenfold. I fully understood the magnitude of the situation at the age of twenty-six, almost twenty-seven, in a way I did not when I was ten.

Mom was trying to be strong, but I knew she was scared. I was so confused by the news, given the fact we had just been at the farm less than twenty-four hours earlier; everything had seemed fine. Mom told me she'd known she had a problem, but she wanted to get all of the crops out before she addressed the issue. That was Mom. She always put everybody else before herself. This was a situation when I wish she'd have sought help when she discovered the lump in early September.

Mom was very persistent and insisted on seeing her oncologist, Dr. Reed, in Omaha the following day. Despite her fears, she felt some comfort knowing that she'd been through this before and knew what to expect. She was so good at finding the positive in every situation. She and Dad packed up and drove to Ro and Scott's house in Gretna, so she could be at her appointment the following morning. It was a bit of a blessing that she was a prior patient because she was able to get in right away.

I went back to the office and straight to Mike's office to explain the situation. Through my tears, he could tell my life had just turned upside down. In the past, I had briefly shared Mom's history with breast cancer but never the details. Mike is a religious man and an understanding person. He is very busy, but he always takes time for his employees. He comforted me, referring to his religious background. I do not remember the rest of the day, but I made it through.

The following day was tough. I knew Mom was in good hands in Omaha, but I am not good at waiting for the phone to ring. I knew she would be put through a series of tests to see just how advanced the cancer was. (Unfortunately throughout the next few years, I became very accustomed to waiting for my caller ID to say "Mom Cell" and hearing her reassuring voice on the other end of the line.) We texted each other throughout the day, but I could not wait to hear her voice. The doctors were running behind as usual, so the texts would let me know they were in the waiting room or did not yet have results of the numerous tests.

I went home after work, but I could not stand sitting around waiting for the phone to ring. I gathered Bryson and Holden, and we drove around. I was focused on staying strong for my kids, but inside I was crumbling. Chinese food is my default comfort food when I am feeling down. I was not hungry, but I needed something to distract me from the awful feeling I had. The boys and I drove through Panda Express, and I ordered way too much food but ate it anyway. Finally at about five thirty that evening, my phone rang and "Mom Cell" appeared on my screen.

I picked up the phone and heard typical Mom—"Hey, honey, what are you up to?"—as if nothing were going on.

I told her I was indulging on Chinese and then jumped right to it: "What did you find out?" I asked.

She and Dad said the results of the biopsy would not be back for a few days but based on the ultrasound, her doctor was 99.9 percent sure it was cancer. Mom and Dad sounded very optimistic. Thanks to their persistence, Mom had an appointment that Friday to get a port put in so she could start chemo therapy the following week. Despite the fact she had to have an outpatient procedure performed, Dad and Mom confirmed the weekend camping trip to Mahoney was still on. Incredible! Not many people would be that strong, but once again, Mom wanted normalcy for her family.

We had a very good conversation about disclosing Mom's health situation. Dad and Mom both expressed relief that they could be more open than they had been seventeen years before. There was no need to hide information from Ro and me, now that we were both adults and had families of our own. I was comforted by this because I do not handle the unknown very well. I am a pessimist by nature, and I let my mind wander. I would much rather learn the facts so I can deal with them rather worrying about the unknown.

That Friday, Josh and I headed to Nebraska after work. We stopped in Gretna to help Ro and Scott pack the food for the weekend. We headed to Mahoney shortly after five o'clock. Once again the doctors were running behind due to an emergency, so they bumped Mom's surgery to a later time. I am sure Mom was anxious about the delay, but she later said she was grateful the emergency was not hers; she said there was always somebody worse off than we were. Once again, the faith this woman had was profound. We finally got the call around seven; they were on their way to the campsite. By the time Dad and Mom arrived, we had set up the cozy cabin for the weekend.

Mom was such a trooper. She was a little sleepy from the procedure, but she put on her happy face and had a great time. A couple of hours after arriving at the cabin, she ate a little supper and kicked back and watched TV. We had a great weekend at Mahoney. We spent time on the wildlife safari and hiking through the wilderness.

It was Halloween weekend. We ate breakfast at the buffet each morning. The first morning, the employees wore Halloween masks. Anisten and Bryson were afraid of the masks, and one of the waiters realized this. He was a typical teenager, looking to have a good time. He continued to walk by our table wearing his mask, so the little ones would be afraid. Mom's feathers got ruffled after he passed by the third or fourth time. She tracked him down and told him to take off his mask so the kids could see he was "fake." She was not going to let some kid terrorize her grandchildren.

We all had a wonderful time, but I dreaded our departure more than ever. I knew what was in store for Mom in the coming weeks. I could feel the tears building as we said "see you later" in the parking lot. We all went our separate ways, and I cried most of the way home.

On October 28, 2010, Mom was officially diagnosed with invasive ductal adenocarcinoma, triple-negative breast cancer, the same thing she'd been diagnosed with in 1993. It is my understanding that this type of cancer is the most aggressive and most resistant to several of the chemo medications available.

The course of treatment was different than it had been 1993. Rather than having the mastectomy first and then receiving treatment, the recommendation was to undergo chemo therapy, have the mastectomy, and finish up with radiation. Radiation would only be necessary if a certain amount of the lymph nodes were cancerous; however, we would not find that out until Mom completed her chemo and underwent the mastectomy.

The course of treatment seemed unsettling to me, but how does a twenty-something-year-old argue with the latest research and the best doctors Nebraska has to offer? It seemed counterintuitive to keep the breast intact knowing the cancerous tumor was present. Mom and Dad expressed their reservations to the doctors, who assured my parents that this was standard treatment. They would measure whether or not the tumor was shrinking based on the mixture of chemotherapy given. If the tumor were not shrinking, they would try another mixture of chemo until they got favorable results. Once we received a detailed explanation, we felt better about the decision. If they removed the breast and then administered chemo, they would have to guess whether or not her body was reacting positively to the chemo. If there were cells floating around her body that were too small to detect on the preliminary scans, it would be too late to treat once they became aware of the cells.

Mom was ready to move forward with the treatment once she had her road map. She always felt better once she had a treatment plan in place.

## Chapter 8

# Fight Like a Girl

Unsurprisingly, Mom handled her treatment very well the second time around. She scheduled her trips to Omaha around her work schedule. She received treatment every other Thursday. Her goal was to miss as little work as possible. During the week of treatment, she'd work Monday through Wednesday, and she and Dad would stay with Ro and Scott in Gretna on Wednesday night. A new facility had been constructed in Elkhorn, near Ro and Scott's home. Mom could see her oncologist and receive her treatment within minutes of leaving Gretna. After she completed treatment, she and Dad drove back to Indianola, and she went to work on Friday.

Community Hospital in McCook was in the process of a major construction project during her treatment. Mom was heavily involved in the planning and interior design. The open house was scheduled for January 2011, and Mom was not going to let anything, not even cancer, get in her way of seeing the project to the end. She was also involved in planning the open house.

Mom talked about how bad her joints hurt during treatment. When her counts were low, due to the chemo, she was given a shot of Neupogen to build them up and allow her to receive the next round of chemo. Neupogen helps the body make white blood cells, which prevent infection during chemotherapy. Mom always made it a goal to stay on track with her treatments. Thankfully, she only missed one, maybe two treatments throughout her experiences with chemo. At one point during the hospital's construction, the main hallway by Mom's office was blocked off, and several detours were in place. Despite her pain, she walked back and forth numerous times a day from her office to the new wing to make sure every last detail was right.

Mom really did not complain about her pain and discomfort. She saw the pain as progress, and each treatment brought her one step closer to being done and moving on. She knew she needed the lifesaving-yet-toxic drugs to kill the cancer cells that were living inside of her.

Once again she experienced the side effects of chemotherapy, including a metallic taste in her mouth. The only one she complained about was the joint pain from the Neupogen shots. It must have been pretty bad if Mom mentioned it. The chemo seemed to make her more tired the second time around. This bummed her out a bit because Mom was a woman on the go. I reminding her that she was almost twenty years older than she had been the first time around. I said she could allow herself to be tired this time because she did not have to worry about her ten-and twelve-year-old daughters. I think she found some comfort in this, but she still did not like to be slowed down.

One Saturday morning she was getting ready to go to a bridal shower, and she noticed a lot of her hair was shedding. She asked Dad to shave her head, and he did just that. I am sure Mom was bothered by this to a certain extent, but she was not vain. Hair is a big part of a woman's identity, but Mom knew she would be done with treatment in no time, and her hair would grow back. She knew the chemo was doing its job, and she was thankful she had been given the chance to fight.

Mom completed her last round of chemo at the end of January 2011, and her oncologist reported that, to the touch, the tumor had shrunk in response to the treatment. On February 12, 2011, Mom underwent a mastectomy. Just before the surgery, she was given an injection through her nipple, which, during surgery, would help the doctors detect whether there was lymph-node involvement. Ro reported that Mom cried during the procedure. It breaks my heart to think of all the pain she experienced, but she was a warrior.

Dad and Ro were at the hospital with Mom during her surgery. Mom politely asked me to stay home. She knew she was in good hands, and she was thankful Ro could be there with Dad. Mom always worried about our schedules being disrupted because of her health. We were happy to be there when we could, but Mom wanted normalcy. I anxiously waited by the phone during her surgery. Ro did a great job of keeping me in the loop by periodically sending texts.

The phone rang earlier than I expected, so I picked it up during the middle of the first ring. Ro was on the other end, and she was whispering and laughing at the same time. In that moment, I could not imagine what could possibly be so funny. Poor Dad was having trouble with his front tooth. As he bit down on some food, his front tooth came out. Dad took it in stride. It provided a good distraction, which made the time go by a little faster.

Following the surgery, the doctor reported that all had gone well, but the tumor was still present. In addition, it was not quite as small as they'd initially thought based on the physical exam. They had to wait on the pathology report regarding the lymph nodes. I cannot remember what Mom said when she came out of anesthesia, but Dad was missing his front tooth, and Mom was so witty. I am sure she had something to say about it, and they all had a good laugh.

The next course of treatment would depend on whether there was lymph-node involvement. Thirteen lymph nodes had been taken, and four of them contained cancer. The doctors determined there was enough lymph-node involvement for Mom to undergo radiation. This was a catch-22 situation. Clearly, the best possible scenario would have been no malignancy in the lymph nodes. We had mixed emotions. We wanted the journey to be over, but we were thankful radiation was an option for getting rid of the cancer once and for all.

The doctors discussed the pathology report with Mom and Dad during a follow-up visit. They noted she had advanced right-sided breast cancer. The tumor that had been removed measured 8.5 centimeters. Approximately two weeks after surgery, Mom and Dad made a special trip to our house so we could go to Missys' Boutique at the University of Kansas Cancer Center and she could be fitted for post mastectomy bras. Missys' Boutique is a specialty store for people with cancer. It has a nice variety of hats, scarves, wigs, bras, prosthetics, jewelry, shirts, bags, and so much more. It is my understanding the boutique was named after two young women who both went by the name Missy. The women lost their battles against breast cancer in their early thirties. Prior to their passing, both women asked their family members to help them live on by helping other cancer patients; thus, the boutique was formed.

Mom was excited to get fitted with a bra and find prosthetics after her surgery. She was frustrated because her surgical drains were still in place. There was too much output for them to be removed. She had them for almost four weeks. She felt so free once the drains were removed. Afterward, she had one pocket of fluid near the surgery site. She hoped it would go away, but it was stubborn. I do not recall the time frame, but Mom told me the first time she wore her new black bra from Missys', it really rubbed on the fluid-filled area and was quite uncomfortable. She felt a pop, and the fluid-filled sac disappeared.

Mom received her radiation treatments in Grand Island for six weeks, just as she had in 1994. She was shocked to see how much things had changed in seventeen years. In 1994, she spent her first appointment setting blocks. In other words, the doctors created physical barriers so the targeted area would receive radiation and the remaining parts of her body would not. In 2011, things were very different. Everything was computerized, and there were no physical blocks, only maps. Mom was somewhat uncomfortable about this, but she always trusted her doctors. Her radiation treatment went a little longer than expected because she had to miss a few treatments along the way. As expected, her skin became very burned, and she was forced to skip some treatments to allow her skin to heal.

Mom finished her treatment just in time for a road trip to Marion, Indiana. Ro was being inducted into the National Association of Intercollegiate Athletics (NAIA) Hall of Fame in recognition of her God-given talent, hard work, and success. During her time at Doane College, she was a sixteen-time All-American in track and field.

Josh, Bryson, Holden, and I left Olathe and met Mom, Dad, Scott, Ro, Anisten, and Scott's parents, Jim and Sandi Swanson in Des Moines, Iowa. We parked our vehicle in the garage at Josh's grandparent's retirement home in Des Moines. We visited with his grandparents while Scott loaded our bags and car seats into the twelve-passenger, rose-colored van that would take us to Indiana. That van was a riot. We had so much fun and made so many memories during the many miles between Des Moines and Indiana. We had not been sure how well the three kiddos, ages three, two, and one, would travel but they did great.

Rochelle and her family following the induction ceremony (2011)

On the way home from Indiana, we stopped in Chicago. We enjoyed Chicago-style pizza and swimming at the hotel. The next morning we went to the Navy Pier. Now I understand why they call Chicago the Windy City. Based on our experience, it proved to be just that. The day started out quite cold, rainy, and windy. It became quite obvious we had not dressed for the weather. We had lunch the Navy Pier and went shopping for jackets. We then took a ferry ride so we could see the historical buildings. It was an amazing tour, but unfortunately our teeth were chattering the entire time. Once we got off the ferry, we headed back toward the shopping center at Navy Pier. Thankfully, we had a good hold on the umbrella strollers because the wind gusts would pick them up off the ground. We were laughing so hard we could barely catch our breath. Mom was still wearing a wig at that time, but rather than deal with the wind, she stuffed the wig in her purse and wore a baseball hat. That was a great choice, because I am confident that wig would have drifted for miles.

On our way home from Chicago, we stopped at the Amana Colonies in Amana, Iowa. Jim and Sandi had previously toured the site, and they recommended it to us. We had a wonderful time walking around and absorbing the culture. Mom loved the old buildings. We took several pictures so she could choose her favorites and make canvas prints to hang in her office. We ate lunch at a quaint little restaurant; then we loaded up the van and headed toward Des Moines, where we would part ways.

Our road trip was a celebration in many ways. We celebrated Ro's successes, Mom being in remission, and Holden's first birthday. Life was good. We were so thankful the year was behind us, and we could continue to live life to the fullest.

# CHAPTER 9

# CHECK YOUR GENES

We had a great 2011, and we were excited to see what 2012 would bring. We were busy living life and enjoying some normalcy. Mom and Dad took advantage of every opportunity to get together so they could spoil the grandkids. Anisten had just turned three, Bryson was getting ready to turn four, and Holden was eighteen months. Rochelle was a little more than three months pregnant with Kardyn. Life seemed really good and care free. It seemed as if we had jumped over a lot of hurdles with Mom's health, but little did we know, our biggest, most challenging hurdle was within reach. Mom and Dad spent Christmas at our house. We all enjoyed a tour of the plaza lights in Kansas City.

Plaza Lights in Kansas City, Missouri (2011)

Rochelle had to work on Christmas Day 2011, so we decided to celebrate with my side of the family on New Year's Eve in Gretna. We cooked our very own prime rib that year, and I must say it turned out quite well, that is, if you like your meat cooked rare to medium rare. The meat was too pink for Dad's palate, stomach, and eyes. His typical answer to the question, "How do you want your steak cooked?" is "Well done, no pink." Dad was a good sport and took part in the feast. After supper, we pulled out the New Year's hats and noise makers, poured the drinks, and celebrated. We knew we would not be able to stay until midnight; therefore, we celebrated early.

Holden, Nana, Bryson, Papa, and Anisten
ringing in the New Year (2011)

Everything seemed perfect, and we all had a wonderful time. The theme of normalcy was always present. Mom did not want anyone to worry about her, so she kept her health concerns to herself. We later learned that she'd noticed a small red area developing around her port around New Year's Eve. She also started having problems with lymphedema. She was diligent about attending physical therapy and doing exercises at night to keep the lymphedema under control.

We saw Mom and Dad a few weeks later to celebrate Bryson's fourth birthday. I noticed compression sleeves on Mom's arms when she walked into our house. I did not say anything to her, because I figured she would talk about it when she was ready. She told me she swelling in both of her arms had been caused by the removal of her lymph nodes. She had not had a problem with lymphedema after her first time around, but unfortunately it really set in after her second bout with cancer and the lymph-node removal.

She kept a watchful eye on the red area around her port, but then decided to ask her doctor about it. She called the clinic in Omaha, and the doctor told her it was likely an infection and prescribed some antibiotics. A couple of weeks went by, and the antibiotics did not seem to be doing the trick. She followed up with her doctor, and she was prescribed another round of antibiotics. Mom had a very good gut instinct, and she had a feeling something was not right. In addition, the redness had gotten much worse. That is when she decided to make an appointment.

On February 2, 2012, Mom went to her doctor's appointment, hoping to get to the bottom of the problem and resolve the issue. Her doctor noted bilateral lymphedema and a "recent infection near her port with likely cellulitis." The doctor's note also states that Mom had been on antibiotics for some time. That note is evidence of what an amazing, strong woman Mom was. It also sheds light on the reality of situation and the difficulties she faced. Her doctor described Mom as a lovely fifty-five-year-old woman. Mom had reported that "all in all," she was doing fairly well; however, her lymphedema was causing her concern. She described significant lymphedema in her right arm including her hand and all the way up to her shoulder and also some tenderness in her axilla and posterior axillary area. What surprised me the most was reading that Mom said the infection near her port had started in mid-December and that the lymphedema was affecting her abilities to function. Mom described the infected area as quite dramatic, red, hot, and very tender. She also expressed her discontent with the compression garments. She did not like to wear them as they were unattractive and hard for her to get on and off.

Mom was instructed to follow up in three weeks so doctors could check on the status of the cellulitis surrounding her port. She also was given a prescription for physical therapy and a lymphatic pump. In addition, the doctor removed her port because of the apparent cellulitis.

Unbeknownst to my sister and me, Mom's doctor suggested she meet with a genetic counselor to get tested for the BRCA mutation. Given the fact she had bilateral breast cancers, both of which were triple negative, her doctors believed Mom had a measurable chance of having an underlying BRCA mutation. Rochelle was thirty, and I was twenty-eight; her doctors told Mom if she were a carrier, there was a chance that the gene would affect us as well. They made arrangements for Mom to have genetic testing in April 2012.

The antibiotics did not seem to make a difference, so Mom followed up with her doctor a week later. The doctor noted dramatic changes around the old port scar as well as changes to her chest wall. The doctor referred to the area as cellulitis; however, there was no drainage or infection. At that point, Mom was only seven days into her antibiotics, so the doctor recommended she finish the two-week prescription; if the redness did not subside, they'd do a biopsy of the skin to see if there were any evidence of a potential recurrence of cancer.

Mom and Dad came to Kansas City in February 2012 to attend the National Pheasants Forever and Hunting Expo. Earlier Mom and I had talked about the discolored area around her port but everything seemed to be under control. Mom's description of "a little red area" was much different than my definition. I asked if I could see the redness, and she showed it to me. It was very red with a slight purple tinge. The red area covered a lot more of her chest than I had imagined. Mom portrayed the confidence and reassurance she always did in the past. We were sitting in my living room, and she said she would go to her doctor the following Thursday for a biopsy. When I heard about the biopsy, I felt as though I'd been kicked in the stomach. In my mind, a biopsy meant only one thing: cancer. I was very concerned and scared. Mom sat in our leather chair as she told me this. Once again, I had flashbacks to the time when we were on my waterbed back in December 1993.

I had a hard time enjoying the rest of the weekend. I put on a happy face as Josh, Bryson, Holden, and I attended a birthday party for one of our friends, but I had a knot in the bottom of my stomach. I felt so sad for Mom. She had already been through so much, and it seemed unfair for her to have yet another health issue. It was obvious Mom was in pain. She took Tylenol quite often, and she tried to convince us and herself that it was helping. I felt so helpless. By the end of the weekend, she was walking almost in a hunchback position. She told me it felt a little better to shrug her shoulders forward when she was walking, as it relieved some of the burning. It was so hard to see Mom and Dad leave on Sunday. I hugged Mom and told her everything would be okay with her upcoming biopsy. I got in the car and cried the whole way home. My instincts and pessimistic nature were telling me something was very wrong.

The alarm went off on Thursday morning, and I woke up with a sick stomach. I texted Mom and asked her to call me after her appointment. She and Dad met with the doctor and were reassured there was nothing seriously wrong. In fact, the doctor said, "I'm going to prove to you one final time there is nothing wrong with you. I am 99.9 percent sure it is cellulitis." Mom and Dad left the appointment feeling good about the pending biopsy results, which she would return a week later to get.

I talked to Mom on the phone the night before they went to Gretna to receive the results of the biopsy. She told me about a good friend who was having major health issues; Mom reminded me there is always somebody worse off than we are. She felt good about the upcoming appointment but did not want to be overly confident, because it was potentially something. In these types of repeated situations, Mom learned to expect the worse and hope for the best. It was becoming increasingly difficult to stay positive before her appointments because history continued to repeat itself. We ended the conversation feeling good about the situation and the upcoming appointment.

The next morning Mom and Dad went to the doctor's office, expecting good news about the skin biopsy. Unfortunately, the results indicated an intradermal lymphatic recurrence with involvement of the skin from the chest wall. The primary cancer from her right breast had metastasized to the skin. Arrangements were made to get Mom a metastatic workup within the next two days, so her doctor could recommend a treatment plan. The doctor noted that Mom was very anxious. Mom mentioned her concerns about the pocket of fluid that was present following her mastectomy. As soon as the pocket popped—due to rubbing on her bra—she started having problems with lymphedema. Little by little, the redness started to appear, and she became increasingly uncomfortable.

I had a bad feeling something was wrong but I was trying to think positive. Waiting for the phone to ring is something I am not good at. Each minute without a call meant something was wrong. I left work around 3:20 p.m., and I still had not heard from Mom and Dad. I called my sister to see if she had heard from them. Mom had told me they would not stop at Ro and Scott's house, because they needed to get home. As I was talking to Ro, she interrupted to say Mom and Dad were at the front door. Time stood still. Mom got on the phone, and I could tell she had been crying.

She said, "I didn't get the news I was hoping for." She told me the results of the biopsy and about her appointment schedule the following day. She was concerned because she might have to go to Chicago for treatment.

I was so angry when I found out about Mom's diagnosis. I felt as if we were being treated unfairly, and I could not understand why this was happening yet again. It seemed as if Mom never got good news when she went to the doctor. How could she be diagnosed with cancer for a third time? I made some negative comments, and Mom listened politely. As soon as I was done venting, she reminded me to pray. She was not happy about the news but insisted that turning our backs on God was not an option. I was humbled in that moment. Despite Mom's fears, she focused on the positive rather than on the very negative situation at hand.

The following day, Mom underwent several tests. We had to wait a week to obtain the results of the bone scan and other tests to determine how advanced the cancer was. We prayed so hard that her organs and her bones would be clear. Thankfully, the comprehensive workup showed that the cancer was confined to the skin in her chest. It had not metastasized to her organs. Mom also heard the great news that she did not have to travel to Chicago for treatment. You have to learn to take the good with the bad. We were elated that the cancer had not spread; however, the oncologist informed Mom that she would never be cured. She would have to be on a maintenance program for the rest of her life. She was prescribed oral chemo meds; thankfully, she started seeing positive results. Her oncologist encouraged Mom by saying some of her patients had been on oral chemo medications for years and had done quite well. The side effects of the oral chemo were fatigue and thinning of hair rather than complete hair loss.

A few weeks after Mom's diagnosis, Dad had a minor health issue that required surgery and an inpatient stay. I called and checked on both of them several times a day. At one point, Mom told me she was afraid for Dad, and she would shoulder any illness for her family. Mom was so used to being the patient that it was difficult for her to be on the other side of a health issue. My parents' simultaneous health issues made me think about what I would do without one of my parents. I did not allow my mind to go there very long, because there was no point in focusing on the "what ifs." Thankfully Dad healed quickly, and life went on.

In early May, Josh, the boys, and I spent the weekend in Gretna with my family. I could tell something was on Mom's mind because she had a look in her eyes. As we were visiting in the living room, Mom got up and went out to the truck. She walked back in with a yellow manila folder and pulled out some papers. She told us that she had the results of her genetic test. I did not know what she was talking about. Mom said that given her history with breast cancer, her doctor had recommended she undergo genetic testing. On April 30, 2012, she'd learned she tested positive for the BRCA2 genetic mutation. Mom cried when she gave us the results. She apologized over and over again because there was a 50 percent chance that Rochelle and I would test positive as well. We reassured Mom by telling her there was no need to apologize or feel guilty. We acknowledged her results and I told her that if we inherited the genetic mutation from her, we would deal with it. Knowledge is power, and we were thankful to have this body of information to share with our doctors. The genetic counselor recommended Rochelle and I and Mom's brothers get tested. It was unclear whether the genetic mutation came from Grandma Nettie or from Grandpa Don Ogorzolka. Both of my grandparents had passed away, so there would be no way to determine which side it came from.

Mom and Dad were given a lot of information on what it meant to be a carrier of the BRCA2 mutation. Like many cancer genes, the BRCA gene is thought to be a tumor suppressor. Without these genes, cells grow out of control and develop tumors that can eventually lead to cancer. The information that scared them the most was the fact there was a 50 percent chance the gene had been passed to my sister and me. Statistics show women who carry the BRCA2 mutation have an increased risk of developing breast cancer, estimated to be as high as 84 percent, and a greater chance of getting ovarian cancer, thought to be as high as 27 percent by age seventy. There is also a link to pancreatic cancer and prostate cancer for men.

The recommendation for high-risk women is to undergo monthly self-exams and biannual clinical breast exams as well as annual breast mammograms and MRIs beginning at the age of twenty-five. Some women take Tamoxifen, and others opt for a prophylactic mastectomy.

To reduce the risk of ovarian cancer, it is recommended high-risk women take oral contraceptives. This method has been associated with a 60 percent reduction in ovarian cancer among high-risk women. In addition, doctors recommend removing the fallopian tubes and having a total hysterectomy.

The cost to screen the entire length of BRCA1 and BRCA2 genes is approximately $3,300 in the initial person. If she is found to be a carrier of the genetic mutation, other family members can be tested for approximately $500.

This was a very trying time in my life. It was hard to understand why Mom had been diagnosed with cancer a third time. One time was bad enough, but the repeated diagnoses were very difficult to comprehend. I harbored a lot of anger during this phase. I wanted our seemingly carefree lives back. More important, I wanted Mom to live her life without the fear of cancer, tests, doctors, and the thought that one day she may not win the fight.

Once Mom started treatment, I came back around. The fear of the unknown had interfered with my ability to think positive and remain hopeful. Initially, I was grieving for Mom. I felt as if she had been cheated out of some of the best years of her life. She had been through enough already, and it just did not seem fair. The song "Walk By Faith" by Jeremy Camp talks about having faith even when we cannot see. I did not walk by faith initially; however, I did not turn my back on God. I did not praise Him and thank Him as I should have, but I continued to pray for comfort and strength. I failed to recognize that this was all part of His master plan, and I needed to trust Him. Little did I know, God was preparing our family to walk by faith in the upcoming months.

# CHAPTER 10

# THE CALM BEFORE THE ULTIMATE STORM

The early months of 2012 brought some unwelcome news, but we were learning to come to terms with Mom's diagnosis. Dad healed well from his surgery, and Mom was getting favorable results from her oral chemo. I always enjoyed receiving calls, texts, and e-mails from Mom during the day. It was so refreshing to hear good news when I asked how she was feeling. The oral chemo seemed to be taking control, and life seemed to be getting back on track. Mom continued to follow up in Omaha, and her doctors were pleased with the results.

She and Dad planned a quick trip to Minnesota in June with some good friends. They had planned the trip for a couple of months. It was a big deal to get Dad away from the farm during the summer, so they had to make the most of their trip. In the meantime, Rochelle's C-section was scheduled for June 22, 2012. Josh, Bryson, Holden, and I stayed with Anisten while Rochelle and Scott were at the hospital. On the morning of June 22, we were heading to the zoo to pass time and to distract Anisten from being away from her parents. I called Mom to see where they were on their adventure. I was excited to hear they were just a couple of miles ahead of us on I-80. We arranged a quick meeting with them at a gas station so they could refuel and head north. Everything seemed to be well, and I told Mom how good she looked. She had on a new shirt, and it was very flattering. We greeted one another and said "see you later" in about ten minutes. They planned to stop in Omaha on their way back so they could meet the new baby, Kardyn.

On the day Rochelle and Kardyn were going to be discharged, we all met back at the hospital. Mom and Dad were exhausted from their road trip, but they seemed fine. We visited at for a short time, and then we all went our separate ways so the new family of four could adjust.

It was hard to believe the summer was half over. We kept occupied with swimming and various activities. Bryson was finishing up his first year of T-ball, and we were busy meeting ourselves coming and going. I loved Mom's spontaneity. She called me on a Friday in July to say she and Dad were kicking around the idea of coming to Olathe to watch Bryson play T-ball. It was a rare occasion to get together in the summer, so this was a really special moment. It was a very hot, dry summer, so they could not stay away from the farm for any length of time. They left Indianola before five in the morning to make the noon game. We met at the baseball field, and we soaked in the sun during the game. It was the hottest day of the year—110 degrees! We enjoyed the game but were happy when it was over so we could cool off. We spent a little time at our house, and then they headed back to Indianola so they could tend to the pivots. Little did I know, that would be the last normal get-together we had as a family.

Rochelle, Scott, and the girls spent a few days with us at the Great Wolf Lodge in Kansas City. We enjoyed the water park and evenings at the Legends. After their three-night stay, they went to Indianola to spend time at the farm. I think Rochelle gets her spontaneity from Mom.   Rochelle and Scott are always very busy traveling to spend time with family. They have a lot more confidence in their newborn babies traveling than I had in ours. Anisten was only eight days old when they drove to Olathe to spend Christmas with us in 2008. Kardyn was only three weeks old when they went to the Great Wolf Lodge and Indianola.

They spent several days at the farm. Unknown to me, Mom was having problems with redness on her chest again. She had done well until early July. She asked Rochelle to look at the red spots that were appearing on her chest and back. Dad had noticed redness on her back when he helped her with her daily exercises at home. Mom also was waking up with headaches during the night. She was on a steady diet of Tylenol to help manage the pain. She feared that the cancer in her skin was reemerging, so she called her doctor the following week. As a result of the recurrence, her oral chemo was increased.

I was unaware of the physical problems Mom was facing. I did, however, notice that we did not talk on the phone nearly as often as we used to. In the past, we'd talk at least once a day, if not more. We would also e-mail and text throughout the day. Now, she was a lot slower to respond to my e-mails, and sometimes she did not respond at all. At one point, I was a little upset with Mom. It seemed as if she did not want to talk to me. I could tell she was not fully engaged in our conversations; she would almost cut me off and end the call. I had a feeling deep down that something was not right, but I attributed it to the change in her medication. I established a game to help calm my nerves. I'd send an e-mail first thing in the morning in hopes of a quick response. If she responded fairly quickly, I knew she was having a good day.

Every time I picked up the phone, I'd hope Mom's chipper voice was on the other end, reporting that her medication was working. It got to the point where I did not ask, because I could tell things were not clearing up as she'd hoped. Until this point, Mom had done a great job concealing her feelings about her health; however, I slowly picked up on the fact something was terribly wrong.

One morning in early August 2012, I called her to see if we could get together. I really wanted to see her to reassure myself she was doing fine. In the past, Mom would have jumped at the opportunity and done anything to rearrange her schedule. Her response was "Honey, I don't think I can beat it this time."

I felt numb when I heard this and asked her to repeat what she'd said. She tried to correct herself by saying she simply did not have the energy, and she needed to focus on getting the redness cleared up. I finally asked how it was going. I could sense the fear and sadness in her voice. She said the new dose of medication had not reduced the redness. Her hair was very thin, and her lymphedema was starting to take a toll, physically and mentally. That was a turning point for me. I knew there was more to the situation than Mom was letting on; however, the fact that she admitted she was tired and "not sure she could beat it" made me scared and uneasy. I appreciated her honesty, but I was not used to her being so blunt.

My life changed following our candid conversation. I let my mind consider the thought of losing Mom. I tried to imagine our lives without her, and it was a horrifying thought. Mom was a fighter, and she had conquered the previous battles. Still, something was telling me this time was different. I have always been a bit naïve, but it was hard to ignore how bad the situation had become.

Mom had shown us how to find the positive in the negative, and now was my turn to be supportive and encouraging for her. I could tell Mom was unable to find the positive. When I tried to offer support, she did not reassure me things were going to be okay. I read between the lines: Mom was physically exhausted and emotionally drained.

A few days passed; I could not get our conversation out of my head. I continued my e-mailing game, and there were a few days when I did not hear from her. One evening, Josh and I were at home; Holden had slightly dislocated his elbow. We went to an urgent care clinic and waited our turn in line. I was feeling a whole range of emotions. I was concerned because I had not heard from Mom or Dad for a few days. My motto used to be "ignorance is bliss," but it was no longer working for me. I had been looking for an excuse to call Mom to see how she was doing. I felt bad for Holden, but I took the opportunity to let her know what we were up to. Once again she did not engage me in conversation, and she made yet another comment about her health. I do not remember what she said, but it was negative. She reiterated how tired she was and that she hated her hair because of how thin it was getting. She added that it was her turn to be negative and honest about her feelings. She had stayed home from work for the last couple of days because she did not feel well. I tried my best to cheer her up, but she was not interested. I had selfishly hoped the conversation would go well, and I could focus on Holden's elbow. Unfortunately, I felt much worse after the conversation, and this confirmed my fear that something was wrong.

Mom always said I have a nose like a bloodhound. I can sense when things were off. I refer to it as persistence.

The next day I e-mailed her at work, and I was overjoyed when she responded. She told me that Dad had driven her to work that day because she still was not feeling well. This struck me as odd. I knew Mom was resilient, so it was strange for her not to drive herself to work. I later learned she didn't drive because she was dizzy.

That evening, I told Josh about all of the things that were going on with Mom. I said, "What if the cancer went to her brain?"

I felt as if I were in the middle of a nightmare when those words came out of my mouth. I tried to convince myself that she was having side effects from the increased dosage of medication. I felt comforted that she was on chemo, so in my mind it was impossible the cancer could be attacking her brain. I wiped the tears from my eyes, said a prayer, and went to sleep.

On August 8, 2012, I received a voice-mail message from Mom at work. She sounded so good. I had not seen this side of her in months: "Hi, sweetheart, it's Mom. I thought today might be one of your late days so I was just calling to see how your day was going. Love you, and I will talk to you later." I saved her message and continued to check my voice mail.

The summer drew to an end. I gathered the boys for one final trip to the neighborhood swimming pool. We had such a fun time. On one hand, it was sad to see the summer come to an end, but on the other hand, I was anxious to get Mom back on track and living again.

I was very excited when my phone rang, and it was Mom on the other end. I was getting the boys out of the pool and dressed so we could go home for supper. I could tell my parents were in the pickup and had me on speaker. Dad did most of the talking, but Mom chimed in too. I told them we were at the pool and were getting ready to go home. They said Dad had just picked up Mom from work, and they too were going home. I was a little confused because I'd thought Dad taking Mom to work was a one-time thing, but I was thankful to finally hear from them.

We talked about the weather and how hot it was. Mom said, in a very slow, long, drawn-out voice, "Well, it has to rain sometime."

I agreed and said it would rain when God decides it is time. Mom said that she'd had a really good day. In fact, she said it was one of her better days in a very long time. I felt pretty good about the call but was a little bothered by Mom's slow speech. We talked for a few more minutes, and we ended the call by confirming we would see each other that weekend, August 21, 2012, for Kardyn's baptism.

Rather than going to Gretna on Friday, Mom and Dad decided to wait until Saturday morning to leave. Dad wanted to turn the pivots off before they left home. I spoke with Rochelle that evening, and she told me Mom and Dad would stay at a hotel rather than their house. This was hard for me to understand. Mom and Dad *always* stayed at our houses.

That Saturday, we expected Mom and Dad to arrive in Gretna at a decent time. It was going to be a quick weekend, so we wanted to get in as much visiting as possible. The morning turned into early afternoon, and we had not heard from them. Rochelle called, and they were just outside of Lincoln. They said they'd stopped in Arapahoe, and they were there longer than they expected.

When they finally arrived, Mom seemed a little out of sorts. She told us that she had an incident that morning when she got out of the truck. Her legs felt like they stopped working, and she fell into our family friend, Doug. This concerned me greatly, but once again I attributed it to the increase in her medications. Rochelle, the ortho-neuro nurse, had seen this type of symptom quite frequently, so clearly she expressed great concern. Mom looked tired, and she just did not seem like herself. The rest of the day went on as well as it could, but there was definitely a gray cloud looming over our heads.

The next morning we attended church and the baptism followed. We met Mom and Dad at the church. Tears built up in my eyes when they walked in and found a seat. Mom seemed to be clinging onto Dad. I prayed so hard that Mom would bounce out of whatever was going on, but I could not help notice her downward spiral.

I had a really hard time when it was time to start packing up. All of the signs were there, but I refused to believe there was something wrong. I tried to think positively, but it is difficult to ignore your gut instincts. I held back the tears most of the way home. I told Josh that I had a bad feeling something was wrong. I couldn't grasp the magnitude of the situation, but I knew it was not normal for her legs to quit working. Mom had a difficult time going up and down the stairs at Ro and Scott's house. I followed her up and down the stairs both times and noticed how winded she was. In addition, her appetite was not very good. She felt very nauseous after attempting to eat an English muffin at the hotel.

Les and Nancy Schmidt, Scott, Anisten, Rochelle, and Kardyn Swanson, and Jim and Sandi Swanson following Kardyn's Baptism (2012)

It is obvious that she did not feel well. She was tired and worn out. It was hard to see how quickly Mom went downhill between that hot day in July at the T-ball game and Kardyn's baptism a month later. Bryson took a close-up picture of Mom and Dad. I tried to hold back the tears as he was taking it because I was thinking, *I want to get as many pictures of Mom and Dad as we can because we may not be presented with many more opportunities.* These thoughts were coming more frequently and I was entering the territory of "not if but when" and imagining life without Mom. It seemed impossible and real at the same time.

I did not want the boys to see me upset, so I took an extra-long shower so I could cry as long as I needed to. The thought of Mom being sick really bothered me, and it consumed a lot of my day. I was not very focused at work or at home. I wanted things to be normal and for Mom to say that she'd bounced back and was doing well. Unfortunately, I never received that reassurance from her. I checked in on her on daily, but most of my messages were unreturned.

I knew that whatever was going on was in God's hands, and we had to trust Him. I did not like the way the things were going and wanted to change the story, but I realized it was not my story to write. I trusted God to see us through, even though the situation was far from the ideal. I reminded myself, *the situation is what it is*. I was sickened by the thought of Mom being ill again, but I also knew I could not control what was going to happen. It was difficult to let go, but it was a waste of energy and emotion to fixate on things that could not be changed. We had to stick together and be strong for Mom. It was time for her to retire her cheerleading outfit and pom-poms. We needed to step up and encourage her through whatever challenges she was facing and had yet to face. During this trying time, never once was I angry at God. I leaned on Him even more to help guide us through the storm. I accepted God's will and tried to find peace.

I grew very familiar with the song, "Help Me Find It" by Sidewalk Prophets. Every word of the song spoke to me during our time of despair. The song asks God to help us accept His will and to have faith that He will see us through any difficult situation. As a type A personality, I wanted desperately to take control, but I was at peace when I finally let go. The following lyrics from the song spoke loud and clear to me:

> I lift my empty hands (come fill me up again).
> Have your way, my King (I give my all to you).
> I lift my eyes again (was blind but now I see).
> 'Cause you are all I need.

## CHAPTER 11

# TERMINAL DIAGNOSIS

After Kardyn's baptism weekend, I felt more sad and worried than I had before. Mom did not respond to some of my early morning e-mails, so my worry radar was on high alert. I called her in the evening and asked if she'd had any more spells with her weak legs, like she had the weekend before. Mom assured me she had not, but she had stayed home because she was not feeling well. She said she needed to catch up on her sleep and shake whatever she had.

I was excited when Mom responded to my early morning e-mail on Wednesday, August 29, 2012. She was having a good day and reminded me she had physical therapy later on in the morning. My stomach knots were a little better after receiving that e-mail. Little did I know that would be the last one I ever receive from my mom.

On August 31, I walked back into my office as my cell phone was buzzing. I quickly grabbed it and saw it was Dad. I felt all of the emotions possible in the split second before I answered the phone. I wondered why Dad was calling me during the workday. I grabbed my phone and shut my door. He was calm but informed me they were on their way to Omaha. My knees began to wobble, and my hands were shaking. I tried to control the tremble in my voice, but I was truly afraid. Dad said Mom was pretty dizzy, and her neck was very swollen. Her doctor recommended they travel to Omaha so Mom could be seen. They were trying to get there as quickly as they could, knowing the Labor Day weekend meant time off for the doctors and select staff.

As we learned later, they decided to call the doctor after Mom barely made it to the field to pick up Dad. She had been resting in the chair at home, and Dad was in the field. He said he would call and let her know when he was ready. Mom fell asleep, and when she woke up to the phone ringing, she was a bit frantic, knowing she had overslept. She stumbled her way through the kitchen and out the door. She got in the truck, backed out, and headed north to Frontier County to meet Dad. She was dizzy and could hardly see when she was driving. By the grace of God, Mom made it to the field safely. At that moment, they decided it was time to call her doctor. The dizziness and headaches had gotten out of control, and it was time to figure out what was going on.

Dad and Mom stopped in Gretna to pick up Rochelle so she could go to the appointment with them. When they got to the hospital, they were told no one there could access her port to give her the contrast she needed before she had an MRI. They had to make an appointment, hopefully on Tuesday because Monday was a holiday. Rochelle is a very good nurse and a great advocate for her patients. This time the patient was Mom, and there was no stopping Ro's fierce drive to look out for her number-one patient. The hospital found somebody who could access Mom's port, and off to the MRI she went.

I felt hopeful and anxious as I sat around waiting for the report from Omaha. I needed a distraction, so I called my in-laws and invited myself and the boys over. Josh was not able to get of work until ten thirty at night, so it would be a while until he got home. As we were eating at Bob and Linda's house, Josh let me know he was leaving work early. I had called him earlier in the day to let him know Mom was on her way to Omaha. Josh and Scott are both very supportive and are always there for my sister and me.

My phone rang again; it was Rochelle. She was crying on the other end of the line. She told me she was scared and had a really bad feeling that the cancer had spread to Mom's brain. I was scared too, but I refused to believe this. In Rochelle's line of work she sees brain tumors often and she knows the signs and symptoms. Given Mom's history with breast cancer, she knew there was a strong possibility she was correct. Rochelle told me that

Mom could not walk without assistance when they got to the house. She was very weak and dizzy. She had to hold onto Dad and needed to use the couch and walls to brace herself. We talked a few more minutes and ended the call. Rochelle promised to call again as soon as she knew something.

We finished eating dinner and headed home. I had the boys in my car, and I prayed and cried the whole way home. My instincts told me Mom had a very serious problem, and maybe this time she could not beat it. We got home and put the boys to bed. Josh and I were in our room talking about the day. I told him about the call from Dad and the call from Rochelle. As we were talking, my phone rang, and it was Rochelle. I took the call and went to the extra bedroom. I closed the door and nervously awaited the news.

Rochelle calmly said, "There are spots on her brain."

Time stood still. "What?" I asked in disbelief.

Rochelle said Mom wanted to talk to me. I did my best to keep calm, but I was crumbling. Mom told me that wasn't the news she expected. I felt like I was experiencing déjà vu. This call was strikingly similar to the one I'd received from Mom in March 2012, when she had reported that the skin biopsy was malignant. I am sure Mom was terrified, but she calmly explained that was why she'd been feeling the way she did. There was a sense of relief in her voice, now she finally had an answer. I think she was still in shock as she had just finished talking to one of the residents.

Rochelle got back on the phone and said that the resident had called to talk to Mom. She handed the phone to Mom, and the doctor reported there were small spots scattered throughout her brain, but the majority were concentrated on her cerebellum, which is responsible for balance and controlling movement. This explained why Mom was having a terrible time with balance and walking. The staff helped Mom get an appointment with Dr. Reed on Tuesday, September 2, 2012. We knew that would be a very important appointment, and I wanted to be there for Mom and my family.

After I talked to Mom and Rochelle, I went back to the bedroom to let Josh know. I will never forget the conversation. In a very matter of fact way, I told him that Mom had spots on her brain. I was numb and in shock, so I could not comprehend what I was saying. Miracles happen all the time, so I did not accept that this was a terminal diagnosis. Josh and I agreed to get some rest, as it was close to eleven thirty, and we would head to Gretna on Saturday morning.

That trip was the longest, most dreaded trip we have ever made. Usually, we drove with excitement, knowing the weekend would be packed with fun and adventure. This trip was going to be somber and filled with sadness. When we arrived, everybody was in the basement. We did our best to act happy when we got there. Surprisingly things were calmer than I'd anticipated, but there was definitely a large gray cloud hanging over us.

Mom wanted to stand up, so Rochelle helped her with the walker. They walked to the other end of the basement and looked at a quilt. Scott's eyes filled up with tears, and he gave me more specific details about Friday evening. Mom was unable to walk, and she spent a lot of time hanging over the back of the couch, trying to get reoriented. They decided a walker would help with her mobility, so Saturday morning they'd purchased one from Gretna Drug.

Scott said they all had been crying when they got back to the house on Friday night. He said that Mom told him, "This is not going to end well." That was another defining moment for me; it confirmed that Mom essentially doubted she could beat it this time.

Scott and Josh took the kids upstairs, and we had a private family meeting in the basement. Mom, Rochelle, and I sat on the end of the bed, and Dad knelt on the floor in front of the walker. We all lost it. We shed several tears as we grasped the reality of the situation. Mom kept looking at Dad and said, "I just wanted to live to be seventy years old." At that moment, I experienced true sadness for the first time. Don't get me wrong; I had been sad in the past, but this situation took it to a level I never knew existed. We were still holding onto hope and praying for a miracle, but I think we all knew we were coming to the end of the road. I'd never imagined life could go on without Mom. I did not know what I would do without her. She was our pillar, our rock, and to see her cry tore me up inside.

The timing of small things matters. We were at the depth of our sadness, when all of a sudden, we felt the bed teeter-tottering. Rochelle, Mom, and I made the front of the bed come off the floor, and it made us laugh a little. We hugged and cried a little more and agreed we would face this head on. We did not want to jump to conclusions before we met with

Dr. Reed on Tuesday. We agreed to try to enjoy the weekend as much as we could given the circumstances.

Jim and Sandi Swanson, drove to Gretna, and we spent Sunday afternoon visiting, eating, and reminiscing. Mom seemed to enjoy the weekend. She was glad to see all her grandkids, and the noise of the children playing and laughing was music to her ears and medicine for her soul. We would try to quiet the kids, but Mom insisted on letting them be kids, once again emphasizing the importance of normalcy.

During the weekend, we watched the video of Rochelle and Scott's wedding. They would celebrate their seventh anniversary on September 3, the day after Mom's appointment. There was not a dry eye in the room, except for Mom's, when the portion of the video showed her dancing with Dad at the reception. It was hard to imagine that seven years earlier, life had been normal. We never expected to be sitting around the TV, watching how good life used to be and wishing we had those moments back. Life is put into perspective when sadness and tragedy strike. All of the little things seemed meaningless when we were faced with the reality of Mom's health.

We spent some time talking about plans for Mom and Dad. Rochelle and Scott graciously opened their house up to them so Mom could be close to her doctors. Mom felt more comfortable in Gretna, but she did not want to be a burden to Rochelle, Scott, and their girls. It was also the end of the farming season, and harvest was right around the corner. Mom was conflicted because she knew they need to be at the farm, but Dad needed help to care for her. After some discussion, Mom and Dad accepted Rochelle and Scott's invitation. What a blessing that was. It was comforting to know Mom and Dad always had somebody around to help. It was also nice to know they were only a little over three hours away from Josh and me, rather than seven. Mom and Dad were thankful and appreciative.

We were encouraged on Sunday when Mom suggested we get out of the house. She was not one to sit around, so she was ready to get outside. We drove to Lake Mahoney, the same place we'd gone camping in October 2010, when Mom got her port. We drove through the wildlife safari so the kids could see all of the animals. Mom enjoyed getting out, but the motion and bumps made her dizzy. She was a trooper, but she was glad to be back home, sitting still. When we got home, we enjoyed delicious lasagna, courtesy of Chef Scott. The kids enjoyed the outing, and it was a nice way to distract us from the upcoming appointment with Dr. Reed on Tuesday. Mom joined us at the table and ate really well. She was on steroids, so the doctors had warned us she would eat more than normal.

Josh, Bryson, Anisten, Holden, and I stayed at the Holiday Inn Express. Mom and Dad were in the extra bedroom in the basement, and we decided it would be nice to have a little more space. The kids were excited to stay at a hotel. They remembered the trip to Chicago and all of the fun hotels we stayed in. I was dreading the trip to Dr. Reed's on Tuesday. We knew we had to go, but it was nice to live in denial for a short time because we knew the appointment on Tuesday would likely change our lives forever. I tried my best to soak in all of the time I could with Mom and to stay as positive as I could.

I did not sleep well on Monday night. I tossed and turned and had an upset stomach. I prayed, asking God to give Mom at least one year. I finally fell asleep around two in the morning, and the alarm went off at six thirty. The kids and I went to the dining area for breakfast. I could not eat, due to my nerves, but the kids enjoyed gooey cinnamon rolls and all the other great breakfast items. We checked out of the hotel, loaded up the kids and headed back to Rochelle and Scott's house.

Scott and Josh stayed with the kids at the house, and the rest of us piled into the truck and headed for Omaha. The ride was very quiet. I tried to fill the quietness with a comment on how good Dad's driving was. He used to despise city driving but had become well acquainted with the city thanks to all of the trips to and from the University of Nebraska Medical Center throughout the years. We made small talk during the car ride to the dreaded appointment.

As we pulled up to the medical center, I had another déjà vu moment. The campus had changed quite a bit since the last time I was there in 1994. The feelings I'd had then came rushing back, except this time I knew what we were walking into. In 1994, I had been eleven, and Rochelle was thirteen. Memories I thought had vanished came rushing back. I stood there for a moment, trying to comprehend what was going on. We found a wheelchair for Mom, and valet parking took care of our truck.

Rochelle did not miss a beat. She got behind the wheelchair and navigated our way through the large medical center. I am usually a fast walker, but I could not seem to keep up. I was trailing behind, trying to get the tears out of my eyes. It was a sad scene. Obviously, there were a lot of sick people—adults, children, and every walk of life. Cancer does not discriminate. I had tunnel vision, focusing on Mom in the wheelchair in front of me. For a split second, I had a flashback of walking though the airport, trying to find our gate so we would not miss our flight. I snapped out of it, remembering we were in the cancer center looking for Dr. Reed's office so we could hear Mom's fate.

We checked in and had a hard time to find a place to sit. It was a fairly large waiting room, and it was filled with people with cancer and supportive family members. I had so much anxiety that I excused myself and went to the restroom. I received a text from my good friend Lucy. She told me she was praying for our family. I thanked her and said we needed a miracle.

Mom's name was called, and we walked down the long hallway. It was the longest walk of my life. We were put in one of the rooms at the very end of the hallway. The nurse took a brief history, and we waited for Dr. Reed. Mom was calm and explained that her skin seemed to be getting a little better. Dr. Reed knew we were hopeful, but I could tell by the look in her eyes that she had news she did not want to deliver.

The doctor noted Mom's neck was not very swollen, but her rash was more extensive. She described the newly formed rashes as purplish and thickened and the older rashes as pale and not as thick. New rashes were forming on her upper right abdomen and midback.

She'd had a chance to review the final radiology report, and it was not good. The official diagnosis was brain and leptomeningeal metastatic breast cancer, triple negative. She explained in layman's terms that several spots were scattered throughout Mom's brain; the cancer also had made its way into the sac that protects the brain. That sac is constantly being washed by spinal fluid, which runs from the brain, through the spinal cord, and back to the brain. In Mom's case, the cancer cells would eventually make their way to her spinal cord and ultimately take over her body.

"Nancy," Dr. Reed said, "from the beginning the tumor was a bad actor."

We asked about the treatment options, and she said this could not be cured. We had an option to put a port in her head and run chemo through her brain. But when she was asked what the success rate was, Dr. Reed said 0 percent among her patients. Mom said she wanted "quality of life"; therefore we declined the treatment. The doctor also noted that the disease in Mom's chest wall did not seem to be responding to chemotherapy, and she did not believe Mom would benefit from chemo to treat her new diagnosis, leptomeningeal metastatic breast cancer.

This led us to the next question: what was the prognosis? I dreaded to hear what she would say. I had prayed so hard for one year, and I hoped we could have at least one more year with Mom. Dr. Reed estimated Mom had a year to live. We discussed comfort-care options and hospice, and Dr. Reed wrote a letter of disability. Once again, life is a matter of perspective. I was so excited to hear Mom had one year. I was sad but I felt a sense of calmness. I felt as if my prayer from the night before had been answered.

Dr. Reed referred us to the Radiology Oncology Department to discuss treatment to minimize the symptoms. We left her office and headed to the cafeteria first, stopping in the restroom on the way. Mom and Rochelle went in, and Dad and I were in the hall. We shed some tears. Dad was crumbling, but he was being brave for our family.

"We have to be strong for Mom," he said. "It's all going to be okay." People passed by us in the hall as we were crying.

We went to the cafeteria, and Mom chose broccoli cheese soup; the rest of us had a salad. Then we moved to the waiting room in Radiology Oncology, and Mom told us to find the business card for the genetic counselor in her purse. She insisted Rochelle and I meet with her genetic counselor and get tested for BRCA2. Despite her grim situation, Mom was looking out for Rochelle and me. Mom and Dad remained in the waiting room, and Rochelle and I went to the genetic counselor to get tested. All of our questions we answered, and then the nurse drew our blood. We were told we would get the results within a couple of weeks.

We went back to the medical center to meet up with Mom and Dad. We met them in the lobby. Mom was sitting in her wheelchair, holding a large plastic mask. She was fitted for a mask for her face and head, so she could start full brain radiation the following day. She was scheduled to have a total of thirteen treatments. The radiology oncologist confirmed the diagnosis and agreed with the prognosis of one year; however, he was brutally honest, indicating that he did not expect her to live for one year.

The goal of the radiation was to minimize her dizziness and headaches. It was, he said, simply treatment as opposed to a cure. Mom was so brave.

We decided it was time to head home so we could be ready for work on Wednesday. It was so incredibly hard to get in the car and head for home. I wanted to be with my family, but I knew Josh and I needed to get back to Kansas. My boss is amazing. I called him as we were leaving to report the sad news. He did not hesitate and told me to do whatever I needed to do. He was very caring and understanding about our situation, and I will be forever grateful.

Rochelle, Mom, and Dad trekked back through the facility to their truck. They went back to Gretna and spent the night so Mom could be ready for her first radiation appointment the following day.

# CHAPTER 12

# PALLIATIVE CARE

It was hard to be in Kansas City, away from my mom, my dad, and my sister. I wanted to be there for them and with them while Mom went through her first full round of brain radiation. I worked Wednesday, Thursday, and Friday, and as soon as I got off work, we headed to Omaha for the weekend.

Once again God's timing was perfect, and He delivered yet again. Josh and I had worked flex hours to minimize daycare costs. When Bryson was born, I worked Monday through Friday from 5:00 a.m. to 1:00 p.m. Josh worked Monday through Friday from 2:00 p.m. to 10:30 p.m. We were like ships passing in the night. Our daily ten-minute conversation focused on Bryson's feeding schedule and sleeping schedule. We never saw each other, but we valued our one-on-one time with Bryson. We continued to work opposite hours after we were blessed with Holden in May 2010. We were so thankful to spend quality time with the boys. We worked those hours for approximately four years.

A position became available at Josh's work in a different department, which would allow more family time. The hours would be Monday through Thursday from 9:30 a.m. to 8:00 p.m. with Fridays off. We were very excited for this opportunity because the odd hours we had been working were starting to take a toll. We felt more like roommates rather than a married couple. If Josh got the position, I would be able to work 7:00 a.m. until 3:00 p.m., and we would get to spend more time together as a couple.

It also meant I would not have to go to bed at 8:00 p.m. so I could get up at 4:00 a.m. Josh applied for the position late spring 2012, but unfortunately there was a hiring freeze, and his application was put on hold.

Finally, Josh was offered the new position—the same week Mom was terminally diagnosed. Our prayers had been answered, and Mom was thrilled when we told her. We were so excited, and of course he accepted the position. Since he no longer had to work on Fridays, we now could travel to and from Omaha to see Mom as a family. That made life a whole lot easier. We could leave home a lot earlier on Friday afternoons, and we no longer had to be separated from one another. Having Josh at home with me during the evenings also helped because he provided emotional support during Mom's illness. How awesome it was to watch God's perfect timing play out right in front of our very own eyes! His timing is always perfect.

We were all so grateful for Rochelle and Scott's generosity; they had opened their home to Mom and Dad and my family as well. Dad is a very capable man, but I am not sure he could have cared for Mom by himself at their home in Indianola, given her rapid decline in health. There is no doubt in my mind that our neighbors, family, and friends would have helped, but there was something very special about spending as much time as possible as a family during Mom's final days. Mom was at ease, knowing her doctors were minutes away; however, she expressed concern about leaving bad memories in the home. Rochelle and Scott were not worried about bad memories. They were just happy that Mom was comfortable enough to spend her final days in their house so we could all be together.

Not surprisingly, my boss accommodated our situation very well. He told me to do what I had to and spend as much time with Mom as possible. I worked Monday through Wednesday, and after I got off work on Wednesday, I'd drive to Gretna. At times, Josh took off from work and went with me, and at other times, I took the boys, and Josh came up on the weekends. We stayed until Sunday afternoon and then head back home so we could be back to work on Monday. Rochelle's coworkers and boss accommodated her schedule as well. They switched her days so she could spend time with Mom.

Fall was Mom's favorite time of the year. She loved winter and Christmas, but fall was her favorite. When she was terminally diagnosed, she mentioned that because it was around the holidays, we would always associate the holidays with her diagnosis. Typical Mom, thinking of others rather than herself. We reassured her that would not be the case.

Mom was concerned about the farm and the upcoming harvest. It was clear there was no way she could drive the combine, and Dad was not going to leave Mom's side. God blessed us with the most amazing neighbors. Once again, the farmers stepped in and took care of the farm, providing time and equipment. We periodically received text messages with pictures, and they were breathtaking. Multiple combines, tractors, grain carts, semis, and other equipment were in the fields, ensuring the crops got out before winter set in. Our family will be forever grateful to those who lifted the burden of harvest from our shoulders, so we could spend time with Mom. These generous people put their own farms and livelihood aside so they could help our family.

It is definitely a lot easier to help than to be helped, but we were overwhelmed by the acts of kindness toward our family. That was the first time in thirty-five years Dad did not participate in corn harvest. It was hard for him, but he knew the farm in the hands of some of the most talented, caring farmers around. He was so thankful to be blessed to spend every second of the day with Mom, knowing her time on earth was limited. It was sad to think that just a year prior, Mom had been running the combine, and life was "normal"; then to fast-forward a year and see Mom in the position she was in. It still brings tears to my eyes to think about how quickly life can change and how often we take life for granted.

We got into a routine rather quickly. Mom and Dad's belongings were set up in their space in Rochelle and Scott's basement. The large, walkout basement—with its king-size bed, full bathroom, and sitting area—was the perfect setup for Mom and Dad. They had their own space, but they also had the convenience of around-the-clock help from Rochelle and Scott. Mom's radiation appointments were scheduled for midafternoon, so the goal each day was to get her up in the morning and move to the main floor. Mom had to tackle the stairs each day. One person would walk in front of her to help guide her up the stairs, and another person would stand behind her in case she lost her balance.

Each day became more of a struggle than the day before. She got tired quickly and she had a hard time breathing. The lymphedema became more intense, which compromised her breathing. Once we got her upstairs, we positioned her in the recliner in the living room so she could catch her breath and gain enough energy to eat breakfast. We made her a small bowl of oatmeal and a cup of hot tea for breakfast. Occasionally, she requested fried eggs with toast and jelly. It took her quite a bit of time to eat because she was pretty weak. Her eye-to-hand coordination was affected because of the cancer attacking her brain. Typically, she took a short nap after breakfast, and then we would bathe her.

I am so thankful Rochelle is a nurse. Things were definitely calmer when Rochelle and Dad were helping Mom. The situation was a bit chaotic when it was Dad and me. Dad did fine, but I added nervous energy to the situation. I freeze under pressure, and my mind turns to mush. I am happy to gather the supplies, make meals, and various other tasks, but I do not have it in me to be the primary caregiver. I do not have the God-given talent caregivers have.

There were times I failed to gather the supplies. The first time I helped Dad with the morning routine, he told me to make some breakfast for Mom. I was more than happy to help and thought there was no way I could mess up instant oatmeal. I scrambled around in the kitchen and threw open every cupboard, looking for the box of oatmeal. I couldn't find it anywhere! I yelled for Dad and he directed me to it. I remember thinking that I was pathetic because I could not do something so simple, but after the first couple of days I became more comfortable and confident with my limited role as a caregiver. Mom appreciated our efforts, and I am sure she was entertained to see us run around like chickens with our heads cut off. She always remained calm during the hectic situations. It seemed as if she did not have a care in the world.

I was nervous about the schedule for Mom's pain medications, given the fact she had so many. We still get a good laugh when we talk about our system for keeping Mom on schedule. It was very overwhelming to determine when to give which medication, and the schedules and medicines were always changing in response to Mom's needs. Dad developed a system, and it worked quite well most of the time. He came up with his own names for each medication so we'd know what each prescription was for. He wrote the made-up names on the bottles with a black sharpie. I cannot remember all of the medications that were prescribed, but I can vividly see "Mec," "Dec," and "Itch" in Dad's handwriting written on the bottles.

You had to be there to appreciate the humor, but we laughed. Dad did a phenomenal job of managing Mom's pain and her schedule. He faithfully wrote down the times medications were given. We joked that he should have been a pharmacist.

One evening we were upstairs; Rochelle gave Mom her blood-pressure medication after supper. We headed back downstairs to settle Mom in for the evening. She wanted to sit in the recliner and watch TV before bed. I was sitting on one of the sofas and talking to Mom. Dad was at the table, laying out the pills for the evening and night. He gave her some of her bedtime medications. Mom never questioned what she was taking. A few minutes later Rochelle joined us downstairs, and she and Dad had a conversation about Mom's meds. I could tell something was wrong but I wasn't sure what. All I could see was Rochelle laughing and Dad stressing out. He paced back and forth and rubbed his forehead. I tried to maintain a normal expression and continue the conversation with Mom. Rochelle signaled to me that we accidentally doubled Mom's blood-pressure medicine.

Later on, Rochelle warned us to be careful if Mom wanted to get up from bed during the night. Because we'd increased her blood-pressure medication, her blood pressure was likely to be very low, making her feel light headed and even more unstable on her feet. Thankfully, the night went well, and Mom did not have any issues. Once again, you had to be there to fully appreciate the situation, but it was funny.

A few days later we told Mom what had happened, and her response was "Oh, well." She grinned and shrugged her shoulders. "What's the worst that can happen?" she asked. Mom had a great sense of humor, and she never lost it during her illness.

We had a lot of laughs, despite the rough situation. We also had a lot of tears, but I definitely remember laughing hard at nothing. Mom joined in during our outbursts of laughter. We did our best to make the most out of what little time we had. We never really slept very well, so I am sure a lot of the laughter was a result of sleep deprivation. We never lost hope for a miracle, but knew science was saying she would not survive.

My anthem during this trying time was "One Thing Remains" by Kristian Stanfill. I downloaded it on my iPod and put it on repeat. I listened to it most of the way to Omaha and back as well as at my desk at work. I felt an overwhelming sense of comfort when listening to "One Thing Remains." The song was a constant reminder that God's love is always present and unending, no matter what situations we face.

I still hold this song very close to my heart. I continue to listen to it; last time I checked, iTunes showed I had listened to the song more than three hundred times! I know it is borderline obsessive, but I feel a strong connection with Mom when I listen to it, so I will continue to do so, especially on the days I really miss her.

Mom went downhill fast. When we first learned she had a year to live, I was naïve, thinking we would have nine to ten months to go on vacation and live a normal life, and then the last couple of months would be a struggle. Unfortunately, that was not the case. Each day, she became increasingly weaker. Physically, she was completely dependent on us to care for her. Mentally, she was sharp, and she could converse, but she had no fight left. She knew where this was going, and she felt defeated.

At one point she told us, "I knew cancer would hurt, but I didn't know it could hurt this bad."

Mom also lost her ability to make a decision. We would give her choices, and her response more times than not was "I don't know. What do you guys think?" Mom had been a decision maker who stuck to her guns. It was sad to see her lose the functions we all take for granted.

I would receive regular updates from Rochelle and Dad every Monday, Tuesday, and Wednesday morning, letting me know how Mom's night was and how she was getting along. She was absolutely miserable. Her skin was so red, almost purple, and like the texture of leather. Mom described the pain as an overwhelming stinging, burning, and itching. We put a special lotion on her, and as long as we were applying it, her skin was somewhat soothed. The lotion had menthol in it and, honestly, I hope to never smell menthol again. It brings back terrible memories.

On September 11, 2012, Mom had an appointment to discuss her skin condition. Her right arm was causing her severe discomfort. She'd tried numerous lotions and ointments for the itching, but nothing seemed to work. By this time, she had an extensive rash over her entire right arm, and it was more intense in the axilla and medial arm. The rash on her back and stomach were also getting worse. Mom was given a prescription for pain and a sleep aid.

Rochelle quickly recognized the decline in Mom's health, so she recommended getting palliative care, the step before hospice. The goal of palliative care is to relieve pain without treating the underlying cause of the pain. That was very difficult to hear and accept, but we all wanted the best quality of life for Mom. The pain medications were not working as effectively as they had been, and we wanted nothing but the best for her.

To get Mom started with palliative care, Rochelle contacted the Visiting Nurse Association (VNA). The VNA immediately gave Mom pain patches and additional medicine to help control the pain. That seemed to work pretty well for the first couple of weeks. We had a brief meeting with the VNA, and the nurses briefly touched on the dying process. Most of the time, they told us, the patient will get a burst of energy in the days leading up to his or her death. It was hard to imagine how somebody so close to death could get a burst of energy. They are the experts, and they have seen it time and time again, so I had complete trust in what they were saying.

Mom got stuck in her routine, and she wanted to go to bed at seven thirty every night. Before her illness, she liked to plan, but she was very good at doing things at the spur of the moment. Dad was such a trooper. He was not ready for bed at seven thirty, but he did not want Mom to be alone. The good thing about going to bed at such an early time was they had a lot of time to visit. Mom and Dad talked about several things. One thing Mom was worried about was Dad being alone on the farm. She did not want Dad to be alone for the rest of his life.

One evening, Dad asked, "Honey, when you get to heaven, can you please give us signs so we know you are okay?"

Mom's responded, "I will give you guys signs if God allows me."

CHAPTER 13

# NUMEROUS, MORE THAN FIFTY

Monday, September 24, 2012, is a day I will never forget. It was a very emotional day for many reasons, but mainly because I received two faxes within minutes of each another that contained information on Mom's situation and the results of my genetic testing. I trembled as the faxes came in, one right after the other. I have a direct fax line at work, and most of my faxes come from area codes 816 and 913, which are in the Kansas City area. The two faxes I received on September 24, were both from area code 402. I felt as if I had been punched in the gut, kicked in the shins, and slapped in the face, among a whole host of other feelings. My stomach was in a knot because I knew the faxes contained personal health information from the University of Nebraska Medical Center. I dreaded looking at the documents because I had a strong feeling the information was not going to be good.

I'd been handling the paperwork for a cancer policy Mom and Dad purchased. In July 1992, a sleazy salesman showed up at our door in the-middle-of-nowhere Nebraska, trying to sell a cancer policy to my young parents. The man was abrupt and rude. Mom and Dad did not buy his sales pitch, and Dad eventually kicked him out of our house after he looked at Mom, put his finger in her face, and said, "You are going to die of cancer." A few days later, a nice, clean-cut salesman showed up at the door, wanting to sell Mom and Dad a cancer policy. This man was from a different company and was professional. Mom and Dad decided to listen and ultimately purchased a policy. It is one of those policies that you never want to have to use, but you are glad it is there should you need it.

Dad said that the insurance company kept denying Mom's claims. She was too tired and unwell to deal with the insurance company. I finally felt like I was doing my part because I was able to help process the claims. I am a paralegal at a law firm that typically defends lawsuits, but in the situation with Mom, we were on the other side. It was awesome to see how God paved the path and led us to our careers so we could help out in a meaningful way during Mom's illness. Rochelle is a nurse and helped with caretaking, talking to doctors, and understanding the medical jargon. She also had access to awesome social workers who could provide support and advice. I helped file claims and did what was needed to make sure the insurance company did not deny claims that had been submitted correctly. It was helpful to have access to my boss, who is an attorney, when the insurance company denied claims that never should have been denied. After a lot of phone calls, faxes, and resubmissions, the insurance company eventually processed the claims as it should have in the beginning.

The insurance company required copies of the pathology reports and the diagnostic test results. Rochelle and Dad contacted Mom's providers to request this information.

The first stomach-turning fax I received was the dictated report of the MRI of Mom's brain on August 31. Until I read the report, I'd had a lingering hope that Mom would win the battle once again. I know it was wishful thinking, but I never wanted to give up hope or the possibility of a miracle. It was an uphill battle, but Mom was a fighter, and she had won prior battles. Every ounce of hope was crushed when I looked at the fax.

I went straight to the findings and saw "numerous, more than 50"; at that point, I quit reading the report. I did not need to see the details, because I knew the report contained nothing positive. I was crushed and heartbroken. At that moment, barring a miracle, I knew there was no hope: Mom was going to die.

Within minutes, I received the second fax. Before I could read it, my office phone rang, and surprise, it was from a 402 area code. The genetic counselor was calling to let me know that I'd tested positive for the BRCA2 genetic mutation. I honestly was not surprised, but it was too much information at once. I could still see the words "numerous, more than 50." I was not devastated by the news that I'd tested positive, because we had a much bigger problem at hand. During our genetic-counseling session, Rochelle and I were told we each had a 50 percent chance of carrying the mutated gene. My intuition told me I would test positive. Still, I was more focused on Mom and how I would deliver the news about the MRI and the genetic testing to my family.

Shortly after I got off the phone, Rochelle called. She was excited and wanted to share some news with me. She said she'd tested negative! I was elated for her, but then she asked the obvious question: "Did you receive your results?" I had played out the scenario in my head a thousand times of how I might respond. *What if we are both positive? What if we are both negative? What if I am positive and she is negative, or vice versa? If I am positive, should I tell my family?* The obvious answer was yes, if Mom had not been dying. If life were normal, I would have no problem telling my family the news. All of a sudden I was in the middle of a moral battle with myself. It seemed like time stood still when Rochelle asked me about my results, and I could see all the scenarios playing out. I decided to tell her I'd tested negative. She was very excited and quickly passed the phone to Mom.

I could hear her telling Mom and Dad I'd tested negative. I felt terrible. I had always been honest with my family, but I could not tell my dying mother and grieving father the truth.

Mom got on the phone, and she was crying tears of joy. She expressed so much happiness and relief that both of her daughters had tested negative. She asked me several times, "Are you telling me the truth?"

When we were growing up, our litmus test for determining whether someone was telling the truth was to ask, "Do you swear on a stack of Bibles?" I fully anticipated this question from Mom. And, of course, Mom asked, "Do you swear on the stack of Bibles."

I gulped and answered: "Yes."

The rest of my day was ruined. I felt so torn about my decision. Telling her that I'd tested positive would only bring her agony, but lying to my mom was such a hard thing to do. I do not like to refer to it as a lie but as a selfless act to protect Mom. Rochelle and Dad said they could tell Mom was at peace when she learned that both of us had tested negative. I knew at some point I'd have to tell my sister and father the actual results, but I also knew that when Mom got to heaven, she would know and understand why I did what I did. That evening, when Josh got home, I shared the results with him and told him of my decision not to share the results with my family; he fully supported me.

It was not up to me to hide information about Mom's health from my family, but I also knew there was no benefit to telling them about the numerous spots found on Mom's brain. I was having a hard time coping with the fact I just swore on the stack of Bibles to something that was not true. I carried the burden of the results of the MRI for a couple of days, and then I finally told Rochelle. Her response was the same as mine—devastation. Being in the health field and seeing this daily, she'd known the situation was bad, but hearing about Mom's MRI confirmed just how bleak the situation was. Rochelle shared the results with Dad.

To justify not telling Mom the actual results of my genetic test, I knew I had to be proactive with my health. I immediately made an appointment with my ob-gyn for a consultation about the BRCA2 mutation. I learned from her that my risk for breast cancer would significantly increase by age thirty, and my risk for ovarian cancer would significantly increase at age forty. During our discussion, we agreed to focus on breast cancer prevention because of the immediate risk. I told her about Josh and my wishes for a third child. My doctor approved our plan and said I would undergo surveillance—blood work to check my CA125 levels and pelvic ultrasounds—every six months. She gave me a lot of information and referred me to the Breast Cancer Prevention Center at the University of Kansas Medical Center.

She also supported my decision not to report the positive results to my family. She made me feel at peace about my decision, telling me it was a selfless thing to do to protect my dying mother and grieving family. I am a procrastinator when it comes to medical issues. I have lived in Olathe for nearly eight years, and I still do not have a primary care physician. I get nervous when my biannual dentist appointments roll around, and I seldom take any over the counter medications. I knew if I delayed calling to make an appointment at the prevention center, it might not ever get done. The day after my consultation with my ob-gyn, I made an appointment for my initial consultation. My appointment was scheduled for October 24, 2012.

Josh and I spent a lot of time discussing and researching what the positive results meant. He supported my decision to have preventative surgery; however, I was not mentally prepared for an extensive operation during my mom's illness. The conversations were very emotional because I was scared. I wanted to spend as much time with Mom as possible, knowing she was on borrowed time, and I wanted a third child. At that time, I did not feel I could possibly have preventative surgery and then proceed with the pregnancy. It just did not feel natural at that point in my life.

Josh expressed concern about me waiting to have surgery. He knew I was a master procrastinator when it came to medical issues, and he feared that if I did not have surgery right away, it would never happen. He also was concerned that I would develop breast cancer. We already had been blessed with two healthy kids; to him, it did not make much sense to try for a third and potentially leave him as a single dad to three kids. I appreciated his concern and his support, which showed what kind of a man he was. He did not care what I looked like after the surgery, but he did want me to be around to share our lives together. I was so grateful for his support, but I just was not mentally prepared at that moment. I was only twenty-eight years old, and our family was dealing with losing Mom. Josh and I knew we had time to discuss our options. We knew we would have a lot more information after my initial consultation on October 24.

Our family never lost faith or hope. We were never angry, but we were incredibly sad. This is not how we imagined our lives would turn out. A very dear friend of mine experienced a lot of sadness and loss in her life. She lost her brother in a tragic accident, and she was grieving. When we learned about Mom's terminal diagnosis, I let her know. I value our friendship and am so thankful our paths crossed. She warned me that at some point I would be mad and that it was all part of the grieving process.

I was very sad and felt helpless, but I can honestly say I was not mad at God. I have always had faith, but during Mom's illness, I developed a much closer relationship with Him. In the past, I'd heard people talking about accepting God, but I never really understood. I now know, and I am so thankful I have a new found relationship with Him. Josh Wilson's song, "Fall Apart" is a very meaningful to me. The song speaks about the situation I found myself in when I found God during Mom's illness:

81

... my whole world is caving in
but I feel You now more than I did then.
How can I come to the end of me,
and somehow still have all I need?

I still worry, but not like I used to. I have accepted the fact that we are not in control of our lives; we have to trust that God will see us through and that everything happens for a reason. Sometimes it is hard to see during the middle of the storm, but it is reassuring to know that God has planned our lives. All we have to do is trust Him. I am at peace with everything that has happened, and I am prepared to be at peace with situations I face in the future.

All of this was happening for a reason, and I knew we had to walk by faith, not by sight. I dreaded the day Mom would pass away, but her strength during her illness confirmed her faith, and we knew she was going to go to a much better place. I believe we were being tested, and I feel our family passed. We remained faithful and continued to pray for peace and comfort for Mom during her final days and her transition to eternal life.

# CHAPTER 14

# MIRACLES HAPPEN

Mom's full brain radiation treatments continued as planned. She believed the radiation helped with her headaches and some of the dizziness, but her balance was still very off. With each passing day, it became more difficult to get her from the bedroom to the restroom, up the stairs, and into the chair in Ro and Scott's living room. She was so weak that it took quite an effort on everyone's part, especially Mom's, to navigate her throughout the house, much less to the vehicle and to radiation treatments.

It was especially shocking for me to see how quickly Mom's health deteriorated, because I was not with her 24/7 as the rest of my family was. They called me each morning to let me know how Mom struggled to get up the stairs. She had shortness of breath, and it completely wore her out to go up and down the stairs. She dreaded morning because she could not breathe very well when she first woke up. The fluid in her lungs would slowly fill up, and the inactivity during the nighttime hours seemed to make it worse. We would get her to the side of the bed, but she would panic. It took her some time to catch her breath, but she was determined to get out of bed and get on with the day. Mom got somewhat anxious near bedtime because with night comes darkness and silence and the dread of the impending morning struggle. We found ourselves in a perpetual cycle, but we still managed to get through it the best we knew how.

When we arrived at the treatment center, we would pull up front and immediately find a wheelchair. We got Mom out of the vehicle, which one of us would park. It was too taxing on Mom to walk, considering how weak and tired she was. I remember one radiation treatment in particular. Dad, Bryson, Holden, and I were waiting for Mom in the common area. We tried our best not to get down, but it was really hard not to, especially in a cancer-treatment center. An elderly lady rang a bell as she walked through the treatment door. The bell symbolized the final treatment. She was walking with her daughter and wearing a radiation mask like Mom's. Her prognosis appeared to be great, and they were celebrating. Of course, we were excited for her, but at that moment it did not seem fair.

The woman was probably close to eighty, and here was Mom, fifty-five years old, fading before our very own eyes. Dad and I had a conversation about how much easier it would be to accept Mom's diagnosis and prognosis if she'd been elderly, but it was unimaginable that she had to endure such suffering at her age. The conversation made sense at the time, but looking back it seems selfish. We were so thankful Mom had been given almost twenty more years on earth with us because she might not have made it through, or even to, the clinical trial following her diagnosis in 1993. Had we faced the same situation, but with Mom at age eighty, we would have wanted to keep her longer. Life is a matter of perspective. The parents of pediatric cancer patients would love to see their children live to fifty-five or more, but in many cases that does not happen. It is not fair that children have to endure so much pain and suffering at such a young age. In that moment we had to remind ourselves of how blessed we were that Mom had survived her first round with cancer and that she was able to see us graduate from high school and college and marry our college sweethearts, and meet four of her grandchildren.

While we were feeling sorry for ourselves, one of the boys had to use the restroom. As I was helping one, the other pulled the emergency cord. Before I could comprehend what was going on, a team of nurses and staff barged in. We found humor in the situation, and it redirected our focus from our pity party. The next thing we knew, Mom was waiting for us in her wheelchair.

The weekend before Mom's final radiation treatment she suggested we go to the farm in Indianola. She knew Dad would enjoy getting away from the city and wanted to see how the crops were doing. She was persistent, so Dad finally agreed. The plan was to leave immediately following Mom's treatment. We were a little hesitant to leave the Omaha area because we had a routine in place. It was a bit scary to know we would have to modify the way we did things. Regardless, we were determined to make it happen.

Mom completed radiation on Friday, September 21. As the nurse wheeled her through the doors, Mom signaled to Holden to ring the bell for her. It was a bittersweet moment. I asked myself, *Is this really an accomplishment?* It was in the sense that Mom never verbally complained about going to treatment, but we knew this was the final one. There were no more options available for Mom; all we could do was focus on keeping her comfortable. I kept a smile on my face as Holden rang the bell, but I was crumbling inside. Mom received a certificate for completing radiation, and we left the facility.

Before we headed to Indianola, we stopped at Walgreens to make sure we had enough lotion for Mom's skin and to refill her medications. Dad went into the pharmacy, and Mom, Holden, and I waited in the truck. Mom was in the front seat and I was in the backseat, diagonal from her. I could tell she wanted to talk but wasn't sure if she were having a hard time finding the words due to the disease or due to the content of the conversation. I finally broke the silence by saying something; then Mom took over.

She started crying and she said, "I don't want you guys to be sad."

At that moment, I knew where she was going. I could feel the tears building up, but I refused to let them out. This was Mom's moment, and I needed to be her rock. My voice trembled, and I said, "Of course we are going to be sad. We love you!"

She responded, "If this is all that is left for me on this earth, I don't want it."

That was another defining moment for me. We all knew Mom's health was declining but she was letting me know she was aware what the final outcome would be.

She said, "I don't want you guys to be sad and miss me every day. I want to you continue to live and be happy. I want you to be there for your children and love them every day!"

I was lost for words, but once again, God's timing was perfect. I wiped my tears and I looked up and there was Dad, who had gotten what he needed in the pharmacy. He hopped in the truck, and off we went.

I gathered myself in the backseat, and Holden was a great distraction. Mom liked going to McDonald's for a caramel frappé and fries after her treatments. We made our usual stop at McDonald's and headed west toward Indianola.

The trip went as well as it could have. We were unsure whether the movement of the car would make Mom nauseous or if her skin would burn and itch so much, we'd be unable to make her comfortable. She slept most of the way home. We pulled over a few times so we could calm the burning and itching with lotion. Once we made it to the farm, we took Mom inside and made her comfortable in her recliner. Rochelle, Scott, and the girls arrived shortly thereafter. As we pulled into the drive, some wonderful neighbors stopped by and unloaded groceries and paper goods from their vehicles. We opened the refrigerator to find all of the essentials and then some. I cannot overemphasize how awesome our neighbors and friends are. It was very humbling and very much appreciated. Mom had been talking about potato salad. I'd never made it but was determined to do so for her. I planned on making it the following morning so we could have it for lunch.

It was bittersweet to be home. The house had the same welcoming smell it always had. The pictures were the same, and the living room looked like it always had during our previous visits. Everything was where my parents had left it when they headed to Omaha on August 31. Things had been picked up, for the most part, and were in their places, but it was evident that Mom had not been feeling well for quite some time. There were things that were just not characteristic of her. For example, there were piles of clean clothes in the kitchen, office, and bedrooms. She would do the laundry but not put it away. Some of her clothes were hanging in the spare room; others were folded on the bed. Rochelle and I got busy and put the clothes away. Mom never liked piles, but her magazines were piling up, which again was uncharacteristic.

Friends and family stopped by that evening, and we had a good time reminiscing. It was a nice distraction from reality, and Mom thoroughly enjoyed being at home and seeing familiar faces. Dad spent his time both in the house and around the farm. It was comforting for him to know people were taking care of Mom.

At one point, Mom told Rochelle to make sure Dad's suit was ready. Rochelle knew what she was getting at and assured her we would take care of it.

Anisten and Holden kept busy being typical kids. They found all their toys in the basement and took them upstairs. There is nothing like having toy lawn mowers and other noisy toys on wood floors. Mom loved the noise, and not once did she get upset by it. She wanted normalcy for her grandchildren, and she was happy she could watch and listen to them play. Kardyn was only three months old, and Josh and Bryson did not make the trip.

Several times during Mom's illness I had to remind myself that what we were experiencing was real, not a nightmare. I would dream Mom was dying and would wake up, thinking, *Whew, I am glad that was only a dream.* It took a few seconds to snap out of it and realize it was our real-life situation. I would lie in the darkness and wonder why all of this was happening. I am not a patient person, and I wanted to know the answers. I was not angry but curious and extremely sad at the thought of losing Mom. In my mind we had a year, but it was becoming obvious there was no way she would live another year at the rate she was declining.

During our first night at the farm I told God I would love to see Mom walk again: "If it is your will, please let her walk." It was wishful thinking, but I also believe in the power of prayer. Mom was such an independent woman, and it was very hard on her to rely on others to take care of her and help her get around.

The following morning, I was peeling potatoes for the potato salad. It was hard being in the kitchen because I desperately wanted things to be "normal." In the past, Mom would have had her apron on, music would have been playing, and we would have been musing about life in general. It was almost as if my life were on a reel of tape. I had so many flashbacks of our childhood and the wonderful memories we shared in our home. The tears were building up in my eyes, when all of a sudden I heard "click, click, click" in the hallway. I stopped what I was doing and ran to see what was going on. Mom was walking down the hallway! She was using her walker, but she was walking!

I ran to her and asked, "What are you doing?"

She responded politely. "I had to go to the restroom, so that is where I am headed." Mom explained that she had been yelling for me, but apparently I did not hear her. Her voice had become somewhat raspy, but that is not why I did not hear her. I was not supposed to hear her. God answered my prayer by allowing Mom to walk. She had not been able to get herself out of bed for several weeks, and that was the last time she got up without assistance from us. Coincidences do not happen; God happens, and God gave Mom the strength to get her weak body out of bed and down the hallway by herself. To this day, I am still in awe of this miracle. As Mark 11:22 states, "Have faith in God."

The rest of the weekend went well. We found it was a lot more difficult to care for Mom at the farm because of the layout of the house. The stairs were difficult at Ro and Scott's, but once we got Mom upstairs, their home was very accommodating. Their shower had a built-in area where she could sit. Whenever Mom got weak in the shower, she could sit, so she did not fall. That was not available at the farm. Mom and Dad were always very appreciative of Ro and Scott, but being at the farm confirmed over and over again just how grateful they were. Mom required around-the-clock care and immediate access to her healthcare providers. They knew Gretna was where they needed to be.

On Sunday we packed up the vehicles and headed to Gretna. Ro drove my vehicle, Scott and Anisten followed, and Holden and I rode with Mom and Dad. We stopped in Lincoln so I could take my vehicle home, and they could return to Ro and Scott's house. Each parting was harder than the last. Mom was not a crier, but as we hugged, she squeezed me, and I could tell she did not want to let go. She hugged me tight as she was crying. I think she knew her time on earth was coming to an end. We told one another "see you later," and Holden and I left for Olathe to reunite with Josh and Bryson and get ready for another three-day workweek. The rest of the family headed toward Gretna.

Mom was a planner, and she was also very witty. She fooled us all. We put our heads together after she passed away and realized she wanted to go home one final time. Mom knew her health was declining, so she made the most of the opportunity when it presented itself. She used farming as an excuse to entice Dad, but there was also a genuine desire for him to get back to normal as well. Mom's plan was very well thought out.

## Chapter 15

# The End Is Near

Mom had a follow-up appointment with Dr. Reed on Friday, September 28, 2012. Rochelle was working, so Dad and I took Mom to the appointment. We went to the same facility where Mom underwent full brain radiation. It was difficult returning to the facility because we did not know what the doctor was going to say. When we'd received Mom's terminal diagnosis, Dr. Reed mentioned the possibility of chemo for Mom's skin after she completed the thirteen rounds of radiation for her brain. Rochelle, Dad, and I discussed whether we felt the chemo was necessary. Barring a miracle, we had come to terms that Mom was not going to beat the battle this time. Dad believed there was no way Dr. Reed would start chemo given Mom's state of health. Rochelle asked Mom at various times whether she wanted to undergo treatment, but she never gave a definitive answer. I am not sure if that was because she had lost the ability to make a decision or because she knew there was no point. Right after Mom was diagnosed, she emphasized she wanted *quality* of life.

During the appointment, we reviewed Mom's medication list with the nurse and discussed her health. I was sad because Mom tried so hard to convince the nurse that her skin was doing better, but it obviously was not. Her skin had gotten so much worse over the course of the month. Dad spent several hours—both day and night—rubbing lotion on her skin to soothe her. Mom told me she could handle the dizziness and headaches, but the burning and itching were driving her "over the edge." The purplish rash spread with a vengeance. The cancer in her skin covered the right side of her chest, arms, and back.

I was heartbroken because Mom had to struggle to speak. For the most part, she spoke very well, but there were days when she could not come up with the right words. It was frustrating for her because she recognized each time it occurred. Once she was in the shower she told Rochelle to wash her shoes when she really meant her feet. Most of the time she got close enough, so we knew what she was talking about. In the doctor's office, Mom looked right at me, and I knew she could not think of my name. She stumbled and finally said "my daughter." I felt a pit in the bottom of my stomach but smiled and continued to help her find her words.

Dr. Reed and her assistant spent some time talking with and examining Mom. The radiation had made some of Mom's hair fall out. Mom was not concerned about her looks. We all knew she was as beautiful as ever, and we continued to remind her of that. She had a variety of cute hats to wear to her appointments, and she definitely rocked them. While at home, she did not wear a hat. Her hair was very thin and patchy, but she did not want to shave her head. We asked her a couple of times if she wanted us to trim her hair, and she always said no. Dr. Reed wrote an order for a "cranial prosthesis for chemotherapy/radiation-induced alopecia," known as a wig to the general public. Dr. Reed did not suggest starting chemo during that office visit.

I continued to keep my BRCA2 status quiet because I did not believe that bringing it up would accomplish anything except unnecessary worry and increased anxiety. I had decided to share the news only after Mom passed away, but it is so much easier to tell the truth. I wish the circumstances had been different and I could have been open about my results but I could not break Mom's heart by telling her I was a carrier of the mutated gene. I was paranoid that my BRCA2 status would come up during Mom's appointments because my genetic testing had been done at the University of Nebraska Medical Center. The medical staff were very professional, and that did not happen.

After Dr. Reed exited the exam room, I chased her down the hallway. I told Dad I needed to ask her a question about the prescription for the wig, but I wanted to tell her I'd tested positive for the BRCA2 genetic mutation. I asked to speak to her in a room so our conversation would not be overheard. Dad had perfected the art of packing after appointments, so I had to get straight to the point. Dr. Reed responded, "I was wondering. Does your Dad know?"

I told her about my decision to not share the news with my family until the right time. She agreed and supported me 100 percent. She told me Dad would be devastated when he found out, but she agreed not to burden him with this information. I thanked her for her time and returned to the room, where Mom and Dad were waiting patiently for me. Mom had an appointment with Dr. Reed scheduled for October 12, but she would not be well enough to make it.

Once again, we put two and two together after Mom passed away. Dad believes Mom wanted to see Dr. Reed one final time. Mom and Dr. Reed had a nineteen-year history, and Mom wanted to see her. She did not want to start chemo for her skin, and she knew Dr. Reed would not order it. There was no point. Mom's wishes had been for quality over quantity when she received her terminal diagnosis. It all makes sense now.

Each passing day became more of a challenge, but we all stuck together and made it work. Faith is believing things will work out according to God's will. We knew God had this situation under control, and we had faith that he would see us through it. We faced each hurdle as it presented itself and moved on to the next challenge. As the days passed, Mom spent a vast majority of the day sleeping. She started eating and drinking less. She would wake up for her pain pills and would visit for a while, but she was worn out. She would finish a conversation by letting us know she wanted to take a nap. Occasionally she would sleep talk. We tried to make sense of it, but most of the time it was jumbled. When Mom was terminally diagnosed, one of her worst fears was that she might lose her mind. During her illness, she was able to keep track of the conversation approximately a vast majority of the time. God performed another miracle by allowing her to be mentally active and engaging most of the time during her final days on earth.

As soon as it was seven thirty, Mom would be ready for bed. She might have just woken up from a deep sleep, but if it were close to seven thirty, she would announce she was ready for bed. Dad would playfully roll his eyes but obliged. We'd help her out of the recliner and to her walker. We had a system; we would get her to the edge of the recliner and

91

count, "One … two …" and when we got to "three," that was the signal for Mom to stand and let us pull under her arms and help her out of the chair. One evening, Rochelle and Dad were counting in sync, but Anisten chimed in, counting at her own pace. Mom was also counting to her own beat. It was so confusing to have so many counters that we lost track. We were laughing so hard, we had to give ourselves time to regroup before we could try again. Mom laughed too. You have to make the most out of the situations in which you find yourself.

Each night, when we tucked her into bed, a tear rolled down her cheek. It became increasingly difficult to get Mom down the stairs and into the bed. At times, she would say, "I don't want to do this anymore." She was tired and worn out and, knowing Mom, she was hurting much more than she was letting us know. We continued to encourage her and make her as comfortable as possible. We had to make sure she was near the edge of the bed so we could get her up and down when she had to go to the restroom during the night. We tucked her pillows in the right places, and gave Mom her medications for the night.

When my family stayed over, Josh and I slept on an air mattress in the basement living room, and the boys slept on a futon in the office next to us. We were down there to help get Mom to and from the restroom during the night. We slept with our ears open to make sure we were there when we were needed. I could sense when the light was turned on in the adjacent bedroom and would go to help get Mom out of bed. Her walker had some blue plastic pieces on the front. One night, the walker rubbed against the wall in front of the toilet and left a small blue smudge. Rochelle says she will never paint over the smudge. When we visit Gretna, I think about Mom and smile when I see the blue mark on the wall.

Saturday, October 6, 2012, started out much like the previous thirty-five days had, except Mom did not want to go upstairs. She took her time getting from the bedroom to the recliner in the basement. When we told her it was time to go upstairs to take a shower, she said she did not want to. She drank her hot tea and watched the local news. It was a nice change of pace not to struggle with the dreaded stairs. Later that morning, we received a call from a wonderful group of family friends. They asked if Mom was up for company, and when we asked Mom, she declined. She'd had some very restless nights and she was not focusing as well as she had. She needed her sleep, and visiting would be too much for her.

I was upstairs making tacos when the doorbell rang. Our friends decided to come see Mom anyway because they really wanted to see her and our family. They were very concerned about her. The day went really well, and Mom enjoyed the visit. The women spent time in the basement, and the men were upstairs. At one point during the conversation, Mom looked at me and said, "I'm not tracking, am I?" I told her we knew what she was trying to say, which we did, and we moved on. The group left for lunch and to do some shopping. They planned on bringing supper back before they headed home. We could tell something was on Mom's mind. She finally said she was not up for company that evening. We believe Mom knew she'd seen her friends for the last time, and she did not have the emotional strength to say "see you later" a final time.

That night was Mom's worst night during her illness. The wonderful VNA staff did their best to meet her needs, which were always changing, as were her medications. We were frequent customers at Gretna Drug due to the amount of medicine Mom needed. The nurse practitioner gave her Ativan along with a sleeping pill. She said to start with one and if that did not work, it was okay to give Mom a second dose.

Dad and Mom were in bed by seven thirty, and Rochelle, Scott, Josh, the kids, and I were in the basement watching TV. We thought Mom was tucked into bed and comfortable, but we kept seeing the light turn on and off through the crack under the door. Rochelle and I went to see what was going on. Dad said Mom was restless, but she could not express what the problem was. She was moving a lot and talking in ways we could not understand. Dad needed a break, so Rochelle and I tried to settle her down. She kept asking us for help and begging us to take her out of the room. She looked at us with eyes like I have never seen. This was very unusual behavior for Mom, but we tried to understand and make her as comfortable as possible. She continued to beg us to get her "out of here!" We could not talk her out of it, so we got her out of bed and to the recliner in the basement living room. Once we got her settled there, she began the same requests and behavior. She tried to throw off her blanket and told us she had to go.

"I have to go. I have to get out of here," she said, as she kicked her legs and moved her feet. She seemed to be extremely panicked. She begged us to help get her out of the situation she thought she was in. This went on and on until we decided to give her another dose of Ativan, per the nurse practitioner's instructions, to calm her down. After a couple of trips between the two rooms, she could not walk because she had worn herself out. We used the office chair as a makeshift wheelchair to get Mom around the rest of the night, which seemed like it would never end.

Around midnight, Dad told us he was going to contact the hospice facility in the morning so we could get Mom checked out and likely admitted. He knew there was no way we could continue to provide for Mom the way she deserved, considering her new onset of symptoms. It was emotionally painful to make the decision to admit Mom to hospice because she'd made it clear early on she did not want to die in a facility. She was more comfortable in Rochelle and Scott's home, but we knew she would understand that we needed assistance from professionals. We finally calmed her down and got her to sleep around three thirty in the morning. I slept on the floor in the bedroom.

That morning, Mom woke up around nine o'clock, and her eyes were glassy. We wheeled her to the basement living room, and she chose to lie down on the loveseat rather than the recliner. She still did not make a whole lot of sense, but she was not acting as if she was scared and wanted to leave wherever she had been the night before. We honestly thought the disease had finally overtaken her brain. It broke Dad's heart, but he told Mom we were taking her to the hospice facility. As soon as Mom heard "hospice," she started to snap out of it. She did not want to go, and she worked hard to express this using body language. We slowly got her in the recliner and gave her some breakfast. Little by little, Mom made a comeback. She started making sense and carrying on conversations that we could understand.

Later that morning, we concluded Mom had experienced delirium, an adverse reaction to the new combination of medications. We had assumed the disease had progressed to the point we'd all dreaded and feared the worst. I cannot imagine the mental torment she went through for that night. She begged us for help, but no matter what we did to try to alleviate her anxiety, it did not seem to help. The look in her eyes is one I will never forget.

Around midafternoon, Mom told us she was ready to make her way to the main floor. We told her it was almost evening, and we tried to convince her to stay in the basement. Mom was persistent and clear: she wanted to go upstairs. She tackled those stairs with a determination I had not seen before. It took some time to get her to the top, but she did it. Once she made her way upstairs, we got her settled in the recliner. At one point, she commented on how well she'd rested the night before. We never gave her any indication that it was a horrific night. We all just smiled at one another and moved on.

We decided it was time to gather the troops and clean the house. We needed a fresh start to the day, considering the night we'd had. Mom rested in her chair and Dad tended to her needs; Rochelle, Scott, Josh, and I were ready to clean. There was still frost on the trees and ground, and it was sleeting on and off during the day. The kids were a bit stir crazy but we could not send them outside to play while we cleaned. We turned the TV to their favorite channel, Nick Jr. We were all a bit surprised to find out that Nickelodeon was celebrating National Play Outside Day. The network did not air any shows that day but rather played a continuous cycle of birds chirping and a clip that said it was time to take a break from the TV and play outside! We got a good laugh out of it, and every year on National Play Outside Day, we laugh and reminisce about the network's timing in 2012.

That evening Mom was hesitant to go back to the basement, and we were not that excited about taking her back down. On the chance that we had to take her to an outside facility, it would be easier to get her out of the house. We were thankful she had made her way to the main floor, because if her health continued to decline at the same pace, it would be impossible to get her out of the basement. Once again, we think Mom had a plan. She knew she could no longer make her way up and down, so the determination we had seen earlier was her way of letting us know that was the last time she would navigate the stairs. We credited divine intervention as well.

Rochelle and Scott graciously offered their room to Mom; it was perfect, very accommodating. Dad could watch TV in the evenings and afternoons when Mom was sleeping. The master bathroom was right there, and the living room was steps away. Rochelle and Scott relocated to the spare bedroom downstairs. Kardyn stayed in her crib as she was only three-and-a-half months old, and Anisten stayed in her bedroom upstairs. When I visited, I slept on the living room couch so I could assist during the night. During the week, Rochelle slept on the couch. Our family agreed that this was the best situation and were so thankful Rochelle and Scott never thought twice not only about offering their home but about giving up their bedroom. We also agreed it was time to call the VNA to get a wheelchair and other items to help care for Mom and her increasing health needs.

On Sunday, October 7, 2012, a nice couple from the Gretna Catholic Church came to the house to give Communion to Mom since she could not go to church. They are a very neat couple, and they were genuinely sad for our family. Before they left, we decided to pray the Our Father. As we began, Mom started saying a Hail Mary, so we all joined in. Dad shared with us that Mom prayed every morning on her way to work. She enjoyed the peaceful twenty-minute drive while praying for the living and deceased.

That afternoon, Mom wanted to nap in bed rather than in the recliner. As she and Dad slept, the kids played in the basement, and the adults were in the living room. We were worn out physically and emotionally from the previous night. We barely got any sleep and we were sad to see Mom in such a state. I will never forget the conversation we had during Mom's nap. Rochelle said that she believed Mom had started the dying process. Unfortunately, Rochelle had experienced this on more than one occasion. She was tuned into the signs, and her instincts were correct.

# Chapter 16

# Hospice

During Mom's illness, we met some wonderful caregivers, and we developed lifelong friendships with some of them. Dad was Mom's primary caregiver but there were times he needed to step away so he could relax. Rochelle scheduled an appointment for him at Skilled Touch and Massage in Gretna. At his first appointment, he met the owner, Jean, a very compassionate woman who understood firsthand what we were going through. Her daughter was getting ready to undergo a stem-cell transplant in November due to leukemia.

Dad and Jean connected as caregivers, and Jean asked if she could give Mom an oncology massage at Rochelle and Scott's. Dad was grateful for the offer, and he took her up on it. Mom thoroughly enjoyed the massages from Jean and her staff. The sessions relaxed her, and she always looked forward to the next one.

One day, Jean called Dad to see if she could give Mom a massage. Mom did not have an appointment until later in the week, but Jean had a strong need to see her. Mom welcomed the extra massage, and after the session, Jean said she wanted one of her staff members to try a technique called Reiki on Mom. Reiki is a Japanese technique for stress reduction and relaxation and also promotes healing. It is administered by a practitioner who lays his or her hands on the body and is based on the idea that an unseen life-force energy flows through us and causes us to be alive.

Following the Reiki session, we asked Mom how she felt, and she said, "I feel like I am moving in the right direction."

The nurse practitioner from the VNA visited Mom again on Monday, October 8, 2012. Mom was sleeping in the recliner in the living room, and Ro and Dad were sitting behind her at the kitchen table, telling the nurse about the adverse reaction to the medications on Saturday night. The nurse practitioner changed Mom's medications and answered all their questions before she left.

Apparently Mom had been sleeping with her ears wide open during the house visit from the nurse practitioner. Later she said to Rochelle and Dad, "I guess I was a pain in the butt the other night." She shrugged her shoulders and grinned slightly. We spared her the details but reassured Mom that she had not lost her mind and those medications would not be given to her again. Thankfully, she did not remember a thing about that night, just like she did not remember much of the clinical trial in 1994.

It was much easier for Mom on the main floor. It was a huge relief that she did not have to go up and down the stairs daily. Rochelle also found it very comforting. On the days she worked, she missed Mom terribly, but she knew that Mom would be waiting for her when her shift ended.

Rochelle and Mom had a conversation about dying. One night, Rochelle asked if she were afraid to die. Mom paused and said she was not afraid but was sad to leave her family. Mom adored her family, and she would do anything for us. She once said she would take a bullet for her family. She was used to being the patient, and if anybody had to be in that position, she was thankful it was her and not one of us.

The thought that we would not be able to have our daily phone calls, exchange daily e-mails, or schedule weekend visits started to sink in. Selfishly, we wanted to hold on to Mom and not let her go, but we knew this world had nothing left to offer her, and she would soon make the journey to heaven. As a family, you want to do everything to keep your loved one just one more day but it is sad to see your loved one suffer during their terminal illness. As hard as it was to accept, we were ready to let Mom go so she could be at peace.

The calls on Monday and Tuesday morning were hard to hear. I was told Mom was having a hard time breathing, and her lungs were taking on fluid. She was so weak that moving her from one space to another was more of a challenge than ever. The only food Mom consumed was a little bite of pudding so her pain pills could be swallowed. Her throat was weak, and her appetite was nonexistent.

During our phone conversation on Tuesday, October 9, I was not prepared for what Rochelle was ready to tell me. She and Dad had talked and, with Mom's support, they decided it was time for hospice. I did not want to hear the H word because I knew that was the final step before death. I knew the day was drawing near, but it all seemed to happen so fast. No matter how prepared you think you are, it is not easy when the dreaded day finally comes. I knew this decision was in Mom's best interest; therefore I had to put my selfish desires aside. Once hospice took over, we would no longer interact with the palliative care nurse practitioner and the VNA staff. We had developed strong relationships with the palliative care staff in a short time, and we will be forever grateful for the wonderful care they provided to Mom. Dad and Rochelle called the VNA to let them know Mom was ready for hospice.

On Wednesday, October 10, Dad called me fairly early at work. I could tell he had been crying. He reported that Mom had a rough night, and the morning was not going well. She could not catch her breath, and she was panicking, which made it worse. They had been in contact with hospice and they were going to start Mom on morphine to make her comfortable. He believed the morphine would be administered that evening, so he suggested that if I wanted to have a final conversation with Mom I should probably get to Gretna as soon as possible.

I got off the phone with Dad and told my boss what was going on. I did not have time to log off my computer, because my coworkers were handing me my purse and coat and pushing me out of the door. I was very appreciative, and I cried as I pulled out of the parking lot. I called Josh to let him know what was going on and that I needed to leave town immediately. I went home and threw a few items in a suitcase before I rushed out the door. The magnitude of the situation had not set in. I packed some comfy clothes and toiletries. A thought crossed my mind about packing something for the funeral so I quickly selected an outfit but chose to leave it in my closet. Right before I left the house, I decided to pack the outfit just in case.

As I was driving on I-435 North toward Omaha, I felt the need to call somebody. My heart was racing, and I wanted to snap my fingers and be in Gretna with my family. I called my dad's brother, Brett, to update him. I am so thankful he took my call during his work hours. We had a good conversation. We talked about how he was twenty-one when his dad, my Grandpa Cliff passed away and how difficult it was to see him suffer. I was only twenty-eight, and I could not imagine losing Mom. I was terrified. I started feeling like I was having a panic attack. I had never experienced one, but that is what was happening. My heart was beating hard, my body was numb, and all of a sudden I could not focus on the road. Everything started going black, and I looked down at my speedometer: I was traveling well over eighty miles per hour. I thought I might pass out as I was traveling down the highway. I was driving in the left-hand lane and quickly pulled over and stopped. I did not pass out, but I sat there for several minutes before continuing to drive. Brett stayed on the phone with me the whole time, which was very comforting.

I turned on my iPod and listened to "One Thing Remains" until I got close to Omaha. I finally turned to K-LOVE for a change of pace, and the song "Even If" by Kutless was playing. It was the first time I had heard that song, and it was fitting and timely. I believed God was speaking directly to me. He was telling me it was not His will for Mom to beat the battle, but we had to continue to have faith and trust Him. At that very moment I came to terms with the fact that Mom would soon pass away. The song by Kutless addresses the question of what we do when we feel our prayers are unanswered. The lyrics that caught my attention during my trip to Gretna are:

> Even if the healing doesn't come.
> Life falls apart and dreams are still undone.
> You are God, you are good
> Forever faithful One.
> Even if the healing doesn't come.

While we may not understand why we must endure certain events in our lives, we have to know they are part of God's plan.

The thought of losing Mom brought me to tears, but I was at peace with it. I knew she would soon walk through the gates of heaven and be greeted by God and her friends and family who had gone before her. It was comforting to know she would no longer have to endure the pain she had experienced throughout her multiple battles with cancer. She would leave this world and be welcomed in a place with no sadness or worrying and be greeted by angelic choruses. I was comforted knowing we would have our personal guardian angel and it brought me tremendous peace to know Mom would walk with each one of us every step of every day.

As I drew near to Gretna, Rochelle called and asked me to stop at the store to pick up some supplies for Mom. Close to the store, I had a strong urge to call Bruce Bohlen. He is a very spiritual man, and I knew he would have great insight and would provide comfort during such a difficult situation. I had been a nanny for Bruce's family during a summer in college. I also lived with his family from the summer through October 2006. They are such a wonderful family, and I grew close to each of them. I called Bruce, and we greeted one another; he told me that he had been driving a few days prior and felt the need to pray for me, so he did. I was very humbled during our conversation. I told him about Mom. He was the person I needed to talk to at that very moment. He provided words of wisdom, and I will be forever grateful for meeting Bruce and his family. Our paths crossed for a reason, and it was so comforting to visit with him.

I finally arrived at Rochelle and Scott's; there was an unfamiliar vehicle in the drive way. As I walked to the house, a lady introduced herself as a respiratory therapist from hospice. She was delivering Mom's oxygen supplies. This was very surreal; it was hard for me to put on a brave face. I wanted to curl up in a ball and cry, but I had to be strong for Mom. God gave me the grace and strength to get through that very difficult time.

I went inside and hugged Mom, who was patiently waiting in the recliner. She smiled and was glad to see me. The respiratory therapist hooked her up to the oxygen machine and explained it to us. Rochelle was very familiar with it, so I did not pay close attention to the instructions. I sat and talked to Mom, and she seemed at peace. She did not look scared or afraid. She acted as if this was how it was supposed to be, and she seemed confident in her decision to welcome hospice into the home. Before the respiratory therapist left, she confirmed that another nurse would stop by soon to put in a catheter. Mom was getting too weak to use the restroom, and when the morphine was started, the catheter was necessary. Mom seemed very comfortable and relieved once she was hooked up to the oxygen. When the nurse arrived for the catheter, I went to the basement with Scott and the girls.

Scott and I had a good conversation. We shed a few tears as we discussed the situation. The procedure seemed to take longer than it should have, and I was becoming very impatient. Rochelle came downstairs, and she was upset. She too was frustrated about how slow the process was going. Rochelle is a very good nurse, and it was difficult for her to stand back and let someone else take care of Mom. The nurse eventually got Mom settled and he left for the evening.

It was surreal to see Mom on oxygen, but it was nice to see her more relaxed. The oxygen provided more mental support than physical support, but she no longer struggled and panicked when she tried to breathe. We all take breathing for granted, but when you wonder where your next breath is coming from, that is a very scary thought.

We had supper and were sitting in the living room watching the DIY channel. Mom had been fairly quiet most of the evening, as if she were processing information. All of a sudden, Mom sat up and said, "We need to have a family meeting." Dad, Ro, Scott, and I gathered around the recliner. I wish Josh could have been there, but he was at home taking care of the boys.

Mom wanted to address several items, and she had quite the agenda. Shortly after the meeting started, all of us except Mom started to cry. Not once during the meeting did she shed a tear. She was very matter of fact, and she definitely controlled the conversation. She told Dad not to be "stupid" at the farm. She worried he would have an accident during harvest and the late nights. Rochelle and I promised to call Dad every day to make sure he was okay. Mom also told Dad that she did not want him to be alone. At that time, it was hard for Dad to imagine being with anyone other than her, but he listened to what she had to say. Mom looked specifically at Scott and told him to take care of our family. She really loved Scott and Josh and she trusted them to look after her family. Scott agreed to keep Dad and the rest of us in line.

Mom told Rochelle and me to be proactive about our health. She emphasized the importance of getting our baseline mammograms and staying on top of things. She told us she never wanted us to experience what she had, and we promised to take care of ourselves. Rochelle told Mom that she would get her baseline mammogram once she had been cleared by her ob-gyn. Her doctor wanted her to be at least six months postpartum before she ordered a mammogram. I told Mom I had already made my appointment and I could tell she was pleased about our preventative measures.

She told us to enjoy every day with our children. She reminded us about the importance of letting them be kids and to be thankful they are active. She told us to hug and kiss them every day and to let them know how much they are loved. Mom said we should not go to bed mad. She told us that when she and Dad had disagreements, they always made up before bedtime. Mom and Dad stood by this rule for the thirty-three years they were married. I believe they were a couple who were admired. Mom and Dad had something very special, and it was beautiful to see them together during the time they had.

Through the tears, Scott had a very heartwarming, genuine visit with Mom. We were all still in the room, but it was as if it were only Scott and Mom. I do not remember everything that was said, but Scott said how much he loved Mom and was so thankful to be blessed with such a wonderful mother-in-law. Had Josh been there he would have said the same thing.

Once everything that needed to be said had been said, Mom said she was done. She sat back in her recliner and took a brief nap. Shortly afterward, she was ready for bed. We got her to the room and positioned into bed for the night. Once again, tears rolled down her cheeks. We kissed her, told her we loved her, and that we would see her in the morning.

Mom was so strong, both mentally and physically. We concluded that she made it through the family meeting without shedding a tear by the grace of God. We feel that divine intervention had taken place, and Mom was at peace with what was to come in the very near future. We also wondered if the burst of energy Mom exhibited during the family meeting was the same energy the nurses told us about. We knew we were heading into more unfamiliar territory, but we were thankful that hospice was there to help us through the process.

On Thursday, October 11, we met with the hospice nurse assigned to us through the VNA. Mom rested in her recliner, and Dad, Rochelle, and I sat at the kitchen table with the nurse. She brought a booklet and discussed hospice's role with us and what to expect. It was uncomfortable talking about sensitive subjects in front of Mom, but they needed to be discussed.

We talked about contacting the local funeral home and arranging transport from Gretna to the funeral home in McCook. We also received instructions for the emergency kit of medications that was kept in the refrigerator. The nurse discussed in detail the physical signs of end of life. She told us Mom eventually would start sleeping more and ultimately would quit eating. The nurse also emphasized that patients need reassurance and permission to pass away. I am sure Mom had her ears open, just as she had in the past, but never did she seem uncomfortable. I occasionally got up from the table and sat by her to distract her from the conversation in the kitchen. Mom was a realist and very matter of fact. If she were listening, she would have agreed these items needed to be discussed, and the planner in her was probably thankful we were talking about them in advance.

# CHAPTER 17

# GATES OF HEAVEN

Thursday, October 11, 2012, was another day Mom was given on earth. She did well through the night; thankfully, it was fairly uneventful. She woke up a couple of times to take some pain medications and was able to rest comfortably. We chose to have Mom take oral morphine rather than administer it through an IV. We did not want to burden her with more lines and cords. We wanted her to be as comfortable as possible during her final days.

Dad and I were with Mom that morning. Rochelle and Scott were working, and the girls were at daycare. We had a difficult time getting Mom out of bed. She was so weak. We sat her up in the bed, but she was having a terrible time breathing despite the fact she was using her oxygen machine. We tried our best to remain calm. She eventually caught her breath, and we got her in the wheelchair. At this point, she was too weak and tired to shower, so we arranged with hospice to come to the house the next day to give her a sponge bath. In the past, Mom had liked to shower in the morning and at night. She probably was not a fan of the sponge baths, but I am sure she was thankful for the effort.

It was clear that Mom was not very comfortable in her recliner. Her catheter was bothering her, and she seemed restless and in pain. We gave her the scheduled pain medications, and she eventually calmed down. The rest of the day went fairly well, as best as I can recall. Dad and I called Mom's boss, Jim, to let him know she was in hospice. Jim had just visited a week or so earlier. He was in Omaha for meetings and wanted to stop by. She was excited but hesitant to see him. She knew she could not return to work, and she did not think it was fair for the hospital to hold her position. Mom knew the demands of her job, and she knew they needed to start looking to fill it. Tears built up in her eyes as she talked to Jim. He took the news well but also reassured her that the job was hers as long as she wanted it.

Scott's sister, Andrea, and her husband, Ryan, brought us supper that evening. Mom did not eat, but she thoroughly enjoyed the company. They also brought some food prepared by coworkers, and a prayer blanket. I think Andrea was taken aback by Mom's state of health. She had declined so rapidly it, and it was hard for Andrea to see Mom that ill. Andrea gave Mom the beautiful blanket made by some women at her church. She also read a very nice message to her. Andrea teared up as she read, but as usual, Mom did not shed a tear. She graciously listened and smiled. As the women were making her blanket, they had prayed for her the entire time. It was so humbling to know complete strangers were praying for Mom during her time of need.

During the evening, Mom slept a lot, and sometimes she would sleep talk. She seemed to do more sleep talking than normal, but we were prepared for this. The nurses warned us that morphine can make people hallucinate. Mom would come in and out of the conversations between her naps. I was sitting in a kitchen chair to the right of Mom's recliner. When she woke up from one of her naps, I could tell she had something to say because she kept looking at the wall and then back at me. She had a grin and she said to me, "See those bugs. Look at all of those bugs. They are crawling around everywhere." I didn't know whether I should play along or tell her there were no bugs.

Mom always told me she could tell exactly what I was thinking based on my facial expressions. Clearly I did not do a good job of hiding it because she said, "You don't believe me, do you?"

I smiled and told her there were no bugs.

Rochelle got home from work and joined us for supper. There was a country-folk-themed sign hanging above the television in the living room. It was a long sign that had the alphabet across the top and a farm scene as the main center point. Mom woke up when Rochelle came home, and once again she started staring at the wall. She pointed out to Rochelle that one of the letters in the alphabet sign was missing. Mom really had us going. I had looked at that sign several times but assumed all of the letters were there. Imagine a room full of adults looking hard to make sure all twenty-six letters were properly painted on the sign. We agreed no letters were missing, and Mom joined us in the laughter.

Mom stayed up a little past her bedtime that night because she was enjoying the company. Around eight thirty, we started getting her ready for bed. Thankfully Scott was in the living room that evening, because it took all four of us to get Mom up. Her legs were incredibly weak and she did not have the strength to get out of the recliner. We barely got her to stand at her walker and immediately got her into her wheelchair. As we were wheeling her to her room, she started talking in ways we could not understand. Her speech was jumbled, and it did not make sense. We wheeled her into the room and began the nightly routine of getting her ready for bed. As we were positioning Mom into bed, she said, very clearly, "Heaven." Rochelle and I looked at each other, and Rochelle asked what she'd said. Mom did not answer. It was a very special moment, and one I will never forget.

Mom was lying on her left side and Rochelle, Dad, and I were standing in front of her by the bed. Mom looked up toward us, yet beyond where we were standing. At first we did not think she could focus on us due to the disease. She continued to look beyond us and asked, "Who is that woman with a cup?"

Rochelle, Dad, and I looked at each other to try and figure out what Mom was talking about. She asked again, "Who is that woman with long hair who keeps trying to give me a drink?"

We thought she was confused and referring to Scott's sister. We reminded her that Andrea and Ryan had left, and her response was, "I know Andrea, but who is that woman with a cup?"

What Mom was seeing was real, and we believe she was starting to cross over. We kissed her, told her we loved her, and we would see her in the morning.

I did not sleep well that night. I was nervous about Rochelle and Scott being at work and I was not confident Dad and I could handle Mom alone, given how weak she had become. A hospice nurse was coming to the house to give Mom a bath, but I was very uneasy. It had taken all four of us to get Mom out of the recliner the evening before, so I was not sure how Dad and I would handle it alone. Anisten did not sleep well that night either. She woke me up as she was passing by the couch on which I was sleeping. She was crying because her throat hurt. I walked with her to the basement to let her parents know she was not feeling well.

Friday, October 12, is a day our family will cherish forever. I rubbed the sleep from my eyes as Scott passed through the living room. He asked if I thought if it would be okay to go into the bedroom to get his lapel pin. October is Breast Cancer Awareness Month, and the teachers at Scott's school had decided to wear their pink ribbon lapel pins that Friday. Scott went into his room to get the pin, and when he came out he had a look on his face.

He said, "It smells like incense in there."

I said, "What?"

He said, "It smells just like a Catholic church."

I asked him if he was sure it wasn't the lotion, which has a very distinct smell.

Scott said, "No. It definitely smells like incense."

I got off the couch and went into the bedroom. As I walked through the door, the smell of incense hit me in the face. The smell was strong, and it was undeniably incense. We woke Dad up so he could share the experience, but he was disappointed because he could not smell it. He had been in the room all night, so he could not distinguish the smell. Dad took a shower downstairs, and when he came back in the room the faint smell of incense was still present. We felt so incredibly blessed.

Scott left for work, and I called Rochelle at work. I explained the situation, and she was blown away. She was excited but disappointed that she did not get to experience it. We knew with the events from the night before, God was really giving us strong signs that he was close to welcoming Mom to heaven. After I got off the phone with Rochelle, I called Josh to let him know what had happened. I told him the end was near, and it would be a good idea if he and the boys headed to Gretna to be with us. I also called hospice to see if Mom could be seen first thing for her bath. The hospice nurses rearranged their schedules, and they confirmed Mom would be the first patient.

That morning was very unusual. During the previous forty-one days, Mom would nudge Dad around seven o'clock to wake him and let him know she was ready to get out of bed. Mom did not do that on October 12. She slept well into the morning. We tried to wake her, but she did not respond. She was resting comfortably, and we were satisfied. The aide showed up around ten o'clock, and Mom was still sleeping. The aide was very kind and gentle. Mom slept during the duration of her sponge bath. Another hospice nurse arrived around ten thirty to help us get Mom out of bed and into the recliner. As we were getting her out of bed, Mom sat up with ease, and her breathing was not labored. She did not have the look of panic in her eyes that she'd had the previous mornings. She sat on the side of the bed for a short time, and we got her to her wheelchair and the recliner in the living room.

I could tell by the look on the nurse's face that she knew Mom was dying. Rather than filling the pit in the bottom of my stomach, I was showered with an overwhelming sense of peace. I knew Mom was starting to make her final journey to heaven, given the miracles we experienced the night before and that morning.

Before Mom's health took a turn for the worse, she told Rochelle and Scott she did not want to leave bad memories in their home. She also told them she did not want to die in their bed. Rochelle and Scott were happy to have Mom and Dad there, and they did not worry about the details. What mattered is that they were able to spend a lot of quality time with Mom by having her at their house rather than in Indianola or in a hospice facility.

Mom's typical pattern during her terminal illness was to take her pain medications every few hours during the day. She was resting comfortably in the recliner, and she did not wake up around noon to take her next round of pills. Dad and I decided it was time for lunch, so I took orders and drove to Runza Restaurant in Gretna. I also stopped by Gretna Drug to pick up more prescriptions for Mom. I called my good friend Dena to see how her mother was doing and to let her know about our situation. I was very upbeat given the multiple spiritual experiences we'd witnessed in less than twenty-four hours.

When I was at Gretna Drug, I noticed some beautiful angels near the cash register. I purchased three of the angels with purple wings to symbolize Mom's birth month. I wanted Rochelle and Dad to have one to hang on their mirrors in the vehicle to remind them of Mom.

When I returned from Runza and Gretna Drug I expected Mom to be awake, but she was not. Dad said she'd slept the entire time I was gone. Dad and I sat at the kitchen table and ate lunch while Mom rested in her recliner. After lunch, we started working on thank-you notes to send to all of the generous farmers and their families who had taken over the harvest and gotten all of our crops out, which allowed us to spend as much time possible with Mom. She continued to rest comfortably and did not wake up to take her scheduled medications.

Around two in the afternoon, Dad said he really wanted Mom to open her eyes just one more time. Just then she took a really deep breath, and it was silent for what seemed like an eternity. We looked at each other. Dad said, "This is it."

Mom eventually started breathing again, but it seemed different after she took the one big breath. Dad has been present when other family members have passed away, so he knew what the deep breath meant. We decided it was time to call a priest so Mom could receive the sacrament of the anointing of the sick.

We called the local church to see if the priest would come to the house. We were told the priest had left for vacation earlier in the day and were given a different phone number for another priest. We called the second number; that priest was getting ready to leave town to go to his niece's wedding but made arrangements to stop by the house on his way out of town. Dad stepped outside and started calling Mom's brothers and our close friends to let them know the end was near. Mom and I were the only two in the house, and I sat at head and told her how much I loved her and what an honor it was to be her daughter. Just as I was kissing her on her forehead, Josh and the boys walked through the front door. Shortly thereafter the priest pulled up in his red Volkswagen bug. He gave Mom the last rites, and we held hands and said a prayer over Mom. As we said Amen, she opened her eyes and looked at us. Once again, God delivered. Dad wanted to see her eyes, and there they were. Mom hadn't opened her eyes for several hours but when she heard amen, her eyes immediately opened. She then closed them and continued to rest comfortably.

Throughout the day, Rochelle called from work to check on Mom. We told her about the situation, so she was somewhat prepared when she got home. Scott got home too, and we shared with him what had occurred that afternoon. Mom's brother Lloyd came to the house to be with us. He brought meals and desserts, some of which Aunt Mary had made and some that had been sent from friends in southwest Nebraska. We all gathered around Mom and comforted each other in conversation. Mom's brother Eldon and his wife, Carol, arrived, and they too joined us in reminiscing. The fire place was running, and we circled around Mom.

We did not think that Mom would make it through the evening, much less the night. Mom's brothers and their spouses stayed until around midnight, and they asked us to call if she passed during the night. Her breathing continued to worsen, and she did not wake up. Hospice was informed of the situation, and they told us to keep them updated and call with any questions or concerns. Not once did we leave her side. We had had very little sleep, but our adrenaline was running high and we wanted to be right there to hold Mom's hand.

Around two in the morning, a thunderstorm developed. The lightning and thunder were very intense. We decided Scott and Josh should try to get some sleep so they could care for the kids in the upcoming days. Before they went to bed, they each leaned down, kissed Mom on the cheek, and told her they loved her. We all held hands and prayed around Mom.

Around two thirty, Mom became restless. She continued to exhibit signs of the end of life. We called hospice to assist us with her care. The next hour was emotionally painful. Mom opened her eyes, and she looked similar to the way she had a week earlier, when she'd had a reaction to the Ativan. She acted as if she needed something, but she could not express it to us. She moved her right hand and seemed to point to her stomach. We took this to mean she was itching, so we found the lotion and started rubbing her stomach, arm, and back. Time stood still. It was if the hospice nurse had forgotten we had called, and we felt abandoned. We called back, and the woman on the phone referred us to the emergency kit in the refrigerator. She told Rochelle how much of which medication to give to Mom. She also assured us the nurse was on the way. We continued to tell Mom we were prepared for her to go to heaven. We promised her we would be fine, and we begged her to go pass.

We were growing increasingly frustrated because the hospice nurse had yet to show up. We reminded one another that the nurse probably had been delayed because another person was in a situation similar to Mom's. At a quarter to four, a hospice nurse finally showed up. It was the same nurse who had initially visited the house on Wednesday. Rochelle was relieved when the nurse showed up because she no longer had to be responsible for administering medication to Mom during the intense moments.

Only God knows when it is someone's time, but it is nice to have medical professional give you a general time frame so you can prepare yourself. We were not sure how much longer Mom could continue down this path. The unknown was one of the worst parts for me. The thought of losing Mom was terrifying, but I was mentally prepared for her to pass. I prayed for her to pass during the night so her suffering would end and we could take care of the planning and logistics with the funeral home before the kids woke up. The nurse listened to Mom's lungs, and he told us they were filling up and she would not be able to hold on too much longer.

I was almost delirious. The last six weeks had been emotionally taxing and physically draining. The worry alone was enough to tire somebody out. I felt bad stepping back to take a quick nap, but I had to in order to be prepared for the days to come. Rochelle lay down next to me to rest. Dad stayed by Mom's side. He did not take a nap but instead sat by the recliner and held Mom's hand the entire time.

The long night finally ended, and the sun came up. We called Mom's brothers and our friends to provide an update. Lloyd and Mary came, as did their daughter, Alisa. Once again, we circled around Mom and visited. Thankfully the weather on Saturday, October 13, was a typical fall day. It was nothing like it had been the previous weekend. The children spent most of the day in the basement and outside playing with the neighborhood kids. Rochelle and Scott live in a wonderful community, and they are surrounded by phenomenal neighbors. The neighbors knew what was going on, and they helped with the kids so we could be with Mom.

Mom continued to rest comfortably, and we were so thankful for that. Around eleven that morning, Mom's brother Todd and his wife, Dee, arrived at the house to be with her. We talked and stayed by Mom's side. Shortly before one o'clock, Todd and Dee decided it was time to go. I could tell Todd was upset, and he needed some time. Just as he and Dee were leaving, Josh and Scott decided to make a trip to the store with Anisten, Holden, and Bryson.

I sat in the chair to Mom's right, Rochelle sat at her head, and Dad sat to her left. Dad suggested we pray around Mom. Lloyd, Mary, and Alisa joined our circle, and we prayed. Once again, when we said amen, Mom's eyes opened. We caressed her hands and head and told her it was okay to leave us. I told her, "This is not good-bye; it's see you later."

All of a sudden, Mom's right arm started turning blue. I looked at Rochelle, and she gave me a gentle nod, basically saying, *It's happening.* Mom gave Dad one final glance, and she took her last breath. I will never forget the look on her face. I think she was telling us she was making her journey home. She looked sad to leave the earth and her family behind, but she knew she was making her journey to eternal life. Mom departed her earthly life and was taken to the gates of heaven shortly after one in the afternoon on Saturday, October 13, 2012.

We believe Mom had held on so she could see Todd and Dee. They had been unable to make it the night before, and Mom needed to hear her brother's voice one more time. We also believe Mom did not want her beautiful grandchildren to be present when she passed away. God's plan worked exactly how it was supposed to, and we knew she was in a much better place.

The moments after Mom's passing were a blur. I felt every emotion on the spectrum within a split second. I was so sad to see Mom go, yet I was relieved the pain and suffering had finally come to an end. She was no longer hurting, and we knew she was being welcomed into heaven with open arms. There was a sense of peace but a terrible sense of loss. Mom was our rock, and the unimaginable had just happened right before our eyes.

My sadness and worry shifted from Mom directly to Dad. I no longer had to worry about if or when the cancer was going to come back. My new focus was the horrific loss Dad had just experienced. Mom and Dad had so many plans for the future. It was scary to know that Dad was alone. The thought of him living alone made me almost physically sick.

Dad and Mom spent a total of forty-two days in Gretna at Rochelle and Scott's home. Our parents were amazing role models for us, and Dad continues to be one. When Mom passed, I realized she had taught us how to *live* with dignity and grace and how to *die* with dignity and grace.

Every time I hear the song "Walking Her Home" by Mark Schultz, I remember Mom's life and her final minutes on earth. The song is about a couple who were married for sixty years until the wife passed away in a nursing home at the age of eighty-five. That was how I had imagined Mom and Dad's life together, but that was not part of God's plan. Mom and Dad made the most out of the time they had together. They lived life to its fullest, in good times and bad. They stood by one another and shared many wonderful years together.

The last part of the song really holds true to Dad's role during their thirty-three years together as well as his 100 percent dedication and involvement in Mom's care. Dad was by Mom's side every day and night during those final forty-two days. He stopped at nothing to make sure Mom was as comfortable as she could be. When she passed, he was holding her hand, walking her home.

## Chapter 18

# Funeral Arrangements

A few family members and the hospice nurse arrived shortly after Mom passed away. I was frustrated by the nurse's late arrival because I thought hospice was supposed to be there to help during the process. We later learned the nurse had been with another terminally ill patient, and she simply could not be in two places at the same time. The nurse contacted the funeral home in Gretna and the Sarpy County sheriff. The process was expedited since this was a hospice situation. The sheriff was kind and compassionate. He filled out the paperwork and left.

Two gentlemen from the funeral home arrived to take Mom's body. Rochelle and Scott's neighbors entertained the kids at their homes during this process. The adults went to the basement, and we came back upstairs after the men left. That's when it hit me that Mom was really gone. I found myself glancing in rooms as I walked by, longing to see her there. We knew her soul was in heaven, and it started to sink in that she was physically gone.

Mom was such a planner, and her organizational skills rubbed off on us. Our planning mode kicked into high gear. We started making plans for her funeral. Monsignor Witt was available on Wednesday, October 17, as was the funeral home, so that is the date we chose. We gathered around the kitchen table and drafted Mom's obituary. It almost felt as if we were dreaming and could not wake up. We should have been gathered around the kitchen table with Mom, drinking a cup of coffee, talking about work, kids, family, and life, but instead we were planning her funeral. How could this be?

That evening a woman from the Catholic church in Gretna brought supper to the house. She sat down and visited with us and offered her condolences. When she left, we moved Mom's recliner back to the basement and returned the living room to the way it had been in August, when Mom and Dad first arrived. There was a terrible sense of sadness but also an overwhelming sense of peace. We were thankful the fight was over. We believed Mom was as comfortable as she could have been, and that brought us comfort.

Once we finished Mom's obituary, the funeral director called to confirm a ten o'clock meeting with him at the funeral home in McCook on Sunday, October 14. We started doing laundry and packing. We planned to stay at the farm until the Sunday after the funeral so we could spend as much time with Dad. I was already dreading leaving him by himself. Dad had been with family for forty-two days, so it was sad to think about leaving him alone.

We didn't get to bed until after midnight, and we had planned to leave Gretna by five in the morning. We made plans to stop by the house to pick out an outfit and jewelry for Mom before our ten o'clock meeting at the funeral home. We were exhausted, physically and mentally. We were running on next to no sleep and were emotionally drained.

As soon as my head hit the pillow, I started having flashbacks from the previous twenty-four hours. I cried and cried, knowing I would never get to hug her, call her, turn to her for advice, or even tell her "see you later." Josh and I slept on the futon that night because the boys were already sleeping on the air mattress in the basement by the time we made our way downstairs. I woke up, screaming, and Josh was there, comforting me, telling me it was okay. I was having a nightmare. I do not remember the specifics other than Mom had passed away and her arm was on my head. I screamed, "Get off me. Get off me now!" When I woke up, I realized Bryson had crawled into bed with us, and it was his arm on my head. He started crying, and I felt terrible. I did my best to explain to him I'd had a really bad dream, and I apologized over and over and cuddled with him the rest of the night. I afraid this was the start of horrific nightmares about Mom's illness and passing. It took some time to get back to sleep, and before I knew it my alarm was going off. I rolled off the futon at four o'clock to get ready to leave town.

Rochelle, Dad, and I left at five o'clock, and Scott, Josh and the kids left later that morning. Before we loaded the truck, Rochelle and Dad hung their purple angels in their vehicles. We packed up the truck and left town shortly after five. As we were pulling out of the driveway, Dad pointed out that this was the first time he was making the trip without Mom. It was hard leaving her behind, but once again we reminded ourselves it was only a body and her soul was in heaven. We knew she was riding shotgun in the truck; we just couldn't see her.

Surprisingly, the trip from Gretna to Indianola went quickly. We had a lot to get done in only a few days. The three of us had some really good conversations. We talked about our favorite memories of Mom and how blessed we were to have had extra time with her after her 1993 bout with cancer and to have experienced the signs leading up to Mom's death. We also had some hard conversations about how much Mom would be missed and about leaving Dad alone. Rochelle and I told Dad that we would support him 100 percent if he decided to date or remarry. Dad appreciated us giving him our blessing, but he just lost his wife less than sixteen hours earlier, so dating was the furthest thing from his mind.

We arrived in Indianola just before nine o'clock. It was hard to walk into the house for the first time without Mom. Everything was how we'd left it on September 23, after our quick visit home. Every house has its own smell, and the welcoming smell of Mom and Dad's house was the same as it had always been in the past. I still expected to see Mom in her favorite recliner, kicking back, reading a magazine. Instead, we made a beeline to Mom and Dad's closet to find something for her to wear. We hadn't previously talked about it, and Mom did not tell us her wishes. She was more focused on making sure Dad's suit was ready and that Rochelle and I were mentally ready for what was to come. She must have trusted us to pick out an outfit and plan all of the details.

Rochelle and I picked out two outfits with coordinating necklaces. Dad agreed with our choices and said he wanted Mom to wear earrings. She had a pair of diamond earrings with gold backs. Mom always kept her jewelry in a green antique soap dish in her bathroom. Rochelle and Dad went to the bathroom, but they could not find the earrings. I joined them, and we dumped out the soap dish and separated everything. For the life of us, we could not find the earrings. We decided to look later; otherwise we were going to be late for our meeting.

We drove to McCook, and we were taken to the conference room at the funeral home. The funeral director was very compassionate, and he offered his condolences. We provided a copy of the obituary so they could get it in the *McCook Gazette* on Monday. The private family viewing was scheduled for Monday, October 15. The rosary was scheduled to take place on Tuesday at St. Catherine's Catholic Church, and the funeral was on Wednesday, October 17.

> Nancy Marie (Ogorzolka) Schmidt passed away Saturday, October 13, 2012, in Gretna, Nebraska. She was 56 years old.
>
> Nancy was born on February 21, 1956, to Donald Paul and Nettie P. (Arendell) Ogorzolka. She graduated from Bartley High School with the class of 1974.
>
> On March 24, 1979, she was united in marriage to Leslie L. Schmidt at St. John's Catholic Church in Cambridge. They made their home on a farm north of Indianola. Nancy was an integral part of the farming operation especially during harvest when she helped run the combine. She was also employed at Community Hospital for 33 years.
>
> Family was very important to Nancy. While her daughters where attending college at Doane, Nancy spent hours on the road so she could attend their sporting events. She also enjoyed her four grandchildren. She was a member of St. Catherine's Catholic Church in Indianola and a member of St. Catherine's Altar Society.
>
> Preceding her in death were her parents, Donald and Mariann Ogorzolka and Nettie and Page Voorhees, grandparents Tony and Marie Ogorzolka and father-in-law Clifford Schmidt.
>
> Survivors include her husband, Leslie Schmidt of Indianola, NE; daughter Rochelle and husband, Scott

Swanson, granddaughters Anisten and Kardyn of Gretna, NE; daughter Kirby and husband Josh Smith, grandsons Bryson and Holden of Olathe, KS; brothers, Daniel and Nancy Ogorzolka of Fort Collins, CO, Eldon and Carol Ogorzolka of Lincoln, NE, Lloyd and Mary Ogorzolka of Indianola, NE, and Todd and Dee Ogorzolka of Henderson, NE; mother-in-law, Peggy Schmidt of McCook; brother-in-law Brett and sister-in-law Lori Schmidt of McCook, NE and sister-in-law Brenda (Schmidt) and brother-in-law Troy Hinz of Clayton, IN and numerous nieces and nephews and great nieces and great nephews.

Memorials given in Nancy's name will be donated to further breast cancer research.

We spent most of the day making arrangements at the funeral home. I had no idea there were so many details to planning a funeral. We were presented with many options for every possible aspect of the funeral. Dad, Rochelle, and I wanted it to reflect the beautiful woman Mom was and the life she had lived. We made unanimous decisions on all of the details. Since fall was Mom's favorite time of the year it seemed fitting to select a program with all of the vibrant colors of autumn for the celebration of her life.

The easiest decision of the day was the poem we selected for the inside of the program. It was as if it was written specifically for Mom. The three of us were in tears, and we barely made it through the poem the first time. We loved it so much that we read it over and over. We could not believe how fitting it was, and we knew Mom would be happy with our decision and the plans.

The funeral director asked whether we were interested in putting together a video containing pictures of Mom. At first we were not sure if this was something we could do in time, but we decided it would be a great keepsake item for us and our children. That evening we pulled out several photo albums and sorted through a lot of pictures. I had mixed emotions as I reminisced with family and friends as we went through the pictures. The photos reminded me about all of the fun times we'd shared with Mom, but they also reminded me that no more memories were going to be made with Mom. We stayed up well past midnight to put the pictures in chronological order so the video could be completed the following day during the visitation.

We had an easy time choosing three songs for the video. When Rochelle told us her choices, Dad and I said those were the songs we were thinking about too. The three songs were "Because You Loved Me" by Celine Dion, "Amarillo By Morning" by George Strait, and "You Raise Me Up" by Josh Groban. The video was really nice, and it is a treasured keepsake for our family.

One of the most emotionally challenging parts about planning Mom's funeral was selecting a casket. I really dreaded picking out the casket because it made the situation very real. I kept having flashbacks of shopping *with* Mom for groceries, clothes for school, prom dresses, wedding dresses, cars, a houses, etc. It was difficult to choose a casket *for* her. I was at peace, but I also had the selfish desire for her to be with living with us on earth. The funeral director did a great job, and the process was not nearly as bad as I had anticipated. There were several other things I would rather have been doing at that moment, but that was the situation we were in, and we did our best to get through it.

After we left the funeral home, we drove back to Indianola and met with Father McGuire. We selected the readings and the songs we wanted for the funeral. We also met with Crinda McConville, an organist for the church, and her husband Rick. It was very comforting to visit with them. They offered wonderful words of peace and comfort. Crinda is a very talented musician, and she did a fantastic job of helping us select the music and playing the piano during Mom's funeral.

We were running on adrenaline. We had a very long, exhausting day but did not feel that tired. Around eight o'clock that night, we finally returned to the farm. We were greeted by several neighbors, family members, and friends. Throughout the day, people stopped by to offer their condolences and provide our family with food. We had so much love and support, it was truly overwhelming but in a very good way. Mom was loved by so many, and our little community came together and gave our family more support than we ever could have imagined. Our community is much larger than we realized.

Scott, Josh, and the kids had stayed at the farm during the day while Rochelle, Dad, and I made the arrangements. The guys did a great job of welcoming guests and entertaining the kids. Dad and Mom always said how blessed they were to have such wonderful sons-in-law. Rochelle and I are so grateful to be blessed with loving, supportive husbands.

That evening, several of Mom's coworkers stopped by the house. One of them said Mom had gathered some personal belongings and cleaned up her computer on what ended up being her last workday at the hospital. It was as if she knew she would not return. Mom had very strong intuition, and she was a planner. Still, I was taken back when I heard this because it proved that she believed she would not return to work. I am sure she remained hopeful, but just in case, she wanted things ready for the person who would take over her responsibilities. We also learned from another coworker that Mom struggled to navigate her computer during her final days at work. Mom was skilled at her job, so the fact she could not access basic items on her computer was troubling. Hearing this broke my heart over again because I'd failed to recognize how ill she really was. It upset me to think about the mental agony she likely went through before and during her terminal illness.

Once our guests left, we took a little time to talk with Scott and Josh about the funeral plans. We talked about how busy our day had been at the funeral home, and we informed them about all of the decisions we made. We were disappointed that we could not find Mom's diamond earrings. Scott asked if we'd looked in the green soap dish, "because that is where Nancy always kept her jewelry." We explained that all three of us looked, but they were not there. Scott walked into Mom's bathroom and returned to the living room with the earrings in his hand.

He said, "You mean these earrings?"

We asked where he'd found them, and he said they were in the green soap dish in Mom's bathroom. We could not believe it. The earrings had not been there that morning. We put the earrings on the counter so we would remember to take them to McCook the following day.

Around two in the morning, we decided it would be a good idea to get Dad's suits together, so we didn't have to hassle with them the following day. Dad and I went to the closet and found the tan-colored suit with the shirt and tie; however, we could not find the black pants that went with his black jacket. We panicked at first, but then we remembered the warning Mom had given Rochelle. At the time, we'd figured that was Mom's way of telling Rochelle she knew she was going to die, but it was almost as if she were telling us the suit wasn't complete. We searched the closet high and low, and we could not find the pants. We were not sure what to do.

The following day was booked solid, with more funeral plans and the family viewing that evening. We did not have time to find Dad another pair of pants to match the jacket. We were exhausted and thought we would look for them in the morning. We planned to call the dry cleaners and Garrison's for Men in McCook the following morning to see if Mom had dropped off the pants and forgotten to pick them up.

The next morning, I woke up and headed back to Mom and Dad's room. I wanted to see if Dad was awake, so we could get ready for another busy day. I was so sad when I glanced in the room and saw him alone in the bed. I felt sick. I hated the thought of Dad being alone. He is an independent man, but he and Mom had done everything together. I knew Dad would make the best out of it, but I also knew a lot of tears would be shed, and a terribly broken heart might never be mended.

Later that morning, the three of us went to McCook to pick out flowers for Mom's casket. As we were flipping through the book, we chuckled at some of the choices. We could hear Mom say, "That looks like it belongs at a funeral." We found a beautiful fall arrangement. It contained sunflowers as well as a variety of orange, yellow, and purple flowers. It was vibrant, and it definitely did not look like it "belonged at a funeral." We felt Mom would have been thrilled with our choice. After we met with the florist, we stopped by the cleaners, hoping to find Dad's pants. Unfortunately, they were not there. We walked across the street to Garrison's to see if Mom had dropped them off to be altered, but the mystery continued.

The night before, we had found a navy suit in Dad's closet. It looked nice on him, but he really wanted to wear his black suit but we did not have time to get him another suit. We went home, and he tried on the navy suit, and we all agreed he looked great. To this day, we have yet to find the black pants.

# CHAPTER 19

# CELEBRATION OF LIFE

I do not remember much about Monday, October 15, 2012, other than it was the day of the family viewing. Rochelle and I went shopping because we had not packed properly. The week before, the only thing on my mind was getting to Gretna to be with Mom and my family. I did not think to pack an outfit for the viewing or the rosary. Dad was a trooper, and he went shopping with us.

I found some black patterned pants with a coordinating top and a black jacket. The print on the blouse was red, pink, black, and white. I wanted something to make the outfit pop so I looked for a flower to pin on the jacket. The decision was easy because there was only one option. There was a large red rose, and it coordinated perfectly with my outfit. I got the chills and could not wait to tell Dad about my find. The flower was meant to be!

Mom and Dad treasured red roses, as the rose played a significant role in their lives. When Mom was diagnosed in 1993, a parishioner sent her a folder; inside was the Saint Therese novena. Before they received the generous gift, Mom and Dad did not know anything about the novena. They would say the novena and other prayers on their way to Omaha for Mom's treatment.

The belief is that after the prayer is recited over a period of time, those who prayed the novena would be presented with a rose.

The novena, in part, reads as follows:

Saint Therese, the Little Flower, please pick me a rose from the heavenly garden, and send it to me with a message of love. Ask God to grant me the favor I thee implore, and tell Him I will love Him each day more and more."

This prayer is said in conjunction with other prayers each day.

Following one of Mom's treatments in 1994, she and Dad stopped at Saint Mary's Cathedral in Lincoln, Nebraska. Mom and Dad prayed and lit a candle before they left. When they turned around to leave, there were roses in the pew behind them. This experience reassured then, and they felt very blessed.

After we finished shopping, we went to Mac's Drive-In for lunch. We stopped by the funeral home one final time before heading back to Indianola to prepare for the viewing. We returned to the house and relaxed for a short time. Several of our generous neighbors had stopped in during the day, and once again Scott and Josh welcomed and visited with them as we were finalizing plans.

I was nervous and excited to see Mom for the first time since she passed away. It had been two days since she passed, and I could not wait to see her. This is the best way I can describe how I was feeling: I knew she was gone, but I also had a sense of false hope that we actually would get to talk to her. I know that sounds crazy, but I think I was still numb and exhausted and maybe even in denial.

We gathered in the meeting room to talk with the funeral director. He told us everything was in place and we were welcome to see Mom whenever we were ready. He also pointed out that so many flowers and plants had been delivered, they were running out of room in the viewing area. Some of the floral arrangements had to be placed outside of the viewing area to make room for our family and friends.

We headed back to the viewing room and stood by Mom's casket. She looked amazing! She was beautiful as ever. She looked so healthy, so vibrant and so peaceful. It was really hard to comprehend that she had been so sick just days earlier. Mom looked like her healthy self, and it was hard to accept that she was really gone.

Our grandma Nettie was notorious for taking pictures of bodies at funerals. On a couple of occasions I would came across a random picture of a body as I was flipping through some of her pictures. It made me uncomfortable, and I could not figure out why she would do that. Years ago Mom politely asked Grandma why she took those pictures, and Grandma said she wanted to remember how people looked.

When Rochelle and I were looking at Mom, I turned to Rochelle and said, "Would it be weird if I pulled a Grandma Nettie?"

Rochelle knew exactly what I was talking about, and we agreed I should not take a picture. We laughed a little, and it certainly lightened the mood. Mom looked so healthy that I wanted a picture to remind me of how she'd been before her illness took over. I was still having nightmares about the last couple days of her life, and I thought having a photograph would help counteract them. I took a mental image, and I will remember forever how peaceful she looked.

Our family and friends gathered in the viewing room, and we watched Mom's video for the first time. There was not a dry eye in the room. The video came together so nicely, and it was a wonderful testament to Mom's life and legacy. The pictures were dated between 1956 and 2012. The photographs included Mom when she was little, with her brothers and family; Mom and Dad during their early days as a couple as well as at their wedding and on their honeymoon; and from Rochelle's and my births through the last picture taken of Mom and Dad with the four grandkids at the hospital on June 23, 2012, when Kardyn was one day old. The final picture was of a rainbow with the words "Nancy's Rainbow." A wonderful family friend took the photograph after she learned of Mom's diagnosis in March 2012. She took it as she was leaving Mom and Dad's house. The video was emotional to watch, but it couldn't have turned out any better.

Tuesday, October 16, was visitation for the public as well as the rosary that evening. We stopped at the funeral home to see Mom again and visit with people who had stopped by to pay their final respects. We stayed for a couple of hours. We wanted to see her body as much as possible because we knew the day of the funeral we would have very little time to see her. During the public viewing, many people told us they were shocked when they'd learned of Mom's passing. A lot of people did not even know Mom was sick.

That evening the rosary took place at Saint Catherine's in Indianola. It was difficult to pull up to the church and see the hearse in the parking lot.

I hated the thought that Mom was not with us and the fact we were going to a rosary in her honor. We had a flower ceremony before the rosary. All of the beautiful arrangements from the funeral home were taken to the church, and the funeral director read the cards and words of comfort. The church was a beautiful sight when we walked in for the flower ceremony. Our family was showered with plants and floral arrangements.

It was extremely emotional to walk into the church. From the back, all I could focus on was the casket near the altar. I kept wanting to change the ending of the story, but I knew this was God's plan and I was at peace with it. The last time I stood at the end of that aisle, with Mom up front, was when Dad was getting ready to walk me down the aisle on my wedding day. This time, Mom's body was at the front of the church, but it was for her funeral. How could that be?

The rosary was beautiful. Several people supported us by attending. People traveled both near and far to be there for our family. After the rosary, we played Mom's video on the projector for others to view. It was such a nice tribute to Mom and the life she had lived to the fullest. After the video was over, people offered their condolences. It was comforting to have their support. God gave us strength, and our family and friends provided us with comfort, support, and shoulders to cry on. Following the rosary, several peopled joined us at home, and we continued to reminisce about Mom. She would have loved having all of the people at our house. She always said, "The more the merrier." Our house burst at the seams with all the love and fellowship from our family and friends.

Wednesday, October 17, was the day of Mom's funeral. We had been planning for that day since October 13. We wanted every last detail to be perfect because that is how Mom would have wanted it. She always gave projects her all, and she saw them through, right up to the last minor detail. The mood around our house that morning was better than I expected it to be. We got up and got ready and left the house only a few minutes later than we'd planned. We wanted to get to the church early so we could see Mom one final time. Our family and friends were to gather at the church hall prior to the funeral. We arrived at the church, and Mom's casket was in the back. I looked in and thought, *This is the last time I will physically see Mom's body on this earth.* I could not take my eyes off her. I wanted to imprint her image in my mind so I would never forget. I knew when

I turned to walk away, all I'd have left to remember her by would be photographs. I reached out, touched her hand and said, "See you later."

We walked over to the church hall and waited for ten o'clock. We had time to visit with family and friends. I talked to our family friend, Deb, and her daughter Paige. I told them how much I dreaded leaving Dad on Sunday. I was trying to focus on Mom's funeral, but it was hard to not look beyond it. I was terribly saddened by the thought of leaving Dad. We spent forty-two days with Mom and Dad in Gretna, and the last four days had been filled with regular visits from family and friends. Deb assured us that she and her husband, Doug, would be there for Dad, and they would not leave him alone. They even offered to let him stay with them, but Dad declined because he knew that at some point he would have to learn to live without Mom. The offer was very much appreciated, and Rochelle and I knew our friends would stand by their word and take great care of Dad.

The funeral director came over to the hall to let us know it was time for the funeral to start. We lined up and walked toward the church. It was obvious how much Mom was loved and how many lives she had touched during her lifetime. Saint Catherine's is a large church and holds several people. There was not enough room for everyone to sit. People lined the sides of the church and the stairs to the choir. I have never seen the church that full. It was very humbling and inspiring to see the impact Mom had on so many people. We estimated that well over five hundred people attended. Along with the flowers and plants, we donated approximately $7,500 to the Lied Transplant Center in Omaha from the generous memorials given in Mom's name. The funds were dedicated to breast cancer research.

God continued to give us strength when we needed it most. We were comforted by all of the spiritual happenings that had taken place before Mom's death. We had an overwhelming sense of peace. Dad, Rochelle, and I did not shed a single tear during Mom's funeral. I felt some tears build up as we sang "On Eagles Wings" and "Here I am Lord," but I continued to sing along with the rest of the congregation.

During the homily, we witnessed another amazing spiritual event. Monsignor Witt was describing Mom's final days and how she'd seen an angel the night before she passed away. All of a sudden I smelled incense. It was the exact same smell we'd experienced at Rochelle and Scott's house. At first I thought my mind was playing tricks on me. I looked at Josh and asked if he smelled it, and he nodded yes. I looked to my right, and I saw Scott looking our way, indicating that he too smelled the incense. Dad was to my right, and he told me he smelled it even before I asked him. The scent lasted approximately ten seconds, and it was gone. If you recall, Rochelle was disappointed that she did not smell the incense at her house on October 12. God blessed us with a miracle by allowing all of us to smell the incense during Mom's funeral.

We spoke with Monsignor Witt after the funeral. He jokingly pointed out that we had been talking during his homily. He asked us why, and we told him about the incense. He agreed a miracle had been performed, because the incense was not lit until *after* the homily. He explained that the smell of incense indicated all the prayers for Mom were being lifted up to heaven. We were so blessed to have experienced the two incidents. We had a sense of peace before the funeral, but the second episode with the incense was nothing short of a miracle. It was validation that Mom's soul was in heaven, and she was assuring us that she was more than okay. We talked to other people after the funeral and only a couple of them had smelled the incense. One person had just lost his dad a couple of weeks earlier, and this experience brought tears to his eyes.

I was taken back by the number of people at the funeral. When we walked in, we saw how full the church was, but we were focused on Mom. We embraced the music and saw all of the folks who were there to honor her. People drove from near and far to be there and support us. I was pleasantly surprised to see my boss take Communion. He had an important deposition in southern Missouri that day, but instead he drove seven hours to attend Mom's funeral. Some of Rochelle's coaches from Doane, Mom's friends from grade school and high school, and a host of employees from Community Hospital were there. Rochelle's in-laws drove from Utica, and my in-laws drove from Olathe. Dad's coffee buddies from Indianola and McCook attended. Our neighbors, fellow farmers, businessmen and businesswomen, high-school friends, college roommates, teammates, and countless others attended the funeral. It was so amazing to see how many lives Mom touched during her time on earth.

After the funeral, I was greeted by three of my best friends from Kansas City. I had no idea they were planning on coming, and it meant a lot to me that they would travel such a distance to be there during this difficult time. Our family will be forever grateful to everyone who was there in body and spirit. It meant so much to us to have the love and support of the amazing people we have met during the years.

After the funeral, we made our way to the cemetery. During the car ride there, Rochelle, Dad, and I talked about how nice the funeral was. We all said we did not shed a tear, and we agreed that God gave us the strength. We had shed so many tears leading up to Mom's death, I thought we would be a mess during her funeral, but it was the complete opposite. We talked about how amazing it was that Rochelle was able to experience the incense. We definitely missed Mom, but given all of the spiritual experiences and reassurances, it was hard to be sad. We knew she was in heaven and in a much better place than we were. Mom's earthly life was over, but her eternity had just begun.

After the burial ceremony, we went back to the church hall for a luncheon. It was nice to visit with our family and friends. A woman approached me and said she assumed Mom planned her funeral. She was shocked when I told her Dad, Rochelle, and I made all of the arrangements. She told me it was "so Nancy," and it was perfect. It was such a nice compliment because we wanted it to be the way Mom would have planned. Based on the one comment alone, I think we succeeded.

At the end of the luncheon, our family and friends helped us gather as many red roses as possible from all of the arrangements. Rochelle's good friend gave us contact information for a lady in Tennessee who makes rosaries out of rose petals. We wanted to make sure we had enough to make rosaries for our immediate family members.

That evening we all gathered around the dining table and opened the numerous cards and read the beautiful messages from friends and family. We helped Dad write thank-you notes, and we talked about how wonderful Mom's celebration of life was. Mom's perseverance rubbed off on us. We finished writing the thank-you notes around two in the morning. We were still in awe about the experience with the incense at the funeral. We felt blessed to have smelled the incense a few days earlier, but the fact that we experienced it a second time was breathtaking. Mom lived a wonderful life. She faced her battles as they were thrown at her, and she relied on her unwavering faith to see her through. It was a relief to know she was in heaven, pain free, and worry free.

The following day was very windy. We were so thankful the weather had been perfect for Mom's funeral. We visited the cemetery and some of the flowers were still in place, but others had blown off her grave. It was emotional to stand over Mom's grave. The dirt was freshly piled up, and the headstone was not in place. I thought about how my subsequent visits to Indianola would be so different. I also had a sick feeling in my stomach about the thought of leaving Dad. We were going to return to our homes, jobs, lives, and Dad was going to be by himself at the farm. He was a grieving widower who would be reminded constantly about the terrible loss we just suffered. *Will he be okay living by himself? How will he go to bed or wake up every morning without Mom? Will his broken heart ever be mended? Will Dad ever experience true happiness? Who will drive the combine during harvest?* All of these thoughts and then some rushed through my mind. Before Mom passed away I couldn't imagine life without her, and now that she was gone, I could not imagine how Dad would ever cope without her. I am not trying to shortchange Dad, because he is an incredibly brave, strong person, but he and Mom did almost everything together for thirty-three years. Being alone was something he was going to have to adjust to, and it would not be easy.

We did our best to enjoy the rest of our time at home, but we all dreaded Sunday. Our bosses had been generous to give us time off during Mom's illness, and we all needed to get back to normal. That is what Mom would have wanted. As we pulled away, Dad stood on the front steps and waved. In the past, he and Mom would have stood together, and we would always honk a couple of times as we drove down the blacktop. This time, we tooted our horns and wiped our tears as we drove away. Seeing Dad stand there by himself was something I had been dreading since the day we learned about Mom's terminal illness.

Thank God for wonderful friends and family. They promised to keep Dad company after we left on Sunday, and they did just that. Dad and Doug spent most of that afternoon and evening together. When we arrived home, we called Dad to let him know we had made it. He said he and Doug were out and about. He sounded strong and positive, but I knew he was crumbling inside. He was dreading that night more than any of us. He had to drive home by himself, and go home to a quiet, dark house by himself. His nightly routine was no longer the same. In the past Dad and Mom would watch shows they had previously recorded. They would fall asleep in their recliners in the living room and eventually make their way to bed. Not this time. Dad was alone in the house he and Mom once shared. Everything was there except Mom.

It breaks my heart a thousand times over to think about the emotional pain that accompanied this time in our lives. My sister and I were heartbroken, but I cannot even begin to understand how horrible it was for Dad. He is an independent man, but he was forced to learn to do everything by himself. Dad can do a lot around the house, but cooking is not his forte. Thanks to the generosity of our family, friends, and neighbors, Dad's freezer was always full. They made Dad several meals and divided them into small portions so he could pull meals out of the freezer whenever he wanted. He had plenty to eat for several weeks, which gave us time to plan the menu for the following months.

Mom is always on my mind. I never want to forget how much of an impact she had, not only my life but on the lives of so many. She was such an inspiration, and she really knew how to live. I miss her every day, but I can also hear her say, "I don't want you to be sad. You have to keep living and be happy." We had to get back to normal because that is what Mom would want. Life would never be the same, but I strived to be happy, despite the fact our number-one fan and cheerleader was no longer a phone call away. I had a really hard time wondering how Dad would get back to normalcy without Mom.

The weekend following Mom's funeral Dad drove to Gretna to spend time with Rochelle's family. Harvest was over, thanks to help from our neighbors, and the long, cold winter was ready to set in. I knew Dad would be able to keep himself busy during the week, but I dreaded the weekends. We did our best to book Dad's schedule solid so he wouldn't have to spend weekends alone. Halloween was right around the corner, so Josh and I asked Dad to come to our house so he could see the boys in their costumes and take part in trick-or-treating.

After Mom's death, I grew fond of the song "Homesick" by Mercy Me. The song is about missing a loved one who is in heaven and longing to be with him or her. It also asks for the strength to make it through without a loved one by your side. For me, the highlights of the song are the following lyrics: "In Christ, there are no good-byes. In Christ, there is no end." We are only on this earth for a very short time, but knowing we have eternal life waiting for us is a great thing. I love the thought of being reunited with Mom at the end of my life. I hope she is the angel who appears to me when God calls me home.

# CHAPTER 20

# FULFILLING OUR PROMISE

Monday, October 22, 2012, was my first full day back to work. I was happy to be back, and I was welcomed with open arms from my boss and coworkers. I was ready to get back to normal, but I couldn't help but think about all that had happened in six short yet very long weeks. I could not believe that Mom had been given one year to live, but forty-two days later we were mourning her loss. Mom would have said the way her life ended was a blessing. When she was given a year to live, she was afraid she would lose control of her thoughts, feelings, and actions. I firmly believe that if she'd known her life was going to end, she would not have wanted to rewrite the ending. She did not want to live a year in such poor health. I can still hear her say, "If this is all that is left for me on this earth, I don't want it." She was ready to depart, although she was sad to leave her family behind. She knew eternal life was awaiting her arrival, and she was ready to meet God.

On my first morning back, each one of my coworkers stopped by my office to offer condolences and remind me to speak up and ask for help if I needed it. They know how independent I am; seldom do I ask for help with personal situations. I am incredibly blessed to work for a caring, kind boss and extraordinarily nice people. My work family is definitely my second family, and each and every coworker holds a special place in my heart.

In an effort to be proactive with my health and to fulfill my promise to Mom, I made an appointment at the Breast Cancer Prevention Center at the University of Kansas Hospital. When I made the appointment at the end of September I thought Mom would be alive at the time of my initial consultation on October 23. I wanted to be able to reassure her that I'd gotten a clean bill of health, although she did not know I was BRCA2 positive.

I struggled during my appointment. I was not emotionally prepared: it was only six days after Mom's funeral, and the clinic is located in a cancer center. All the negative feelings came flooding back as soon as I parked and walked inside. When I got off the elevator, Missys' Boutique was right there. I had a flashback. I could vividly see Mom walking around the quaint store with me just eighteen months earlier; she had been shopping for bras and prosthetics after her mastectomy. I saw several people who were very sick along with their family members who were trying to be strong for their loved ones. The sight of wheelchairs, oxygen tanks, face masks, bald heads, and everything medical made me extremely sad. It took all I had to keep walking toward the office and not turn around and leave. In fact, as soon as I saw the sign for Breast Cancer Prevention Center, I stood there and stared at it for a short time. I strongly considered walking away and never going back. I have a bad habit of making appointments and then cancelling them at the last minute, but in this situation I knew I owed it to Mom, Josh, and our boys to follow through and move forward with preventative care.

I pulled myself together, walked into the office, and was greeted by a very welcoming staff. As soon as I filled out the paperwork, a nurse called me into the exam room. I walked two steps down the hall and broke down. I hadn't cried like that in a very long time. I was terrified of being there, and all of the emotions associated with losing Mom just days earlier were overwhelming. I was still processing the fact Mom would not be a phone call away when I was at the appointment. I cried the entire time I was there. I apologized over and over because of the way I was acting. The staff was very understanding, and they reassured me I was doing the right thing by taking the first step in being proactive.

The doctor and the physician's assistant came in shortly thereafter; once again, I started crying. We reviewed Mom's history with breast cancer, and I told them she had passed away ten days earlier. The doctor did a breast exam and reassured me everything was normal. Her recommendation was to have a baseline mammogram and continue with surveillance, which meant a physical exam and a rotation of mammograms, MRIs, and ultrasounds every six months. She recommended women who are carriers of the BRCA genetic mutation to begin surveillance at age twenty-five. A mammogram is important; however, MRIs and ultrasounds are more sensitive and typically pick up things a mammogram cannot. Each test is beneficial, and high-risk women are encouraged to undergo an intense surveillance plan. Some women choose to undergo surveillance while others choose surgery.

I felt a huge sense of relief once the physical exam was over and I understood what the surveillance program entailed. I got dressed, and the doctor asked me to meet her in the consultation room so she could give me a risk assessment. I told her I would hear her out, but I had already made up my mind. She wanted to tell me about several clinical studies and the surveillance regimen. Josh and I, however, had made a decision: we wanted to have one more child, and then I would undergo a prophylactic bilateral mastectomy with reconstruction. Given Mom's strong history and early diagnosis at the age of thirty-six, I was not willing to have anxiety every six months until cancer was found. I told the doctor that breast cancer had destroyed our family once; therefore I was willing to take extreme measures to ensure it would never happen again.

The doctor understood and gave me her recommendation. She wanted me to have a baseline mammogram and an MRI; if both tests came back negative, she would give us her blessing to start trying for baby number three. She assured me that my high risk for breast cancer would not increase until age thirty. Women with a BRCA 2 mutation, she said, have 50–85 percent risk of breast cancer and a 15–40 percent chance of ovarian cancer. She explained that after I reached age thirty, my chances of developing breast cancer would increase by 2 percent every year.

The doctor left a lasting impression on me when she told me that more times than not, daughters follow in their mother's footsteps. She said that if I were between the ages of thirty-five and forty, she would strongly discourage our plan to try for another baby and recommend that I move forward with preventative surgery.

We also discussed surveillance for ovarian cancer since I had an increased risk for that too. She said a pelvic ultrasound with a yearly CA125 blood test is recommended beginning between the ages of twenty-five and thirty-five and until the uterus and ovaries are removed, usually at thirty-five or after childbearing is over. A total hysterectomy reduces the risk of ovarian cancer by 95 percent; however, women who undergo removal of ovaries before age forty-five have an 84 percent chance of having a fatal cardiovascular event and an increased risk of cognitive impairment.

I am embarrassed to admit that my body mass index at that time was well above where it should have been. I'd needed to lose weight before we tried for another baby. I had lost twenty pounds through diet and exercise, but I am a stress eater. As soon as we learned of the extent of Mom's illness, I quit exercising and ate whatever I wanted, whenever I wanted. Given Mom's strong history with breast cancer and my BRCA2 and overweight status, the risk assessment indicated my lifetime risk for breast cancer was 94.5 percent and between 40 and 50 percent for ovarian cancer.

I was on information overload at the end of the consultation; however, I appreciated hearing all of the details. I was relieved to learn that preventative surgery would reduce my lifetime risk of breast cancer by 95 percent. I definitely had a lot to think about, but I was confident about our decision to add to our family before I had any preventative measures. We remained hopeful I would conceive quickly so I could meet with a surgeon. Before I left the facility, I made a November 1, 2012, appointment for my baseline mammogram and one on November 8 for my baseline MRI.

Thinking about the appointment that evening, I was both upset and reassured. Being BRCA2 positive is both a curse and a blessing. I do not like the idea of being at high risk for developing cancer, but I do appreciate the fact doctors pay very close attention to patients with this status. In addition, most insurance companies will pay for genetic testing and diagnostic exams and procedures. I was relieved that my first appointment was over; however, I dreaded the upcoming mammogram and MRI. It was something I had to do to honor Mom's legacy and because I'd promised Josh I would be proactive so we could live to see our children and grandchildren.

As previously arranged, Dad packed up his bag and his black lab, Tess, and they drove to Olathe to spend the week of Halloween with us. The farthest Tess had been from the farm was the gas station in Indianola. We weren't sure how she would manage traveling six to seven hours. I hated the thought of Dad traveling alone, but knowing Tess was with him helped lessen my anxiety. Besides, Bryson and Holden loved the thought of having a dog. They had been asking for one, so we told them they could see what it would be like to have Tess at our house for a week.

The weather in October 2012 was atypical. It was somewhat mild, nice enough to have the windows open. After I got home from work, Dad and I would sit in the living room talking while the boys played out back with Tess. They had fun walking her around on her leash in the backyard. I was a bit uneasy letting the boys play outside, but our backyard is fenced in, and we could see them from our living room. I told Dad that I was nervous about the boys being outside by themselves because of a four-and-a-half-foot window well. We talked about how much Mom had disliked the window, afraid one of the kids would fall inside the well. Josh and I had intended to buy a cover, but although we'd lived in the house for five years, we'd failed to do so.

Dad and I talked about how weird it was that Mom was really gone. It seemed like she had been gone for a long time, but it was only eighteen days. Then I heard a faint cry. My heart stopped when I realized it was coming from Holden. Then I heard Bryson's voice getting closer and closer to our screen door. "Mom! Mom! Holden fell in the window!"

My heart sunk, and my adrenaline kicked in high gear. I was thankful that I could hear Holden's cry because that meant he was alive, but I was terrified to look down into the well, afraid of what we would find. Dad, Bryson, and I looked down the four-and-a-half-foot hole and found Holden lying on his back. His left leg was bent backward and his head was between two large boulders. I jumped down and picked him up. He was crying, but everything seemed to be intact. I asked if he were okay, and he said yes but kept sobbing. I think he was more frightened than anything.

I asked Bryson what had happened, and he said they were playing with Tess, and as Holden was walking backward with the leash, he stepped right into the uncovered window well. He fell flat on his back. We took Holden inside and looked him over from head to toe. It gives me chills to report that Holden walked away without a bruise or a scratch. The two large rocks were less than a foot apart from one another. He could have easily hit his head and broken several bones. We truly believe Mom, our guardian angel, was there and caught him as he fell. There is no earthly explanation for how he walked away without a single injury. The window well is now covered, and we have not had any other incidences with it.

Bryson (General Grievous), Papa and Holden
(Darth Vader)—Halloween 2012

On November 1, I pulled up to the cancer center. Once again my nerves got the best of me. I knew this was something that had to be done, but I did not like the feelings I was having as I parked my car and walked inside. I checked in and waited for like what seemed like forever. Eventually, I was taken to a room with several dressing rooms and given a pink gown. I put the gown on and found a locker to hold my personal belongings. As I entered the waiting room, I couldn't help but notice that I was the youngest woman there by at least ten years. I felt as if the other women were staring at me, but I am sure they were wondering why I were there, considering my age.

I was nervous as could be, and it was obvious the other ladies were nervous too. Nobody talked. We all just sat there, each of us hoping her name would be the next one called. I waited for approximately thirty minutes before my name was finally called. The tech was wonderful. I told her my history, and she listened patiently. As usual, I cried during most of the visit. I was not excited to be there but knew it was what I had to do. Once I was done the tech told me to go to the waiting room. She said it is not uncommon to have to repeat the mammogram, particularly since it was my first and there was nothing to compare it to. I sat nervously in the waiting room expecting to get a call back. A nurse took me to another room. She said the radiologist looked at my mammogram, and everything looked great. She said I could get dressed and to have a good rest of the day. I was on cloud nine when I left. I still had to have an MRI before we could start trying for our third child, but it was nice to check the mammogram off the list.

I called my dad to let him know my baseline mammogram was clear. "Thank God!" he exclaimed. I did not tell him about the appointment the following week for my baseline MRI. If I had, I figured, he would put two and two together and figure out my BRCA2 status. It was not the right time to share the actual results of my genetic testing with him.

On November 8, and the days leading up to it, I was nervous about the breast MRI. I thought it would get easier each time I went, but it never did. I was scared to death to have an MRI. It was my first, and I had no idea what to expect. I sat impatiently in the waiting room, and they eventually called me. I had to wear a gown from head to toe and make sure all of my bobby pins were removed from my hair. The nurse explained the procedure. I had to get an IV so I could have an MRI with contrast. I went to a holding room and an IV was started. The nurse then led me back to the room where I would have the MRI.

The nurse said there was no ladylike way to get on the table. A breast MRI has to be completed with the patient laying on her stomach. I threw open my gown and lay down on my stomach on the table. Once I was situated, the table rolled back into the machine. They gave me a squeeze ball so I could alert the tech any time I experienced any problems. The tech estimated the exam would last approximately forty minutes. They told me to hold as still as possible; otherwise the test would have to be repeated at a later date. I tried to stay positive and as still as possible during the exam, but it was scary. I tried to distract myself by singing songs in my head, but I grew increasingly nervous throughout the test.

At one point, I started panicking. I thought about my poor mother having an MRI just weeks before and couldn't even begin to imagine the fear she must have felt. The thought of that alone over took me. I almost squeezed the ball to have the tech stop the test, but then I decided to pray. I knew if they had to stop the test, I would have to reschedule and do it all over again. The MRI is so sensitive, it has to be scheduled around a woman's monthly cycle. I had a plan, and I wanted to stay on track. I did not want to wait another month to schedule the MRI, because that would delay our goal of conceiving our third baby. After about thirty-five minutes I was advised the test was complete and that I would receive a call in a week with the results. The waiting game was not easy for me. I wanted to know the test was clear so my mind would be at ease and Josh and I could move forward with our plan. I received a call five days later from one of the nurses, who let me know the MRI was clear. I was elated.

Josh and I went out to dinner on Friday, November 16, to celebrate my birthday and the great results from my first two diagnostic tests. We went to the Elephant Bar and Grill and had a nice, quiet dinner. We agreed to move forward with our plan.

The following week was Thanksgiving and Dad's fifty-sixth birthday. Dad and Tess were at our house during the days leading up to the holiday, and we made plans to spend the weekend in Gretna with Rochelle and her family. Josh, Bryson, and Holden led the way to Gretna, and Dad and I followed. I had bought Dad a birthday card but rather than mailing it, I wanted to take it with us to Gretna so he could open it on his birthday. I grabbed the card and unsealed envelope as we left the house. I put the card and envelope in the space below the cup holder in Dad's truck, and away we went. As we were driving, Dad and I heard a strange noise, but we did not think much about it.

As we got close to Gretna, I started feeling emotional. I was very excited to see the rest of the family, but it would be difficult to walk into Rochelle and Scott's house for the first time since Mom passed away. It had only been a little over one month, and I was not sure how I would handle it. This also was the first holiday we would celebrate without her. It was the first of many firsts. In years past, we went to the farm for Thanksgiving, and Mom planned and prepared the entire meal. Rochelle and I would help, but Mom was definitely head chef. We warned the guys that our first attempt at preparing Thanksgiving dinner without Mom would be memorable, because we were not sure if we could pull it off without her guidance. We decided to have fun with it and cook away. Surprisingly, it all turned out well. The only thing missing was Mom.

As we were debating on "how much of this and how much of that" to put in the numerous side dishes, Dad received several texts from family and friends wishing him happy birthday and happy Thanksgiving. The messages were heartfelt, and it was a very emotional day. To distract from the sadness, I asked Dad for the keys to his truck so I could go get his birthday card. I went to the truck, grabbed his card and went back inside. Dad put on his glasses and took the card out of the envelope. As he opened the card, Mom's picture fell out. We all stopped in our tracks. Someone had given us some laminated cards with Mom's picture and a nice poem after her death, and Dad kept one of them in his truck. We were dumbfounded when it fell out of his birthday card. The noise Dad and I heard on the way to Gretna must have been Mom's picture falling into his card. We took that as a sign that Mom was wishing him a happy birthday. We felt blessed, and the somber mood was lifted.

Our family tradition is to take part in Black Friday. Dad was stressed out about shopping for the grandkids for Christmas because that was something he and Mom always did together. Then they went home and wrapped the gifts. We talked Dad into coming along with us to experience Black Friday at its finest. He had gone with us in McCook, but it is a whole different experience in the city. As soon as we pulled up to Walmart in Gretna, Dad started getting grouchy. We had to park out in the middle of nowhere and walk quite a distance in the bitter cold to fight the crowd. Rochelle, Josh, and I were excited to start shopping, but Dad would rather have been anywhere but there. We found what we set out to get and discussed our next stop. Dad interrupted us and told us to take him back home. He had enough shopping after one stop, and he made it abundantly clear that he was done. Rochelle, Josh, and I dropped him off at the house with Scott and the kids, and off we went on our shopping adventure. Several hours later, we returned with all of our Christmas shopping complete.

I was sad to see the weekend end, but we were already planning our next get-together for Anisten's birthday party. Josh and I and our kids headed home, and Dad stayed with Rochelle and Scott for a few more days. He was in no rush to get home because the farming season was over, and there was no point returning to an empty house.

The following day at work, I had to get through several e-mails and voice mails. As I was listening to my voice mails, I noticed I had nineteen saved messages. I decided that was a good time to review the saved messages to see if any of them needed to be addressed or deleted. The first messages were related to cases that had settled, so I deleted them. I would listen to the first few seconds and hit 7 to delete the message. I was flying through the old messages and assumed I could delete the subsequent ones. My right finger was on 7, and a pen was in my left hand, on the chance I needed to write down a message.

All of a sudden I heard, "Hi sweetheart, it's Mom." I almost pressed 7 and deleted the message. I stopped myself just in time and listened to the rest. I was so excited to hear her voice. I don't know what prompted me to save her message, which was from August 2012, but I am so thankful that I did.

I immediately called Dad and Rochelle to let them know about the treasure I'd found. I have the capability at work to convert voice mails to e-mails, and I sent the voice mail to Dad and Rochelle so they could hear Mom's voice. We were all very excited and comforted by the sound of her voice.

On December 18, Josh and I found out I was pregnant. My anticipated due date was August 31, 2013—exactly one year from the day we learned Mom had several spots scattered throughout her brain. December 18 was a big day in our family for another reason. It was the day Rochelle went to the doctor to get her baseline mammogram as she had promised Mom she would do.

## Chapter 21

# Rochelle's Proactive Stance and Unexpected News

Our family got together in Gretna the weekend of December 14, 2012, to celebrate Anisten's fourth birthday and Christmas. Rochelle reminded us about her upcoming appointment on December 18. This was part of her promise to Mom that she would be proactive about her health. Her ob-gyn wanted her to wait six months postpartum before she had her baseline due to all of the changes that take place during pregnancy. I had just learned I was pregnant when Rochelle called to let me know she'd gone to her appointment and was waiting for the results. I wanted to share our exciting news with her, but I was still in shock because we'd found out minutes before.

Papa, Bryson, Kardyn, Anisten, and Holden
celebrating Christmas (2012)

Josh and I spent Christmas day at our house with Dad, Tess, and the Smiths. We had a wonderful Christmas together, but again, it was another first without Mom. She loved Christmas, and it seemed strange not to have her pouring eggnog and singing to Christmas music. When we were kids, she had emphasized the importance of taking time to opening presents. We loved savoring the magical moments of Christmas morning. I could hear her saying, "One at a time." There were several years where we took hours to open presents. We would take many breaks in between gifts so we could refill our glasses with eggnog and get another piece of German stollen bread from Sehnert's Bakery. I could feel Mom's presence, but missed having her physically there with us. In years past, she had thoroughly enjoyed watching her grandchildren open their gifts on Christmas morning.

Rochelle had to work on Christmas Day, so we planned to celebrate New Year's in Olathe. Josh and I also thought it would be a nice change of pace to host a holiday at our house. We had traveled a lot during the previous weeks due to Mom's sickness and funeral. We wanted to get the boys back into their normal routine after weeks of back and forth. Rochelle and Scott planned to drive to our house late on Thursday, December 27, to celebrate the holiday weekend with us. I got up that morning and went to work expecting to come home to a full house.

I told my boss, Mike, that my family was coming to town to celebrate Christmas. Given the caring man that he is, he told me to take the rest of the day off so I could enjoy some quality family time. I was hesitant to take him up on his offer because he had been so accommodating and understanding during Mom's illness. I thought I should stay and try to catch up. He insisted I leave early, however, so I did just that.

I called Dad on my way home to let him know Mike had given me the day off and to ask if I needed to pick up anything at the store. He was excited I was coming home early and thought we had everything we needed at the house for the weekend. When I pulled up to the house I noticed Rochelle and Scott's truck was not parked outside. I was a little confused but assumed Scott had gone to the store. I didn't think much more about it. When I walked through the door, Dad was sitting on the couch holding Kardyn. Anisten, Bryson, and Holden were in the basement playing. I asked Dad where Rochelle and Scott were, and he hesitated.

Dad said Rochelle had received a call from the hospital the day before, but she was working so she missed the call. On Friday morning, while she was getting ready at our house, she checked her voice mail; the message was from a nurse saying she needed to make an appointment for a repeat mammogram. Rochelle called immediately, and there was an opening that afternoon at two thirty. Her other option was to wait until January 7, 2013. She was not excited about having to go back to Omaha for the two thirty appointment, but she did not want to wait another week. The waiting game was very unsettling, so she and Scott decided to head back to Omaha, get the repeat mammogram, and drive back to our house so we could celebrate as planned. They fully expected to get good results, so they left Anisten and Kardyn with Dad.

I was a little taken back but remembered the radiology tech saying that more times than not women get called back when they have their baseline mammograms because there are no earlier films to compare them to. I shared this information with Dad to calm his nerves.

Dad broke down, and he said, "I cannot take another illness."

We tried so hard to be positive, but given Mom's history our minds naturally went down the path to the C word. I felt a little uneasy but knew in my heart it was going to be okay.

Once again, we found ourselves waiting for the phone to ring. We desperately wanted Rochelle to call to let us know she'd checked out fine and they were on their way back. It seemed like an eternity, but Rochelle finally called. She did not deliver the news we were hoping to hear. She let us know that the area of concern was located under her left armpit and that she'd been referred to an oncologist. She was scheduled to have a biopsy to rule out cancer. We tried so hard to be hopeful, but Dad and I both started crying. How could this be? Mom had passed away only ten weeks earlier, and now we were facing the potential of Rochelle having cancer. It didn't make sense. According to *my* plans, life was supposed to get easier, not harder. We were still grieving the loss of Mom, and now another hurdle had been thrown in our paths. The first thing I wanted to do was pick up the phone and call Mom so she could reassure us that things were going to be fine. Obviously that was not an option, so I had to kick into "Nancy mode" and be as positive as I could for my family.

I called Josh at work to let him know what was going on. We decided to pack up and travel to Gretna to be with Rochelle and Scott. They wanted their girls home with them but they also wanted us there for moral support. Kardyn, Dad, and I rode together, and Josh, Bryson, Holden, and Anisten followed us. All of the feelings and memories associated with Mom's illness came rushing back—from the dreaded call to the frantic drive to Gretna. I was not mad at God, but I definitely questioned His plan and why yet another potentially tragic event was looming over us. They say God doesn't give us more than we can handle, so Dad and I agreed that He must have a lot of confidence in our family.

Our trip to Gretna seemed longer than usual. Dad and I had a lot of time to talk, but sometimes there were no words to express how we were feeling. He and I have similar personalities, and we allowed our pessimistic natures to creep into the conversation. I tried my best to handle the situation the way Mom would, calmly reminding him that the doctors knew what they were doing. Hopefully, I said, the biopsy would come back benign. We also hoped that if it were cancer, it would be at the earliest stage. We were very thankful that Rochelle had kept her promise to Mom to be proactive. She felt perfectly healthy, so we hoped this was just a blip on the radar, and we could move on.

We finally arrived in Gretna, and as we pulled into the driveway, I felt uneasy. The situation was all too familiar. I dreaded going inside because I could not stand the thought of seeing my sister upset and scared. We were still grieving after losing Mom, and the thought of facing another battle was frightening to say the least. Scott greeted us outside in the frigid temperatures; he had been crying. I asked how Rochelle was doing, and he shrugged his shoulders and said she was doing as good as she could given the circumstances. Scott said that he'd assured Rochelle that they would get though whatever it was, no matter what it was. He said our guardian angel was looking out for us, so we would be okay.

We carried our bags inside, and as soon as I stepped into the house, I hugged Rochelle. She told me how scared she was, and she was so thankful we'd made the trip to be with them. We carried everything in and sat in the living room so we could discuss her appointment and what to expect the following week with the oncologist.

Rochelle and Scott shared the news with their neighbors. They came over for a while and served as a good distraction. They invited us to their New Year's party the following evening, and we accepted their invitation and offered to take some food. My family still did not know I was pregnant, and I was not ready to share the news. I started having morning sickness so I was trying to figure out how to hide the symptoms from them. The one aversion I had was mayonnaise and onions. My default party dip was a corn dip that contained sour cream, corn, cheese, Ro-Tel, green chilies, mayonnaise, and onions. Scott suggested we bring the corn dip. My stomach turned, and my mouth watered as if I were going to throw up. He reviewed the list of ingredients and asked me if I would make it. I tried to avoid the issue, but he wouldn't let it go. I whispered to Josh that he would have to make it or I was going to throw up. I am sure Scott wondered why I didn't jump at the opportunity to make my famous dip. I found ways to get as far away from the kitchen as possible, so I didn't have to have any more conversations about the stomach-churning corn dip.

The following evening, we joined the neighbors for their party. Rochelle said she wanted to go but was not sure how long she would stay. We told her we would stay as long as she wanted. Before we walked next door, Rochelle started crying, and she hugged Dad. She told us how scared she was. We all shed some tears but reminded ourselves that Mom was looking out for us; we would face head on whatever was lying in front of us. We wiped the tears from our eyes and walked over to the neighbors. When we arrived there was so much food, including the corn dip. I avoided the corn dip and alcohol like the plague. I was offered a beer but declined. Later on I was offered a beer again, so I took a fake sip. Rochelle talked about her situation a little bit, but we tried our best to enjoy the evening without remembering the upcoming appointment.

Rochelle's biopsy was scheduled for Monday, December 31. She and Scott went to the appointment, and the rest of us stayed at the house with the kids. We felt a sense of calmness while they were gone. We asked them to call us so we could hear what the doctor had to say. We were so happy when they called and reported things went well. When they arrived at the house, Rochelle had a folder with information. It took my breath away when I saw the words "Cancer Center" on the front of the folder. I tried to mentally bypass that and inquired about the appointment. She said the doctor had pointed out the area of concern on the ultrasound screen. The questionable lymph node was black and enlarged, and the other lymph nodes were white. The doctor said he was not sure what it was, but he hadn't seen anything like this in twenty years. We did not know how to take his comments. We believed that if it were cancer, it would have been obvious, because he saw cancer every day. Furthermore, the fact he hadn't seen this before made us think it was just a freak thing, and all would be well. Rochelle anticipated getting the results of the biopsy later that week. Josh and I packed up our children and drove back to Olathe the following day. We both had to work on Wednesday.

On Friday, January 4, 2013, my cell phone rang, and the caller ID said "Ro Cell." I was anxious about answering the call because I knew our lives could once again change, depending on the message Rochelle delivered.

When I answered the call, she was ecstatic. She reported that the results of the biopsy were benign!

"Thank God!" was my response. I was so relieved. It felt like a ton of bricks had been lifted from my shoulders. We believed the experience happened for a reason, but we were so thankful the scare was behind us. She reported that her doctor wanted her to return in three months for a follow-up ultrasound. The doctor said he expected the questionable lymph node to be gone. Praise the Lord!

I could no longer contain my excitement about being pregnant. I said, "Since you received good news, I want to share our news. I'm pregnant!"

There was a slight pause, followed by "You are? Congratulations!" Rochelle then pointed out how things that happened the previous weekend now made sense. She'd noticed I did not want anything to do with the corn dip and that I was not interested in a new diet plan she had proposed. She and Scott had just invested in Advocare, and they were eager to get their health back on track. She knew I wanted to lose weight, so the fact that I'd declined to purchase the products she was selling confused her. Once I told her the news she said, "It all makes sense now!"

After I talked to Rochelle, I called Dad. The sound of relief in his voice was apparent. He was so thankful, and we talked about how blessed we were that Rochelle's biopsy was benign.

I then said, "Okay. Now it's my turn. I am going to tell you something very exciting."

He paused and asked what it was.

I said, "This is the last time you are going to be told you are going to be a papa!" Josh and I had decided baby number three would complete our family, and Rochelle had a tubal ligation following Kardyn's birth, therefore their family of four was complete.

It took a few seconds for Dad to comprehend what I was saying, and then of course he was very excited. I told him I was barely pregnant, and my due date was August 31.

The rest of the weekend went very well. We felt like the worst was behind us, and we could continue to work through the grieving process of losing Mom but we also could celebrate Rochelle's news and the new life that was developing.

Life continued in the following months. We slowly adjusted to life without Mom's physical presence in our lives. We would find out the gender of our baby at the end of March. We had plans to go to Des Moines to celebrate Josh's grandfather's birthday the weekend of March 17, 2013. As I got out of bed that morning, I felt a gush of blood. I went to the restroom and was terrified because it appeared as though I was having a miscarriage. I was approximately sixteen weeks pregnant and could not stand the thought of another loss in my life. It was too early in the pregnancy to feel fetal movement, so it was unclear to me whether the baby was still alive. I called the doctor's after-hours number and was told to either wait until Monday or go to the emergency room. The nurse on the phone reminded me nothing can be done for a miscarriage. I understood, but I told her that I do not do well with the unknown, so if that was what was going on, I needed to know.

Our friend Jen and her husband met us at the hospital, and they took the boys out for breakfast. Josh and I nervously entered the emergency room and were scared to hear what the doctor had to say. We sat in triage for a short time and then eventually made our way back to the exam room. The doctor walked in, and he said, "Let's get right to it." He wanted to do an ultrasound to determine whether or not the baby was still alive. As soon as he put the probe on my stomach, he said, "It's a girl!" I was so emotionally numb I did not care if it were a boy or a girl. I was so thankful the baby was alive. The little bean was moving all over the place, and the heartbeat was normal for that point in the pregnancy. He instructed me to follow up with my obstetrician the following week. My follow-up appointment went well, and the doctor determined that the baby was doing just fine.

Our official ultrasound was scheduled for March 29. We planned a gender reveal party for the family on Saturday, March 30. Dad watched the boys while Josh and I went to the appointment. As we entered the ultrasound room, the tech asked us whether we wanted to find out the gender.

I said, "We are 99.9 percent sure it is a girl, so please just confirm it." I explained what had happened two weeks earlier. As soon as she put the probe on my stomach, I swore I saw a little turtle head on the top left of the screen. It looked all too familiar, similar to my ultrasounds with

Bryson and Holden. Josh was sitting on my left, and he snickered because he apparently saw the same thing. I turned my head to the right and felt the tears build up. I turned my head toward the tech, and she said, "It definitely is not a girl."

Just two weeks prior we had been faced with the potential reality of losing our baby, and the fact the baby was healthy was all that mattered. After everything we had been through, a healthy baby boy was a true blessing and miracle. We were very excited.

I said, "Well, Laikyn Marie is now Layton Gabriel." As Josh and I discussed later, God's plans are perfect. Because I have the BRCA2 gene, we were meant to have boys. While boys can still be carriers, their chances of getting breast cancer is significantly less than girls.

Our gender-reveal party took place the following day. My sister and her family arrived that afternoon. She said, "I can totally tell it is a girl. If it was a boy, your eyes would be red from crying!"

I chuckled inside and could not wait to see the look on her face when the blue balloons came out of the box. When blue balloons came out of the box, there was a brief moment of silence, then everybody started clapping. We were thrilled to add another boy to our dynamic duo.

That weekend, Rochelle reminded us about her upcoming appointment and ultrasound. Honestly, I had forgotten about it because of the great news she'd already received and the distraction of pregnancy. I was glad she was being proactive, but I hated the thought of her having to experience another ultrasound and potential scare. Regardless, the ultrasound was necessary, so I wished her my best and prayed this would all be behind us once and for all.

The doctors took a "watch and wait" approach because the biopsy results were benign. They hoped the questionable lymph node would be gone. When she was in the ultrasound room, Rochelle quickly picked up on the fact something was wrong. The tech did not say anything as she did the ultrasound. She left the room and returned with a doctor. The doctor looked at the right side to compare it to the left. The doctor said that, unfortunately, the questionable lymph node was larger, and there were more enlarged lymph nodes compared to the previous exam in December. Once again, the doctor recommended a biopsy.

Following the ultrasound the doctor gave a list of potential diagnoses. Of course, doctors always go through the whole list, which ranged from cat-scratch disease to breast cancer to lymphoma. The doctor did not think Rochelle had breast cancer because the ultrasound did not show any abnormalities on the breast tissue, but he did emphasize the need for a biopsy of the lymph nodes to rule out cancer. This was not the news we were expecting. She scheduled her biopsy and was told she would receive the results in a week or so.

I was sitting in the dentist's chair on April 30, when my phone rang. I knew Rochelle had an appointment that day to receive the results of her biopsy. Time felt as it stood still before I accepted the call. I had been talking to the dental hygienist about the rough couple of years we had, with Mom's illness and passing and Rochelle's scare with the biopsies. When the phone rang, the hygienist removed the tools from my mouth so I could answer.

Rochelle asked what I was doing, and I told her I was at the dentist. She said she had been diagnosed with Hodgkin's lymphoma.

"What? What is that?" It was obvious she had been crying, but she was calm—the same level of calmness she'd had when she called to report the cancer spread to Mom's brain.

I felt as if I were dreaming. This was all too similar to what we had previously experienced. I could hear Mom's voice through Rochelle. She said it was not the news she had been expecting, but she had talked to her doctor, who assured her that this was a "good" cancer to have. In my mind, "good" and "cancer" do not belong in the same sentence, especially when my sister is involved.

I lost it. I started crying. The hygienist got the dentist, and he came to the exam room. He was very sympathetic and confirmed that Hodgkin's lymphoma is a "good" cancer. It is very curable and has a very low recurrence rate. I felt better, but I was extremely angry. I was not mad at God, but I was mad at the world!

I went home and talked to our nanny. Jen is a caring woman, and she knew I was upset. She offered to stay and talk for as long as I needed. We sat on our patio, and the boys played outside. It was so nice to have a friend to talk to about this unwelcome news.

I got the boys ready for bed later that evening, and Josh got home around nine o'clock. I did not say much at first, because I couldn't bring myself to deliver the news. As he was sorting through the mail, I said, "Ro has cancer."

He looked at me in disbelief. We talked about it for a short time, and I went to bed. I needed to sleep on it and wrap my mind around what was happening. I tried hard to be positive about the situation, but I was mad and depressed. I knew I would eventually come around, but I had enough.

The following morning, I sent an e-mail to my good friend Gloria. She has experienced a lot of loss and sadness in her life, and she and I really connect. We worked together at the law firm for a short time, but her impact on my life has been monumental. God allowed our paths to cross because he knew we would have similar experiences and would need each other to lean on.

> Good morning. I hope this finds you doing well. Once again I am the bearer of bad news. I am sure people are sick of hearing about the trials of our family. My sister was diagnosed with Hodgkin's lymphoma yesterday. The results were inconclusive last week, so they sent the sample to the University of Nebraska Medical Center for further testing. She had an appointment yesterday and received the news. The good thing is the doctor reassured her that this is the best kind of cancer to have and the survival rate is extremely high. She has to have tests done on Friday, and she meets with her oncologist on Monday to figure out the treatment plan. I am so incredibly sick of the chaos and stress life has thrown our way the past couple of years. I am trying so hard to be positive, but I truly am at a very low point. No matter how hard I pray and no matter how positive I am, it seems to always go the other way. I am really struggling with the "whys." Sorry to be so negative, but I know you understand after being through so many trials throughout your life. I never really hit that low spot with my mom's illness, but I am there now. Just when life starts feeling normal, something like this happens. I

don't know why it can't come in small doses rather than [in] life-changing events. I would love to get together with you sometime to talk. You always make sense of things for me and I appreciate your insight. I feel like I have taken on the role of cheerleader since Mom's illness; however, this cheerleader needs a "pick me up." I will eventually get back on track, but right now I am so angry."

Gloria responded right away, and we arranged to get together that evening. By the end of the day, I was mentally wiped out so I called her and asked for a rain check. She understood, and we arranged another meeting the following week.

Rochelle met with her oncologist, Dr. Tarantolo, the following Monday. A PET scan and other tests were scheduled so the cancer could be staged and a treatment plan developed. Mom's insistence on preventative care helped the doctors catch the cancer early, and she was staged at 1A. Praise the Lord! Life is a matter of perspective. It seemed strange to be celebrating cancer, but what we were really celebrating was the fact the cancer had been caught early and that Rochelle was given a 95 percent survival rate.

At that moment, I had an aha moment. Mom's death was purposeful. It was sad that she was gone, but maybe that is why she passed away when she did. Rochelle and I promised Mom we would be proactive, and we did just that. We both were genetically tested, and we both got our baseline mammograms. Mom saved our lives! Her life was cut short, but it was all part of God's plan. During Dad's surgery in March 2012, Mom made it clear she would gladly shoulder any illness for her family. She gave us life and through her death, we were given knowledge and a second chance to live! Thank you God for allowing us to have such a wonderful mom, and thank you for allowing us to see your master plan come into play.

I debated whether I should tell Rochelle about my BRCA2 status, whether it would help her make sense of the situation so she could have an aha moment. She asked me to attend her first chemotherapy appointment in May 2013. We decided to get coffee before we headed to the transfusion center. As Rochelle turned to grab our coffee from the drive-through window, I said, "I am BRCA2 positive."

She did not respond, so I assumed she didn't hear me. She put her coffee in the cup holder and just looked at me. I explained to her that I'd accepted it and let her know I had a plan. I told her about my appointments at the Breast Cancer Prevention Center and that I planned to have surgery in the near future. I also explained that is why we decided to have another baby so quickly. It took her some time to comprehend, and she was saddened by the news. She felt as if yet another wrench had been thrown at us, and she was sad that I had held in the information for months. I made her promise not to tell Dad, because I did not think he could handle another problem. He was still grieving for Mom and was scared to death that Rochelle had been diagnosed with cancer.

The song "He Said" by Group 1 Crew served as a great reminder during our trying time. At the beginning, the singer questions why bad things keep happening and why life does not always make sense. As the song progresses, we are reminded that God does not give us more than we can handle. There may be times when we feel like we are bending, but God will not let us break. We always must have faith, no matter the situation.

# CHAPTER 22

# ROCHELLE'S JOURNEY: PART 1

Our lives were turned upside down again when Rochelle was diagnosed on April 30, 2013. We knew we had to face her diagnosis head on just as we had Mom's multiple diagnoses, but it was very unsettling. We thought the worst was behind us when we lost Mom, and we were still trying to accept the fact that she was really gone. We could not understand why we had to face another battle, but we knew we had to trust God, and we had faith that He would see us through Rochelle's journey with Hodgkin's lymphoma. We were reassured by her doctors, and we were so thankful the cancer had been caught in its earliest stage. When Rochelle was diagnosed, we felt as if Mom's early death was purposeful and found some peace. We believed this was one answer to the many whys we had asked ourselves. Maybe Mom's death was part of God's plan to catch Rochelle's cancer early, so she would help Scott raise their beautiful daughters. Maybe that had nothing to do with it? We may never know the real answers to our questions on this earth, but I am confident we will find out when we stand before God.

Rochelle kept a journal during her treatment so she could update people about her journey. It is very clear from reading her entries and from talking to her throughout her treatment that Mom's attitude had a big impact on her. Rochelle's positive attitude during her treatment mirrored Mom's positive outlook during her battles.

Once again, God graced us with incredible strength when we needed it. Although Rochelle had a great prognosis, it was so hard to see my sister, my best friend, go through chemotherapy. No time is a good time for cancer diagnosis. All of the emotions from losing Mom were still so fresh. It was disheartening to see my sister endure multiple appointments and diagnostic tests, play the waiting game, have chemotherapy, lose her hair, and feel uncomfortable and scared. We found ourselves in another unsettling situation, but thankfully God's healing hands comforted Rochelle, and we are so blessed that she is in remission.

My brother-in-law, Scott, is very similar to my dad. He has always been Rochelle's rock, and he definitely was her pillar of strength during her treatment. Scott is a wonderful man, and his unending love for his family was very evident during Rochelle's ordeal. He was the caretaker, Mr. Mom, the cheerleader, and the chef, and he took on many other roles. God knew what he was doing when he brought Rochelle and Scott together that fateful night at the bowling alley in Crete, Nebraska. There is no denying their love.

Here is another story that shows how God puts people in our lives for certain reasons. Dr. Reed had been Mom's oncologist for nearly twenty years, and Dr. Tarantolo became Rochelle's oncologist in 2013. During Rochelle's treatment we learned both Dr. Reed and Dr. Tarantolo were involved in Mom's clinical trial back in 1994. Dr. Tarantolo explained the clinical trial to Rochelle in detail and provided a scientific explanation for why Mom survived and thrived after her battle with breast cancer. It was interesting to hear the scientific facts, but of course we believe God allowed Mom more time on earth to help raise Rochelle and me and pave the way for what was to come in our lives after she passed away. Two doctors who worked on the same study treated Mom and Rochelle twenty years apart. Coincidence? Absolutely not!

Below are portions of Rochelle's entries from her Caring Bridge website. As you will see, the positive energy Mom exhibited on this earth shines through Rochelle's beautiful writing during her journey with Hodgkin's lymphoma. Rochelle remained positive despite the negative situation she was dealing with. Her spiritual strength, physical strength, and mental strength helped get her through that difficult time. She relied on God to light the way. She also relied on her athletic ability and drive, which enabled her to train for a half marathon while she was undergoing treatment.

*My Story, April 30, 2013*

On April 30, 2013, I was given news that I wasn't expecting to hear: "You have a diagnosis of Hodgkin's lymphoma." Initially, I was so mad. Not mad at God, but mad [because] I just had lost my mother to breast cancer a few months before.

My mom saved my life! She paid the ultimate sacrifice for my sister, her grandkids, and [me] so that we could take the preventative measures to get tested and have preventative examinations performed. They staged my cancer as 1A, which is the best diagnosis I could have received. I had a PET scan to determine whether or not the cancer had spread.

To get prepared for chemotherapy, I had to have multiple tests, such as an ECHO and a pulmonary function test because chemotherapy is hard on the body. I also had a bone-marrow biopsy, which involves aspirating bone marrow through my hip with a large needle. I am so thankful my bone marrow results were negative. After four of my treatments, I will have another CT-PET scan, and the cancer should be gone. The standard of practice is to do another 4 treatments for preventative measures.

Dr. Tarantolo is my oncologist and is awesome. I have a receptor called CD 20, which is favorable for me and my treatment, because they can give me an additional chemo drug. Only 20 percent of the patients with Hodgkin's have this receptor. This disease has a 95 percent curable rate!

*May 18, 2013: First Treatment Done*

The day before my first treatment I chopped my hair off. I knew I was going to lose my hair, so I decided to cut it off and to try out some bangs. It was a very emotional experience for me. I made it through my first treatment, and I feel great! The first day was the longest because they have to do test doses of the chemo drugs to make sure that I wouldn't have a reaction. I was at the treatment center for nearly ten hours. During a portion of the first part of the treatment I started to have an adverse reaction to the Rituxan; therefore they gave me steroids and Benadryl through my port and it helped instantly, except it made me extremely tired, and I was saying things to my sister that were not making much sense. We had a good laugh about it.

Throughout the course of the day at the infusion center, we got the opportunity to get to know the wonderful staff. My sister and I shared our story about Mom and how I found out my diagnosis. Our story brought them to tears.

Now that I am undergoing treatment, I have to be on a lot of medications. I went from taking no medications to [taking] six different ones! I am on a schedule of medications to prevent nausea, pneumonia, shingles, kidney stones, and gout.

Thanks for all of your wonderful support and comments. It really does help to know that I have a lot of prayers and great friends and family standing behind me. I plan on running the Omaha Half Marathon in September, and I think I have a few people convinced to do it with me.

*May 24, 2013: Second Treatment on the Books*

Today I finished my second treatment! I made it through week one without any problems. I was able to work my three 12-hour shifts. I feel completely normal and hopefully it continues that way. It felt good to get back to work. I truly believe that continuing as I did before I was diagnosed is the best thing and going to work is actually great therapy. This week Scott was able to go to my treatments with me. The entire ... treatment lasted only four hours instead of ten. It is amazing the number of patients that come in and out of the cancer treatment center. I see some older people but unfortunately a majority of patients are relatively young.

Each week I get my labs drawn to determine whether or not I can have treatment. If my labs get too low, I have to get an injection called Neupogen, which stimulates my bone marrow help generate my white blood count. Chemo kills both good and bad cells; therefore it can damage the bone marrow if the levels get too low. Before I started chemo, my white blood count was 10.6 which is considered normal. This week [it] dropped to 4.6, which is on the low end of normal. It is expected that around day 10 of treatment, my numbers will drop to their lowest point.

I have to mention that I am so positively overwhelmed with everyone's thoughts, prayers, and generosity. I want to thank the staff at Gretna Public Schools for everything you all have done. The other day I came home, and Scott showed me the number of gift cards to restaurants we were given. Also, thank you to those teachers that filled in for Scott when he had to be with me during my various appointments. Thank you also to the staff and my neighbors who set up a meal train. I am speechless! You all have been so accommodating and giving, I cannot even begin to thank you all enough. The track athletes that made it to state dedicated their T-shirts to me by putting on the backs of the shirts "Running for Ro!"

God definitely works in mysterious ways. Right after I was diagnosed, I went to the Nissan dealership to get an oil change as well as some general maintenance. They asked how my week was going, and I proceeded to tell them about my diagnosis and how my cancer was discovered. I knew I was in trouble when they asked me whether or not I had an extended warranty, and naturally,

I did not. I was told the maintenance was going to cost approximately $1,200. The man excused himself and returned shortly with some great news. "We can't do this for free, but we can do it for $50." I immediately started to cry in both shock and excitement and hugged him. That same day, I decided to go get a pedicure. The owner of the spa, Kathy, knows me quite well. She was asking how I was feeling, and I was talking to her about my diagnosis. When I went to pay, I was told another woman in the spa overheard my story, and she paid for my pedicure. All of these experiences so far just prove that there are a lot of good people out there in this world.

*May 31, 2013: Done With Third Treatment*

Treatment number three was uneventful. My white blood cells dropped to 3.4, so I received Neupogen the day before I received chemo. The drug works overnight, and today my white count went up to 7.1. I have felt great through my treatment. I feel as normal as I did before I was diagnosed. I think the thing that I have learned the most is patience. Being the patient is makes me see things differently and makes me more aware what patients really go through. I have gone through the same testing and waiting just like them.

So far, I have not noticed any hair loss. When I start to notice hair loss, I am going to go with the "GI Jane" look. It will be hard, but I know it is short term, and my hair will eventually grow back.

*June 8, 2013: It Was a Hairy Situation*

The big topic of the week is my hair. I started noticing my hair was falling out around day 17, especially when I was in the shower and when I would brush my hair. I wanted to be able to get through this workweek with my hair so I could have some time to get use to my new hairdo. I know that it is just hair, but hair is part of our identity, especially for women.

I was lucky to have a coworker who is going through chemo treatments help mentor me and give me advice. I was able to try on different styles of wigs, anything from short and medium lengths, a white tensile one (they made me try on), to super-long ones like the Kardashians. I found the perfect one. Each wig has a name, and I chose "Courtney." It is longer than my hair was prior to cutting it off, but I feel like me and very comfortable in it. I also have a variety of fun and colorful scarves to wear.

Today after my treatment, I decided to buzz my hair. The clinical cosmetologist had my back facing the mirror so I couldn't see her take all of my locks of hair off. With each pass of the clippers my head felt much lighter and cooler. As she was doing it, I was reading Scott's face, and he was doing nothing but smiling. He said, "You look hot Mama!" He also said how I looked just like my mom. I have best husband in the whole wide world. I turned around and looked at my new self in the mirror. I was pleasantly surprised with how I looked. When I got home, Anisten said, "Mom! I like your hair!" Kardyn is so young ... she cannot tell a difference.

I had my labs drawn again today, and they are almost bottomed out. I have to take extra precautions such as good hand washing and avoiding sick people if possible. I have to call my doctor immediately if a start running a temperature because I am more prone to get an infection now that I am immunosuppressed from the chemo treatments. I had to pick up Neupogen injections to boost my white blood cell count. I have learned to give to myself the Neupogen injections in my stomach. Monday, I have to get my labs drawn again to check my white blood cell count. The past couple of days I have felt a little tired, and it is due to my counts being low. This past week I have been trying to get prepared for the Omaha Half Marathon in September. I ran a total of seven miles this week. I am not doing it for time, but rather doing it to achieve a goal—to finish.

I want to conclude by saying I am blessed to have some of the best coworkers and doctors. They surprised me with a goodie bag with an overwhelming amount of gifts, such as cash, gift cards to my favorite places such as Target, Applebee's, and Maurice's. I also received body spray from Victoria's Secret, lip gloss, colorful socks to wear to work, bags of my favorite candy, magazines. They are also so thoughtful and included things for the girls to keep them occupied.

Rochelle's buzz cut (2013)

*June 14, 2013: Fifth Week Done*

This week I needed to get my counts up therefore I had to get four doses of Neupogen to boost my counts. I experienced the most common side effect of terrible joint and muscle pain. This means that the medication is working by boosting my bone marrow by generating more white blood cells. This week my white blood cell count was 30 (normal is 5 to 10), and my Neutrophil count was 18 (normal is 1 to 8). It definitely worked, and I was able to get my chemo as scheduled. I have been battling a bad sore throat and earache this week. I was prescribed an antibiotic, and I am much better. Aside from feeling a little fatigued, I feel great, and I am actually able to get some miles in on the running trails. It is good therapy.

I have to share a funny story. I had one of my head scarves on, and a patient that just came up from recovery was barely opening his eyes and was looking around the room and said, "I see that we have a pirate in the room." I was laughing so hard and thought that maybe I should carry an eye patch in my pocket to sport the look, or maybe not because we do have a lot of confused patients and I would be a true hallucination!

I met with Dr. Tarantolo today, and he felt in my left axilla and he reported he couldn't feel my lymph nodes like he could before! It is so nice to finally receive some good news. All of your uplifting thoughts and prayers must be working, so keep it up! Dr. Tarantolo is confident that I will be cancer free after all of this is said and done.

Getting around in the mornings has been so easy with my buzz cut. Some people ask if I regret cutting and buzzing it off, and the answer is no. I do not think that I could stand slowly losing my hair. My hair was very thick, and I think it would have been upsetting to see parts of my scalp and my hair look thin. I made the right decision for me.

*June 21, 2013: Sixth Week of Treatment, Done and Finished with Rituxan!*

There is light at the end of the tunnel. I am completely finished with my six Rituxan treatments, and next week I will be done with two cycles (four treatments) of chemotherapy. As usual my counts are low again, but this is to be expected. I will get my labs drawn on Wednesday and probably get Neupogen to boost my white blood cell counts before my next treatment on Friday.

Today, my good friend and coworker Rachel kept me company during my treatment. It is amazing how fast time passes when you are in good company. She brought me an amazing breakfast from Panera, and she surprised me with an awesome frame with photographs of my family that she took before I started treatment.

We continue to be graced with cards, care packages, and meals. Everybody has been truly amazing and so thoughtful. It means so much to know I have so many people thinking of me and my family. Soon this will all be behind us, and we can move on. I cannot believe how fast a year goes by. Tomorrow our youngest daughter, Kardyn, turns one. Last weekend we were able to celebrate with many family and friends.

*June 28, 2013: Halfway Done! Woot! Woot!*

It is Friday, and today is extra special because I am halfway done with my chemo treatments! I cannot believe that it has been two months since I began this crazy ride, but surprisingly it has gone fast. The one thing that I keep wondering and asking is if and when chemo is supposed to slow me down. I feel just as normal as I did before I was diagnosed. Today I met with Danielle, who is Dr. Tarantolo's nurse practitioner, and she said the reason why I have so much energy is because I have kept such a positive attitude and I have continued to keep active by running. I will not let cancer run my life, and I will continue to fight on and push through.

Now that I am halfway done with treatment, I have to have another PET scan. Dr. Tarantolo is confident that my cancer should be gone at this stage of my treatment plan. Regardless if my test is positive or negative, I will have to undergo four more treatments.

Thanks again to my dear friend Rachel Breitkreutz for joining me again at my treatment this week. She brought bagels from Panera, and they were fabulous! Thank you also to my friend Rachel Ideus for being my running buddy this past Wednesday. Like she said, the running part was just a bonus. We were able to catch up and allow life to slow down a little. Thanks everyone for all of the support. I am blessed beyond belief and am so thankful for everyone I know in my life.

# CHAPTER 23

# ROCHELLE'S JOURNEY: PART 2

Never once did Rochelle lose faith or give up. She fought like a champion. God allowed her to be healed, and it certainly did not hurt to have her personal guardian angel guiding her through the process. We gained a second guardian angel on July 29, 2013, when our grandma Schmidt passed away due to complications from pneumonia.

On her Caring Bridge website, Rochelle described the comments people made to her along the way (see below). I remembered the time in 1993 when people approached her at a home game after Mom had been diagnosed. I think that moment prepared Rochelle for some of the insensitive comments people later made to her. Rochelle always maintained a positive attitude and had clever comments in response.

I think about Rochelle every time I hear the song "Overcomer" by Mandisa. When she was going through treatment, she was listening to K-LOVE on her iPod while she was training for the half marathon. A lady called in to talk about how much this song meant to her. The caller from New York was battling non-Hodgkin's lymphoma, and she was also training for a race. This is yet another example of God working in our lives. He reminded Rochelle in that moment that He was with her, and He gave her continued strength to win the war. Rochelle felt very uplifted after this experience.

*July 12, 2013: Cancer Free and Over Halfway Done*

I am so excited, and I cannot hold it back. I am cancer free! I have been waiting three months to say this. I am going to try to sum up the last couple of weeks. When I first started treatment Dr. Tarantolo confidently told me that that all of my cancer would be gone after my chemo and Rituxan treatments. At first I was skeptical but at the same time had the total confidence and faith that he knew what he was doing. I also knew God was in control, and He would see me though this according to His will.

I have the best nurses and staff out at the Midwest Cancer Center. They are absolutely amazing, and they always are looking after me. All of the nurses are wonderful, but I really connected with Ethyl. Every time I see her she tells me that she has thought about me all week. When I came in for treatment today I said that I had hoped that I would get great news today. She smiled the biggest smile you could see. I asked her if she knew the results of my PET scan, and she said, "Just look at my smile." As nurses and techs, we are not allowed to reveal test results. It is the doctor's job to report the results to patients. This eased my anxieties before I went to see Dr. Tarantolo.

I have felt pretty good the entire time but this last treatment kind of took a toll on me. My stomach felt a little uneasy, and I have been tired. The first couple of days after treatment I spent my time taking naps. After a few days, I felt back to normal. My counts are also low again, so I had to get Neupogen shots. Mom was not kidding. Those Neupogen shots really hurt! My joints ached so bad this week. After a little bit of Tylenol, I felt much better. I am still able to work full time.

This coming week, we are going to take the girls to the Great Wolfe Lodge in Kansas City. Next Friday we are going to attend a dedication ceremony at McCook

Community Hospital, where Mom worked for thirty-three years. Our family donated a pergola in the healing garden in honor of Mom. This is going to be [a] special day and a nice way to honor and celebrate her life.

### July 26, 2013: Six Out of Eight Treatments Done

I think that I have finally come down after receiving such great news of being cancer free two weeks ago. I met with Dr. Tarantolo, and we discussed the lab work I will have upon completion of treatment. He informed me the chance of reoccurrence is less than 1 percent. Praise be to God! Once again, thank you all for your continued prayers and support. God is good, and He has heard all of your prayers.

I am still training for the half marathon in September, but I really need to get some motivation and consistency with my workouts. It seems like we have been so busy; therefore I only have been able to run maybe once a week. I got up early today and put in 5.5 miles. I plan on trying to run at least three time a week.

### August 9, 2013: One More Treatment Left

Life has been pretty uneventful the last couple of weeks. My labs have looked great despite having a cold for two weeks. Since my diagnosis and treatments I had to call [sick] into work for the first time this week.

I have really picked up training this week because the half marathon is a little over a month away. I ran on the elliptical on Monday and on Tuesday I ran 5.5 miles. The past two days I ran three miles each day. I have a competitive nature but have come to realize that I might have to walk during the race. My ultimate goal is to finish the race. This year has definitely been a year of obstacles—from losing Mom and Grams [to] kicking cancer's butt.

When we were headed out to Indianola last weekend for my grandma's funeral, I got pulled over by a state trooper. I take after my mom because she had a heavy foot. I think I got out of a ticket because the trooper felt sorry for me because I had my scarf on my head. Remember the story of the patient calling me a pirate? I have had a doctor say, "Nice bandana!" I had another patient say, "You look like a biker." Neither the doctor nor the patient realized I was undergoing chemo treatments for cancer. They, of course, felt terrible about it and apologized over and over. I wasn't offended at all, and I get a kick out of people's comments. Sometimes people do not know what to say so they bring up stories of losing a close friend or family to cancer. I do not think their intentions are to scare me but having this experience makes me think before I say things to other people going through hard times.

*August 24, 2013: A Little Too Confident*

I was unable to undergo treatment this week because my white blood cells [had] bottomed out. I have to get lab work done next Friday, and if my labs are good, he will give me my last treatment. I was so upset just [because] I have to wait a whole week to go through all of this anticipation again. Usually I can tell if my counts are low because I feel more tired than usual. I felt a little tired but I thought it was [due] to all of the running I have been doing to prepare for the half marathon. Last Saturday, I ran 8.3 miles without stopping! I have been running five times per week. It helps to have my good friends and neighbors to help keep me motivated. We get up and are running by 5:00 a.m.

My hair has gotten so thin that my scalp has started to show. I went in yesterday and got all of it buzzed off so it can grow back [evenly]. I cannot believe how many comments I received when I wore a low, loose ponytail in my wig. It felt pretty awesome to be able to put my hair back again. It reminds me how it is the little things that make people happy, and this week it was my ponytail!

I have to keep my port in for three months following my last treatment. I was able to discontinue my gout medication, but [the doctor] wants to keep me on my shingles-prevention medication. The reason for this is because he said even after chemo is through, three months after chemo is the peak/increased risk for developing shingles.

*September 2, 2013: Officially Done With Chemo*

My last day of chemo was bittersweet. I was so thankful to be finishing this journey, but I am going to miss seeing the nurses and Dr. Tarantolo. They were outstanding, and I couldn't ask for anything better. The cancer center staff sent me off with bells, bubbles and whistles.

So much has happened in the past year that I want to take a moment and reflect on it. Last year at this time we got the most devastating news when we received Mom's terminal diagnosis. At the time we were wondering why she had to go through this. Although my family was dealt a bad hand, I feel that God doesn't give you more than you can handle. It all makes sense now that time has gone on. I would have never known I had Hodgkin's lymphoma if it wasn't for my mom encouraging me to go get a preventative mammogram. She saved my life, and I will be forever grateful.

Tomorrow, September 3, is our eighth wedding anniversary, and I am so excited to be sharing this day with the birth of my new nephew, Layton Gabriel Smith. This time last year life was so sad and stressful, but now our lives are full of positive and wonderful things happening. I have had a lot of time to reflect, and it feels good to not be constantly scared of what is going to happen next. One thing I have learned from all of this is that you cannot worry what is going to happen tomorrow. You have to take each day at a time and be grateful for the life you have. Life is precious, so grab a hold of it and seize the day.

I feel that having cancer has changed me for the good. I have gained a better understanding of what a lot of my patients and families have to go through. I also have a better relationship with God. I truly believe faith can get you through an illness or hard times, but having a positive attitude makes a huge difference. I hope that I served as a role model for people going through similar situations.

The best advice I can give you all: men and women, get your preventative exams done! As much as we all dread going to these types of appointments, they can save your life! They saved mine!

*October 25, 2013: Cancer Free and Cured! On With My Life*

I received some great news today, and I wanted to share it with you all. I had my postchemo CT-PET scan on Tuesday and have been anxiously awaiting the results until today. I met with my oncologist Dr. Tarantolo today, and he said that my scan was clean! God is the number one reason I beat this disease. Although my family and I went through one challenge after another, we never lost faith. My mom's persistence [in] pushing me to get my mammogram was another reason I am still here. She saved my life! Everyone's constant prayers and kind thoughts and words of encouragement kept me going and fighting through each and every day.

I am awaiting a call from the oncology surgeon's office to schedule my port removal. We are shooting for December. It is so crazy how this whole journey started last year with my mammogram, and now it is ending with getting my port removed this December! Let's hope that 2014 will be a much better year!

Things are starting to turn around for my family. I am cured of cancer, Kirby had a healthy baby boy in September, and Dad has found a great lady companion whom we love dearly. As much as I love my mom, I know that she wanted Dad to be happy. Life is full of many surprises and heartaches, but the one thing a person cannot lose is faith and hope.

People's comments continue to make me laugh. I walked into a patient's room and said, "How are you doing today?" The patient responded, "I am great *sir*, thanks for asking." Today, I dropped off Anisten and Kardyn at daycare, and a little girl in Anisten's class asked Anisten if I was her mom or dad. The girl proceeded to say that I looked like a boy because I didn't have hair. Anisten said, "This is my mom. Her hair is just short." Anisten asked me to take off my hat to show the girl. I am so proud of my daughter for standing up for me and for being strong for me! I did have a patient tell me that she isn't gutsy enough to get a "haircut" like me, but she has always wanted to do it. I told her that chemo sure is an expensive way to get your hair to look like this. I told her that I will take her comment as a compliment.

Thanks again everyone for being there to support me and my family this past year! I love each and everyone one of you! I hope to pay it forward. God bless you all!

Rochelle running in the Omaha Half Marathon (2013)

# CHAPTER 24

# GRAMS

Mom was a big part of the interior design team at Community Hospital. In the early months of 2012, she and the other team members were sprucing up the healing garden, a wonderful addition to the hospital. It allows patients and their family members to be outside, surrounded by flowers, other plants, and an outdoor fireplace. The space provides tranquility and healing for the soul. Dad remembered Mom talking about adding a fixture to the healing garden so people could have shade while enjoying the fresh air. The team submitted a proposal to add a pergola, but it was turned down due to the expense. They were in the process of finding alternate materials, and contractors so they could put together another proposal. Shortly thereafter, Mom became ill and she never returned to the hospital as an employee.

The people at Community Hospital were Mom's second family. She was an employee there for thirty-three years, and she invested a lot of time and energy working with others to make sure all the details were in place. She really enjoyed being a part of the interior design committee and assisting with the various phases of the hospital's overhaul. During our daily phone conversations, Mom would tell me about the status of the projects and all of the additional services that were being brought to hospital. I could always tell how passionate she was about her job and her involvement in the various committees based on the excitement in her voice when she talked about improvements being made to the hospital.

In the spring 2013, Dad decided he wanted to see Mom's vision become a reality. He knew how excited she was about the pergola, and he also knew how disappointed she was when the proposal was turned down. Mom was very persistent and had her health not gotten in the way, I am confident she would have gotten a bid and proposal approved by the committee. Dad wanted to dedicate the pergola in the healing garden at Community Hospital to Mom for her service at the hospital as well as to honor the woman she was. Dad worked with the hospital foundation, and by early summer 2013 the pergola was complete. Dad kept us updated during the construction project with calls and texts regarding the progress. Dan Remple of McCook built the pergola. We feel as if Mom handpicked Dan from heaven to complete the project. Dan was the contractor who had renovated Mom and Dad's house a few years before Mom became ill. Having Dan build the pergola added a special touch.

During the construction process our family compared calendars to see which dates would work for the dedication ceremony. It was somewhat of a challenge because of Rochelle's treatment schedule and my traveling restrictions from my doctor. Thirteen was Mom's favorite number, and Dad thought it would be fitting to have the dedication ceremony on September 13, 2013. Rochelle and I agreed, but I was hesitant because Layton would be less than two weeks old. Josh and I have not had very good luck traveling with newborns, so I was nervous with the idea of traveling with baby Layton. Dad completely understood, and we all agreed on Friday, July 19.

The week of the dedication ceremony, Rochelle, Scott, and the girls took a mini vacation to the Great Wolfe Lodge in Kansas City. The kids had their own separate area with bunk beds and a TV. During their three-day vacation, we had Rochelle and Scott over to our house for supper. Bryson asked if he could spend the night with them, although Holden was reluctant. Then, as Rochelle and Scott were getting ready to leave, Holden put his shoes on and told Josh and me he was going to stay all night with them. We were not sure how this would go, considering how little he was and the fact he had never spent the night away from us. Rochelle and Scott took four kids, and off they went. Josh and I did not know how to act without kids for an evening. It was a much-needed break because we knew it would soon be back to sleepless nights after Layton's arrival. Both families left for Indianola on Thursday, July 18.

I was thirty-four weeks pregnant, so my doctor told me to stop and walk several times during the drive to prevent blood clots. This trip to Indianola was our second since Mom's funeral. The first trip had been in May 2013 for Memorial Day. I had mixed emotions about traveling home. Of course, I was excited to see Dad and to really feel Mom's presence in the home, but I was also sad to think that Mom would not be there to greet us with a hug and smile as we walked through the front door. I found myself having that same sense of false hope that I'd had the night of the visitation. I knew Mom would not physically be there when we arrived, but I continued to imagine her welcoming us with open arms and living life as we had in the past.

The ceremony was absolutely perfect. Our immediate family arrived early so we could view the pergola, and there was a nice breakfast awaiting our arrival. We had time to visit with some of the wonderful employees of Community Hospital as well as with family members who drove from near and far to be with us. We all met in one of the hospital's new conference rooms beforehand, and we made our way outside just before the dedication ceremony. Our immediate family sat under the pergola. We were overwhelmed by the outpouring support once again. Several employees took time out of their busy day to attend the ceremony, and it was a beautiful sight. Jim Ulrich was Mom's boss at the time of her passing. He opened the ceremony by welcoming everyone and talking about Mom and her contributions as well as the healing garden. Jim had been her boss for approximately ten years. Gary Bieganski and his wife, Donna, also attended the ceremony. Gary had been Mom's first boss at Community Hospital. He talked about her wonderful character traits and all she had done for the hospital during her time there. It was very humbling to see how many lives Mom touched, and it was nice to know she left a positive impression during her employment Community Hospital.

Our family under the pergola before the dedication ceremony.

Pergola in the healing garden at Community
Hospital in McCook, Nebraska.

Following the dedication ceremony, we were given a full tour of the hospital. It was amazing to see how much it had changed, and it was fun to see what Mom had been talking about over the last few years. As we walked the halls, I could see her personal touches and the "fingerprints" she left behind through the colors and design. She would have been so pleased to see all of the changes that had taken place.

We wanted to be sure to see Grandma Peggy (Grams) while we were home. She had resided at Hillcrest Nursing Home since December 2006. Previously, she'd lived in an apartment, but her back started to give her problems. It became increasingly difficult for her to walk up and down the stairs or take care of her daily needs. Grams always liked to stay busy and interact with people. It got to the point where she was unable to drive and could not get around like she wanted. She decided it was time to take the next step. She did not need 100 percent assistance; therefore she moved into the assisted living side of the facility.

Grams did really well, and she enjoyed the facility. She had her own apartment, but she had the convenience of having daily meals cooked for her as well as activities to keep her busy. Grams kept the staff on their toes. She was always trying to make people laugh, and she did her best to keep things interesting with her shenanigans. From late night break-ins to the kitchen and refrigerator to telling her funny jokes, Grams was well known around the facility. Eventually, she had to move upstairs to the actual nursing home. Grams thrived, and she was happy wherever she was.

Dad did a wonderful job, frequently stopping by to visit with Grams. He took part in the daily coffee club and played bingo. Several times I'd call Dad on my way home from work, and he'd tell me he was at Hillcrest. I enjoyed our occasional visits over the phone. During our college years we got handwritten notes and cards from Grams. I recently went through some of my old cards and saw one that said "Sex." It had pink and purple glittery hearts on the front of the card. I could not recall Josh giving me a card like this, so I opened it to see who it was from. The card read "Now that I have your attention, Happy Birthday." It was signed "Love Grams xoxoxo." I laughed so hard. I should have known the card was from her.

After our tour of the hospital, we went to Pizza Hut. Several family and friends joined us for the buffet-style lunch. We had plans to meet Brett and Lori Schmidt and their kids for supper that evening. We wanted to have plenty of time to spend with Grams because we were not sure when our next trip back to Indianola would be. Dad, Rochelle, Scott, Josh, Bryson, Anisten, Holden, Kardyn and I went to Hillcrest and spent the afternoon with Grams. We had a wonderful time catching up with her, and the kids always do a fine job of providing the entertainment! It was sad to leave Grams. Her beautiful light blue-green eyes teared up as she hugged us. She told us how much she loved us and to be sure to stop by next time we were home. We assured her we would, and we said our good-byes. Little did we know that was the last time we would see Grams.

I have had time to reflect on how much of our lives we spend planning. God already has every detail of our lives planned out, so why do we spend so much time worrying and planning? To that point, God's timing about the dedication ceremony was once again perfect! We spent time and energy worrying about finding the right date for the ceremony. We compared calendars and suggested several dates to the family and the hospital. At the end of the day, God knew the date would be July 19, 2013. He knew Grams will become ill and pass away just ten days later on July 29, 2013.

I received a call from Dad on Monday, July 22, and he let me know Grams had been admitted to the hospital. She had a fever and was developing a cough. She had pneumonia at least once a year, but after a short hospital stay, she would return to Hillcrest in her normal manner— ornery! This time was different. Each day, she became less responsive, and the fight in her was decreasing. She told Dad early on during her hospital stay that she was ready to go heaven to be with Grandpa Cliff. The doctors were not optimistic that Grams would pull through this time. Her lungs were filling up, and her breathing machines were maxed out. On July 29, our family gained another guardian angel.

Grandma Peggy (Grams) Schmidt

I talked to Dad about how healthy Grams had seemed when we were home the weekend of Mom's dedication ceremony. Her mind was sharp, and she seemed to be in good health. We were so thankful that we were able to spend quality time with her. The pneumonia came on overnight, and it was more than she could handle.

At the time of Grams's funeral, my doctor was not comfortable about me traveling seven hours. My due date had been a moving target. I was confident that my due date was August 31, but the ultrasounds were showing August 20. Depending on the method of calculation, I was either thirty-six or thirty-eight weeks pregnant, and my doctor strongly recommended I not make the trip. It made me very sad to miss Grams's funeral, but I could hear Mom quietly reassuring me by reminding me how much time we spent with Grams when she was alive. The funeral home videotaped the service so our family could watch it at a later date.

Grams lived a great life! She lived life to the fullest every single day. She was well respected, and she always had a knack for having fun. One memory that sticks out in my mind is when Grams knocked over the twenty-foot Christmas tree at Hillcrest. She was backing up her wheelchair when she accidentally hit the tree, and over it went! When she told the story, she spiced it up by slightly exaggerating to make the story even funnier. She said she yelled, "Timber!" as it was falling. Who knows, maybe she did. I would not put it past her.

Grams tried to hook Dad up with ladies after Mom passed away. Grams had a mild form of dementia so her judgment was not the greatest. During their conversations, Grams would spot a woman and say, "What about that one?" Dad got a good laugh out of it and told Grams he was doing fine and was not looking. We always took what Grams said with a grain of salt. She spoke her mind, and she did not care who was listening.

I was really sad for Dad. He lost his wife and his mother in one calendar year, within nine months to be exact. It seemed like everything was hitting at once. We were still grieving the loss of Mom and dealing with the rollercoaster of emotions associated with Rochelle's diagnosis and treatment when we lost Grams, and we were coming up on the one-year anniversary of losing Mom. It seemed like there was bad news lurking behind every corner we turned. We continued to have faith during the trying times. We trusted this was all part of God's master plan, and we had to continue to believe that He would see us through it.

A few weeks after Grams passed away, Dad met a wonderful woman named Deanna. He was hesitant to tell Rochelle and me at first because he did not know how we would feel about it. We were both very excited for Dad. After Mom passed away, I was not sure if Dad would ever experience true happiness again. He said he would always love Mom and never forget her. Rochelle and I want Dad to be happy, and he is too young to live the rest of his life alone. Mom told us during our family meeting days before she died that she did not want Dad to be alone. She also told Dad in private several times that he needed to move on and keep living.

We are so thankful God brought Dad and Deanna together when he did. Deanna and Dad had not met before. Deanna had seen Dad at her office, but she was unaware that he had lost Mom and Grams. One of Deanna's coworkers was getting ready to move, and as Dad stopped to wish her well on her new adventures. Deanna sent Dad a request on Facebook that evening. Dad recognized her picture, and he accepted her request. They eventually went on a date and have been inseparable ever since.

We know this is what Mom would want. Dad tried hard to be alone, but it was one of the hardest things he has ever had to do. He was constantly reminded of Mom's passing by living in the home they shared. He woke up to nobody and went to bed with nobody. Rochelle and I prepared several meals and froze them, but that is not the same as a home-cooked meal. Dad really missed having a companion. He was so thankful for the lasting friendships and the invitations to dinner, but he had to return to a dark house by himself.

As soon as Dad and Deanna met, the happiness in Dad's voice started resurfacing. He could not talk about Mom without tearing up, but the genuine love between Dad and Deanna was obvious. Deanna has many of Mom's characteristics. She is a hard worker; she is very thoughtful and loving. She has brought life back into Dad, and Rochelle and I are forever grateful.

When Dad told us that Deanna reached out to him on Facebook, we reminded him how much of a struggle it was to get him to sign up. Shortly after Mom passed away Rochelle encouraged Dad to set up an account. We wanted Dad to stay in touch with friends and family and see the updated pictures of the grandkids. Dad was very resistant to the idea, but he eventually gave in. We taught him how to navigate on his wall and send private messages. We had a lot of laughs during Dad's learning curve with Facebook.

One story in particular took place in March 2013 when Dad was at our house for the gender-reveal party. As I was getting ready, Dad hollered, "Kirby!" in a panicked voice. I went to see what was wrong, and he was pacing back and forth like he does when he is frustrated. He rubbed his forehead as he explained the problem. He had been trying to update his profile and when he added the month and day of his marriage, March 24, the year defaulted to 2013 rather than allowing him to enter 1979. I laughed so hard when he told me this. He was worried that people at home would think that he went to Kansas City to get married. It took some time to find the setting to delete the marriage date, but it was so funny. Dad was extremely relieved when we told him the problem had been fixed. He promised to not mess with his settings again and to leave things as they were.

When Mom and Dad first met, Dad had a burly beard. Dad later asked Mom what had attracted her to him. She responded, "Your eyes." Dad's eyes "smile" whether he is happy or sad. Shortly after Dad and Deanna met, Deanna commented on how Dad's eyes "smile." When she said this, Dad felt as if he were receiving a sign that Deanna and he were meant to be together. Only one other person had ever told Dad this, and it was Mom. Coincidence? I don't think so!

Life was starting to feel normal again. Rochelle was finishing treatment, Deanna had entered our lives, and Layton Gabriel was born on September 3, 2013, weighing a healthy nine pounds, fifteen ounces. Layton was born on a very special day—Rochelle and Scott's anniversary.

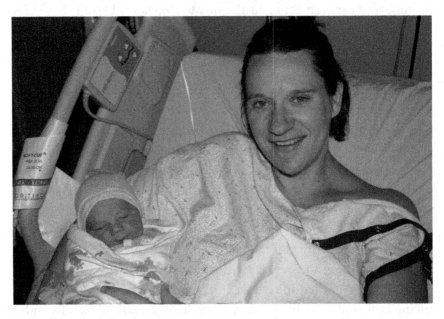

Layton Gabriel Smith and Kirby

It was hard to believe everything that had happened in just one year. We were reminded on September 4, 2013, as we cuddled Layton that a year prior we had been in a hospital receiving Mom's terminal diagnosis. We also reflected on Rochelle's diagnosis and prognosis as well as losing Grams. We also knew that I had to stay on track with my six-month surveillance program and preventative surgery. We were thankful for our experiences, both good and bad, during the last year. It made us all remember just how precious life truly is. We will forever miss a link in our family chain, but we know the God's plan is greater than we can ever imagine.

## CHAPTER 25

# THROUGH THE EYES OF CHILDREN: ANGELS AMONG US

I love the innocence of children, and I strongly believe God uses children in a positive way to open the eyes and hearts of adults. Often adults overanalyze situations or brush them off as coincidences, and have the need to "see it to believe it." Children are able to take things for face value. Before Mom's terminal illness I needed to find a reason for the unexplained things that were happening in our lives. Now that we have lived through Mom's sickness and death, I am able to see situations in a whole new light. We have been showered by signs and blessings from heaven, and we know Mom is with us.

One of the most reassuring and amazing things happened in early July 2013 during Rochelle's treatment. Anisten and Rochelle had an experience that made it very clear that bigger things were happening, and God was in control. Below is Rochelle's version of the story from her Caring Bridge website:

> I have to share an inspiring dream that I experienced this past weekend. As most of you know, we had some spiritual experiences when my Mom was on hospice and since she has passed. A few months ago, when we were on our way to Kansas City to visit my sister and her family, Anisten, out of the blue, pointed ahead and said, "Look, there is

Nana up in the sky right there!" We asked her what she was doing, and Anisten replied, "She is waving at me and smiling and saying that she loves me."

Last weekend we were traveling to our friends' cabin near Yankton, South Dakota, and Anisten once again said, "Look, over there. There is an angel in the sky." That next night, I had a very real and vivid dream, and I truly believe Mom spoke to me. We were walking down some stairs, and Mom had her arm around me and softly spoke in my ear and said, "You know those times that Anisten said she saw me and an angel, IT WAS ME." Then she had her surprised laugh like she was excited to tell me this. I had to wake up to tell this to Scott, so I didn't forget the details. I do believe this was a spiritual intervention.

Another five-year-old girl had a similar experience as Anisten. Our office was handling the case of young man who died in an accident. We received a letter and a drawing from a woman and her five-year-old daughter who had been stuck in traffic as a result of the accident, although they did not know the cause. The little girl started drawing a picture of two angels and told her mother that one was a girl and the other was a boy and they were going to God. The woman later learned about the tragic accident. Unknown to this woman and her five-year-old, the family that lost their son on that day had previously lost their daughter in an accident. Based on this little girl's account of what she saw, I believe the young man was being welcomed to heaven by his little sister.

Anisten has reported seeing Nana on other occasions. Rochelle and Scott have learned to embrace the moments when their daughter opens up about her experiences. She has seen Nana at church in Gretna and during Sunday school. She said Nana sat by her during her first class. She also reported that Nana helped her get dressed one morning. Being the spunky little girl that she is, Anisten likes to pick out her own outfits. According to Rochelle and Scott, she creates fashion statements. Like many five-year-old girls, she goes against the current by choosing colors that may not exactly go together. Once morning Anisten walked out of her room and her outfit matched perfectly. Rochelle and Scott complimented her, and she said, "Thanks. Nana helped me pick it out!" She explained that she'd had her shirt picked out and was trying to decide which pair of shorts to wear. Anisten said Nana pointed to the orange pair and said, "I like those."

Another time she reported seeing both Nana and Grams. She and Scott were outside playing basketball, and all of a sudden she said, "Daddy. There is an angel behind you. It is Nana. I also see Grams." When Scott asked what they looked like, Anisten said Grams was in her wheelchair, but it had wings on the back.

Anisten's experiences reminded me about something Bryson shared with us the morning of Mom's funeral. He said he'd had a dream about Nana. He said we were all sitting in the living room at Nana and Papa's house when, all of a sudden, "Nana walked upstairs from the basement, stopped and said good-bye, and floated out of the front door." I will forever cherish that moment. Maybe it was a dream or maybe Nana really did go to Bryson in his dreams, but it was real to him, and I hope it is something he always remembers.

Mom loved listening to Christmas music 365 days out of the year. She really liked the artist and saxophone player Kenny G. I am my mother's daughter. I love instrumental Christmas music; there are several Christmas songs on my iPod, and I listen to them year round. During the summer of 2014, Holden and I were running errands. We were listening to the car radio as we were driving, and Holden said, "This song reminds me of Nana." My eyes filled up with tears when I told him the song, "White Christmas," was Nana's favorite song; in addition, the instrumental song was being played by Kenny G. There is no way Holden would have known that was Mom's favorite song. The little things are subtle reminders that Mom is walking with us each day. Before her illness we likely would have credited the kids' imagination for their experiences, but now we truly believe children see things adults do not.

After Mom's death, Rochelle and Dad had dreams with positive experiences, but unfortunately I had recurring dreams of her last few minutes on earth. I could see myself sitting near Mom in her recliner in Rochelle and Scott's living room; she would be taking her last breath, and I would wake up. I was reassured by Rochelle and Dad's positive experiences and was hopeful that I would eventually have a good dream or a sign from Mom.

One of Dad's reassuring moments involved the purple crystal angel I had bought at Gretna Drug. He was having a particularly rough day shortly after Mom passed away. He had been in town and driving around the farm when he decided to go home. When he got back in his truck, he noticed something was different. The angel hanging from the mirror was flipped backward and was facing the rearview mirror. Dad knew he'd entered the driveway in the same manner he had many times before, but he thought he might have been going too fast this time, and the angel flipped from the force. Dad fixed the angel and reversed out of the driveway and onto the blacktop. He put the truck in drive and entered the driveway as hard and fast as he could; the angel swung back and forth and did not come even close to flipping over the mirror. Dad said there is no way he'd been driving fast enough to flip the angel. He took it as a sign from Mom to get himself together!

It was some time before Dad had a dream about Mom. He said the dream was so real and comforting. He explained he was praying at Saint Catherine's Catholic Church in Indianola. He was on one of the kneelers at the front of the church, when all of a sudden he heard loud footsteps behind him. He felt hands on his shoulders and heard, "Les. It's me, Nancy. I am okay." When Dad turned around, he woke up.

October 13, 2013, marked one year since Mom's passing. We all wanted to be together to remember her on the one-year anniversary. It was difficult to be home without her, but it was nice to be together to celebrate her life. There were times that it seemed Mom had been gone for years, but at other times it felt as if she had only been gone for days. In the beginning we would count days and weeks. It eventually got to the point when months had passed. When Mom was alive, I talked to her every day, so with the one-year anniversary came the thought that I'd not physically talked to her for 365 days. At times I would find myself picking up the phone and getting ready to dial Mom's number, when it occurred to me she was gone. Old habits are hard to break. It was also strange not going to Hillcrest to visit Grams as we had in the past.

When we were together the weekend of Mom's anniversary, we reminisced about the previous year. We found ourselves saying, "This time last year, we were …" We talked about the many spiritual experiences—the incense in Rochelle and Scott's room and during Mom's funeral; the angel

Mom saw in the hours before her death; the rollercoaster ride of Rochelle's diagnosis and treatment. We were all terribly sad about losing Mom, but we agreed if that is how it had to be, we were thankful the experience was behind us. Our emotions were still very raw, but we all were doing what Mom wanted us to do. We were living each day to the fullest, and we were doing our best to be happy.

The grandkids took part in harvest in 2013. It had been a few years since they were able to help Papa drive the combine. The kids had a blast picking corn from the grandkids' field and taking the corn to the elevator in Bartley. Having the grandkids participate with harvest was a tradition that started in 2009, and I hope it continues as long as Dad is farming.

Rochelle and Scott met Deanna before Josh and I did. They'd met a few weeks earlier when Dad and Deanna took a road trip to Gretna. They had a nice time getting to know her and had very positive things to say about her. Josh and I were anxious to meet Deanna, the woman who brought life back into Dad. Deanna drove to the farm after work on Friday, and we met a very caring, wonderful person with whom we immediately connected. We were all a little nervous to meet for the first time, but it was very easy getting to know her. It felt like we'd known her our whole lives, and it was obvious how happy she and Dad made one another. It was such a relief to know Dad was no longer alone. I could hear the happiness in his voice, and it was obvious he was excited about life again. He will always love Mom but he is doing what she wanted.

On Sunday, October 13, we attended mass at Saint Catherine's. I helped in the kitchen, serving rolls and washing glasses and cups. I spent time with one of Mom's former coworkers. As Sharon and I were talking, I thanked her for giving Mom some of her vacation time, which I'd learned about from Dad. Early on during Mom's illness, she'd received a printout from the hospital showing how much paid time off she had. She was adamant that the printout wrong because it listed a lot more time than she remembered having. It all made sense after Dad shared the story with our family. This was yet another act of kindness that was shown to our family.

After coffee and rolls, we went to the cemetery. Several of us gathered around, and we held hands and prayed Hail Mary and Our Father. The kids found corn leaves and tried to stick them in the ground on Mom's grave. Dennis McConville pulled out his pocketknife and dug out a little bit of the hard dirt so the kids could stick their golden-colored corn leaves on the grave for decoration. Mom would have been delighted.

After we left the cemetery, we returned to Dad's house to pack up and head home. We wanted to give ourselves extra time because Layton was only five weeks old. It was sad to leave Dad but it was also comforting knowing he was not alone. Dad and Deanna had plans to go out that evening for dinner. It had always broken my heart in the past when Dad told me he was eating at a restaurant by himself. Our family and friends did a wonderful job of keeping Dad company and inviting him to dinner and events. We will always be grateful for our lifelong friendships in Indianola and the surrounding area. With fall coming on, harvest would soon be over, and we would get to see Dad more and get to know Deanna better.

# Chapter 26

# Strings from Above

We had fun celebrating the holiday season, and we were ready to see what 2014 would bring. We were planning Bryson's birthday party, and we decided to break tradition. In the past we hosted the boys' parties at our house and celebrated with cake, ice cream, and punch. The parties were not complete until the themed piñata made its appearance. Now, we needed a change, given the year we'd had. Rochelle mentioned it would be fun for the two families to spend a weekend together at the Great Wolf Lodge. We booked a twelve-person suite for January 17–19, 2014, and we crossed the days off on the calendar as we neared the big event.

We had a wonderful weekend celebrating Bryson's birthday, Rochelle being in remission, and the new beginning. The kids spent hours at the water park as well as in the arcade and playing MagiQuest. As always, it was sad to leave our family, but it was reassuring to know that life was starting to feel normal again.

That Sunday night, around eleven thirty, Josh's cell phone rang. We were shocked when "Ro Cell" showed up on caller ID. Rochelle has made late night calls before, so I was not overly concerned, but I did wonder why she was calling. I figured she'd seen something on Facebook, and it couldn't wait until morning. Josh passed the phone to me, and I heard Rochelle crying on the other end. I sat up and asked her if everything was okay, and she said. "No!"

I immediately thought she'd found another lump under her arm, and I grew anxious in the milliseconds that lead up to what she was trying to say. She said, "I'm pregnant!"

I felt a huge sense of relief, but I thought she was teasing. Given the fact she had her tubes tied and she'd just finished chemo, I did not think this scenario was possible. I burst out laughing and said, "No you aren't!" She confirmed she was, explaining that she'd taken two pregnancy tests, and they both came back positive. We agreed that given the year we'd had, this was wonderful news. It was definitely unexpected but this baby was truly a miracle!

Before Rochelle knew she was pregnant, Anisten had been talking about "the baby in mommy's tummy." She made a couple of comments in December and again in January. She even kissed Rochelle's stomach and said "baby." Eventually Scott got stern and told her, "There is no baby in Mom's tummy." Scott believed it was impossible, and he wanted to get the thought out of her head. Lo and behold, a heavenly visitor must have given Anisten insider information about her future sibling.

Because Rochelle had just finished chemo on August 23, 2013, the parents-to-be were concerned about the health of the baby. She had not known she was pregnant; the thought never even crossed her mind. She had a couple of drinks and was not taking prenatal vitamins. She and Scott met with her ob-gyn the following week. The doctor reported there was a less than 1 percent chance Rochelle should have conceived. She was referred to a high-risk doctor due to her situation. She also met with her oncologist for a routine follow-up visit. Her oncologist said it takes approximately three months for the chemo to leave the body following treatment. Based on her due date, Rochelle conceived right around Christmas. The first visit with the high-risk doctor was a bit unsettling, but thankfully the ultrasounds showed a very healthy baby. The high-risk doctor wanted to follow her through the first half of her pregnancy to make sure the baby continued to show signs of normal growth and development.

Rochelle's doctor had a hard time finding the baby's heartbeat during her fourteen-week checkup. Rather than waiting to schedule an ultrasound, her doctor squeezed her into the schedule so they could figure out what was going on. During the ultrasound, the heartbeat was immediately detected, and so were girl parts. They would be adding a third girl to their family. Rochelle immediately called Scott to let him know everything was fine. Scott had said from the beginning the baby would be a girl.

A few weeks later Rochelle and Scott went to their official ultrasound. They told the tech they'd previously found out the baby was a girl. It became quite apparent the Swansons were *not* having another girl. The tech said, "It's a boy!"

They could not believe their ears or their eyes. They were overjoyed that the baby continued to appear healthy on the ultrasound, and they were excited to be adding some blue in their lives. Rochelle called me at work and made me guess. Of course I said "girl," because of the previous ultrasound.

"Nope. It's a boy!" Rochelle was very excited. She said they would have to come up with a new name because Emersyn Faith would not work for their son.

Grady Cruz Swanson was born on September 15, 2014, a healthy ten pounds, nine ounces. Cruz means sign of the cross. When Rochelle's doctor examined the tubal ligation that was performed in June 2012, she confirmed the clips that had been implanted were still in place. She had no other explanation other than this baby was a miracle. God definitely has a plan for this little boy!

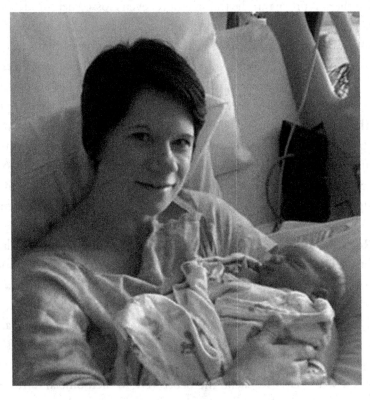

Grady Cruz Swanson and Rochelle

Little by little, I started having good dreams about my mom. In my dreams, Mom played the role of problem solver, much as she had during her time on earth. One dream took place at the church hall in Indianola. A group of us were standing around the fellowship area, and we saw a lady we did not recognize. As we were trying to figure it out, I saw Mom, who was wearing a purple outfit. She was patiently waiting off to the side. Eventually, Mom couldn't take it anymore, and she said, "You guys. It's Ann Vrooman!" She disappeared, and I woke up. Mom always liked solving problems, and she was good at it. Ann Vrooman used to babysit my sister and I and she and her family are good friends of ours.

It has taken twenty-six chapters to get to the point where I can explain the title of the book. "Strings from Above" refers to the random appearances of several pieces of string, which I found beginning in January 2014.

The first string I found really caught my attention. Saturday, January 4, 2014, is a day I will never forget due to the strange events of the morning. I went to Layton's room to get him and headed to the main floor to make a bottle. I put him down in the living room next to Josh on the couch. Josh was fighting a cold, and he slept on the couch so he would not wake me during the night. As I was in the restroom, I noticed a hot-pink string nearly six inches long in my tan-colored underwear. I was puzzled and had absolutely no idea where the pink string came from. I threw it in the trash, washed my hands, and proceeded to make Layton a bottle. I picked up Layton and sat down on the floor. As I was putting the bottle to his mouth, I noticed a florescent green string, six inches long, in the middle of the living room. I reached over and grabbed it. I wanted to compare it to the pink string I had just thrown away. Once I was done feeding Layton, I pulled the pink string out of the trash can and held it next to the green string. They were the exact same length and texture, and the ends on both strings were perfectly straight. I could not believe my eyes.

Josh woke up shortly thereafter. He went to the restroom and when he was done, he came back to the living room with a very perplexed look on his face. I asked him what was wrong and he held out his hand. In the palm of his hand was a shiny dime. I wasn't connecting the dots so I asked him what was up. He said he found it in the band of his underwear! I told him about the pink and green string, and we both agreed both things were weird. We joked, saying it was Mom giving us signs. We had no idea what the significance of the strings was, but we have heard stories about people finding pennies and associating them with loved ones who have passed away.

That evening we were in the basement with the boys, playing video games. The boys like to use the furniture as trampolines, even though they know they are not supposed to. One of my favorite pieces of furniture is a funky-patterned, oversized chair in the basement. The back of the chair has a pillow-like cushion. I couldn't help notice that the boys had been jumping on the back of the chair because the pillow had a large divot in it. As I was unzipping the cushion, a long brown string came off the chair. I held it up and told Josh, "If I find this on me later, I know where it came from."

That evening I took a shower, put on a new pair of pajamas, and went to bed. During the night I woke up to go to the restroom and, much to my surprise, the long brown string from the chair was on the right side of my underwear. I had to wake up Josh to tell him about it. We got a good laugh and went back to sleep. The next morning I called Dad and Deanna to tell them about our findings. Dad and Deanna were also taken back by the strings and coin.

Deanna said, "Maybe the pink string in your underwear is a sign you are going to have a girl!"

We laughed and I said, "Expect the unexpected."

I continued to find random, long strings. I did not keep the first three strings I found, but I held onto the next one and the ones that followed. I took pictures of the strings and shared them with my family so they could take part in the string game that seemed to be going on. I found the next string on February 4. It was very long and similar in color to the first pink string I found. The next string was blue, and I found it on March 4. I shared these stories with people at work, and they were taken back. People said they never found long strings in their houses. They would find short strings hanging off their clothes, but they were able to trace the location of the thread.

On March 6, my friend Lucy and her newborn baby were at our house. As I was telling her about the strings, I glanced over and saw a yellow string balled up on the floor. I reached over and unwound the string, and it was approximately six inches long. I took a picture of it next to the blue string and sent it to my family. Lucy was shocked by this find, and she was glad to have experienced it with me.

On April 3, I found a long pink string on the back of Layton's blue sleeper as I got him ready for bed. I had just boxed up all of his newborn to six-month clothes and replaced them with nine- to eighteen-month clothes. Bryson and Holden were in the shower. As I zipped up the front of Layton's sleeper, I noticed something on his left shoulder. It was another pink string! I added it to the collection and sent a text to Dad and Rochelle. The blue sleeper is one that both Bryson and Holden wore, but it was the first time I had put it on Layton. On May 4, I found two long white strings in our house. One was on Holden's blanket, and the other was on the floor in our bedroom.

May proved to be a very stressful month. I was getting ready to have my diagnostic workup completed on May 9, before my preventative surgery on June 16. I found myself feeling overwhelmed with the mammogram and MRI. I was more stressed about the diagnostic tests than I was about the actual surgery. I do not do well with the unknown, so the idea of having tests with pending results made me worry. On May 7, I found another long string. The strings always provided a good distraction, and I was thankful for the timing of each and every find. I carry the strings with me in my purse along with the rose-petal rosary from Mom's funeral. I never know where a random string is going to show up, and I want to make sure I add them all to the collection.

## Chapter 27

# Spiritual Medium

On March 1, 2014, we had an experience with a spiritual medium. My sister's good friend, Michelle, had a prior experience, and she was blown away by the reading and how accurate the messages were. Rochelle told me some of what Michelle experienced, and the more I listened, the more excited I became about scheduling an appointment for our family. We proposed the idea to Dad, although we expected him to be resistant. Once he heard Michelle's story, he too was on board. March 1 worked with all of our schedules, so Rochelle booked the appointment. She also told Michelle not to share any of our family's personal stories with the medium. Michelle is a very trustworthy and amazing person; she wanted us to have an honest experience, so she did not contact the medium before our appointment.

I went in with very little expectations. Naturally, I was pessimistic going into the reading, but I hoped we would leave with peace. We all had unresolved questions after Mom's death and we wanted to see what the spiritual medium had to offer. Previously, we had been private about our spiritual experiences. We told family and friends, but we did not post personal happenings on social media for everyone to see. Based on the precise details and the accuracy, we are convinced the spiritual medium has a special gift, and we are thankful our paths crossed so we could be provided with answers and closure.

Rochelle and Scott's living room seemed like the obvious place to meet, since that is where Mom passed away. Our appointment was scheduled for six o'clock that evening. Scott, Josh, Deanna, and the kids went on an outing so Dad, Rochelle, and I would be the only ones present during the reading.

The setting was very peaceful and relaxing. Our experience did not involve a gypsy fortune teller, tarot cards, a crystal ball, an Ouija board, or voodoo dolls. The medium's name is Lilly, and she refers to herself as a spiritual counselor and life coach. One would never guess just by looking at her that she has this special gift. Lilly explained that each session is uniquely designed to help individuals evolve into their true selves. Her approach focuses on mind, body, soul, and spirit while communicating with loved ones who have passed away yet continue to surround us. She said she would provide advice and support to us by helping us solve problems and unresolved issues. She would answers from our loved ones to give us guidance and direction in areas where we feel lost and confused. She ended by telling us, "This is a journey of faith and healing for you and your loved ones."

Before Lilly arrived, Rochelle jokingly said she could see Mom saying, "I have an appointment I have to be at six. I can't be late." Knowing how Mom liked to plan, we agreed.

Lilly arrived on time, and we gathered around the table. Dad sat between Rochelle and me, and Lilly sat on the opposite side. As soon as she sat down, she sensed how nervous we were. Rochelle and Dad were somewhat tearful, and I was guarded. I did not know what to expect, but I was anxious to get the three-hour reading underway.

One of the first things Lilly said was, "There is a lot of energy in this house." She pointed out that Rochelle, who was not showing, was pregnant. Initially we thought there was a fifty-fifty chance at getting that right, but we were somewhat taken aback. She then looked at my dad and said, "You have experienced significant loss." Lilly explained she had visions of a heart, and she asked Dad if he lost his wife. Dad was tearful, and he nodded his head yes. Lilly also asked if Dad recently lost his mother. This really caught us by surprise, given the fact that Grams had passed away about seven months earlier. Lilly kept seeing the number three. She said the number three is important in our lives, and we would see it as we move forward. She said that she was getting energy from Mom, who was saying that Dad and I both looked thinner than she remembered. We had both just completed a twenty-four-day challenge and lost thirty-one pounds between the two of us.

Lilly turned to me and asked if I'd had some genetic testing done. I felt my palms get sweaty and my stomach turned a bit. I had yet to tell Dad about the actual results of my BRCA2 test. In the days leading up to the reading, I'd told Josh that if my results were revealed during the session, then the spiritual medium was for real. Lilly said she saw some letters and a number—" …the letters B-R-C-A and the number two."

Dad said Rochelle and I had both been tested and, thankfully, "they both came back negative." I thought to myself, *This could get very interesting.*

We spent a significant amount of time talking about Dad moving forward with his life after Mom's passing. The Catholic Church is important to Dad, and he takes the sacraments very seriously. He was born into the Methodist Church, and he and Mom were married at Saint John's Catholic Church in Cambridge. He converted to Catholicism in 1982 shortly after Rochelle was born. Dad and Deanna met with several priests to discuss getting married in the Catholic Church. Unfortunately all the priests they met with said the same thing in several different ways. Because Deanna had been married previously, they would have to get an annulment before the church would consider marrying them. This news was devastating to Dad and Deanna because they desperately wanted to get married in the Catholic Church. She told Dad to go with his intuition. I cannot remember specifically how it came up during the reading, but Dad asked Lilly how many priests he had talked to. Without hesitation, Lilly responded "five." Dad was stunned. It was true.

Even though my parents spent a lot of time talking about Dad moving on with his life, he wanted confirmation that he was doing the right thing. Mom and Dad's love for one another was such a special thing. Mom knew she would no longer be on earth with Dad; therefore she wanted Dad to move on and to love again. We reassured Dad that Mom wanted him to be happy, and he very much appreciated our approval of Deanna and his desire to love again.

We talked a little bit about Grams during the reading. Dad was tearful during the discussions about his mom. Even though Dad visited her at Hillcrest on a regular basis, he always felt like he should do more. Lilly picked up on energy from Grams and reassured Dad that she was very proud of him and appreciative for all Dad did for her. Grams knew Dad was busy with the farm, grieving the loss of Mom, and visiting his grandchildren. Dad was comforted and confirmed that he'd heard the same from Grams during her time on earth.

Rochelle asked Lilly if she could actually see Mom and Grams or if she was just picking up this energy she kept referring to. Lilly said she could see both of them. She said Mom was standing behind Dad with her hands on his shoulders. Grams was not as apparent because Mom had a lot of messages she wanted to deliver so we could live without lingering questions. We asked what Mom looked like, and Lilly said, "She is very pure, very heavenly and angelic." She described Mom as being in her late twenties or early thirties. She said Mom had dark, curly hair. I immediately thought of a picture that described Mom's appearance. After the reading, I e-mailed Lilly a picture of Mom when she was twenty-nine years old. Lilly confirmed that was how she'd seen Mom during the reading.

Mom's appearance as seen by the spiritual medium

Lilly explained that she can tell the difference between souls who have made it to heaven and those who have not. She said Mom was glowing, almost as if an aura of light was around her. During her lifetime, she has seen souls who have not made it to heaven. They exuded a dark shadow rather than the pureness she saw around Mom and Grams.

She asked Dad if Grams had been outspoken. Rochelle, Dad, and I laughed and said she did in fact speak her mind. Lilly asked if Grams liked to sing. Some of the fondest memories I have of Grams are listening to her sing her catchy jingles and whistling to the tune of songs. It didn't matter where we were—when Grams felt the need to sing she would burst out tunes that would make anybody laugh.

Lilly said she heard Grams singing "Peggy Sue."

Dad paused and tears filled his eyes. He said, "That is what Dad used to call Mom."

We had not referred to Grams as Peggy during the reading nor did I did not know Grandpa Schmidt referred to Grams as Peggy Sue. These were both validating moments for us.

Lilly did not know how Dad and Deanna met. She said she had visions of Mom and Grams pushing Dad's vehicle to Deanna's place of business. It sounds like Mom and Grams tag-teamed and pushed Dad toward Deanna. They had met at Deanna's office three weeks after Grams passed away. Once again, this was another validating moment. We were definitely intrigued and wanted to know more.

Mom's theme of normalcy on earth came out during the reading. Lilly said Mom indicated there was only one Nana but she was agreeable to having the grandkids refer to Deanna as Grandma; they now call her Grandma Dee. Mom also wanted Dad to remember the wonderful lives they had, but she gave him the green light to move forward. Mom's clothes were still in the closet and all of her pictures were still hanging in the house. It was important for Dad to make room for his new life with Deanna.

I could tell Lilly was making headway with Dad over the annulment issue. We were anxious to hear what Lilly would bring up next. Dad opened up because he trusted what Lilly was saying. He wanted to ask a question to which only we would know the answer. Surprisingly, we received an accurate answer.

Dad asked, "What happened in 1994 when I was angry during Nancy's clinical trial?"

Lilly paused and said, "It has something to do with a seat belt."

Once again we were in awe. The chapter titled "Covenant and Mark 11:22" refers to the incident. As Dad was driving back to Omaha to be with Mom, he was angry and under a lot of stress. He asked God to show him He was there. That is when the headlights from the Covenant truck came up right behind him, and Dad slammed on his brakes to signal to the vehicle to give him some space.

Lilly turned to Rochelle and started talking about her unborn baby. Rochelle asked if it was a girl or boy, and Lilly said we had to wait and be surprised. We tried our hardest to get it out of her, but she would not budge. She said an unborn baby symbolizes a new beginning. Rochelle had lived in fear as she worried about the cancer coming back. Lilly told Rochelle she would have a long life with three beautiful children. She said Mom was telling Rochelle to be more aware of her environment, to eat healthy and use "green" products. Rochelle said she and Scott had talked about eating fewer processed foods and using natural household items. Rochelle's doctors were unable to say whether her diagnosis was caused by environmental factors, but before the reading she had felt the need to be more aware of food and cleaning products.

Lilly asked Rochelle if her oldest child was going to start school the following fall. She warned that Anisten would need her hand held a bit as she made the transition. Rochelle said Anisten had a lot of anxiety about going to school because she was afraid of getting shots. Lilly said she could not tell which child but the one with light-colored eyes had the ability see beyond. We decided that was Anisten because of the sightings of Mom she had reported. She was also the one who kept talking about the baby in her mom's stomach before Rochelle found out she was pregnant.

Lilly asked Rochelle if her youngest daughter is strong willed. Rochelle agreed Kardyn is a little "firecracker" and she keeps them on their toes. We all laughed; Kardyn definitely has a mind of her own. Lilly said that Mom was influencing Kardyn's behavior. Due to the timing of her illness, Mom never had the opportunity to really get to know Kardyn. When Kardyn starts acting up we now laugh and say, "Nana!"

Lilly also talked about Mom's gratitude to Rochelle and Scott for opening up their home during her terminal illness. This touched us, and we all started crying. Mom put a lot of thought into whether she could stay in Gretna because she did not want to leave bad memories in Rochelle and Scott's home. Rochelle was so happy this came out during the reading, and it validated their decision to graciously share their home and lives during Mom's illness.

Approximately two hours had passed, and we were anxious to learn more. I was happy Dad and Rochelle had heard everything that we'd discussed, but I felt a bit left out. I asked Lilly if she was picking up any energy from Mom about me. Lilly said I had a shield and it was very hard for Mom to come to me in my dreams. I am not a crier, but this touched me because I knew it was true. I never considered myself a strong person, but as Mom's health faded, I stepped up to be the rock she had always been for me and my family. Lilly pointed out that I always act as though "everything this fine" and "I've got this." Her description of me could not have been more accurate. I tend to hide my feelings and not allow others to know what I really think.

Lilly said Mom was throwing signs in my path, but I was not paying attention to them. I immediately thought of the random strings I had found, but I did not give a hint to Lilly. I wanted to see if she could identify the specific signs I had received.

I asked her "Like what?"

She was seeing something associated with crafts and a coin. I was completely taken back. I told Lilly and I had been finding random strings, and Josh found a coin in his underwear. She said Mom was very good about manipulating earthly items. I am definitely not a person who does crafts, so I was not sure about the significance of the strings.

Lilly said Mom wanted something to be made from the strings. "The strands will be stitched together forever, much like the love she has for you is endless."

She said that Mom loved Rochelle and me equally but differently. We are two different people, and she had to show signs in different ways to get our attention. Years ago, I'd had a conversation with Mom. She'd said that because of our vastly opposite personalities, she loved us equally but in different ways. Now that I am a mom to three children with different personalities, I know exactly what she meant.

We discussed the genetic testing again. I was happy because it was time to let Dad in on my secret. Enough time had passed and since Deanna was in his life, I knew he could handle the truth. Lilly brought up the BRCA2 testing, and I jumped in and said, "I tested positive."

It felt as if time stood still. Dad looked right at me. "What?"

I told Dad not to worry, that I had a plan. I said I had been undergoing surveillance and had an appointment with a breast surgeon on March 18, 2014, to discuss the next step. Dad was not excited about the news. In fact, he was overwhelmed by fear, and he did not know how to respond. He started weeping and asking if I had cancer. I assured him I did not, but I felt as if I had lost credibility with him.

Again, I was telling Dad I had it under control, and Lilly pointed out the shield she'd talked about earlier. She told me it was okay to not have everything figured out. It was hard for me to accept this, but I had unintentionally created a barrier by not allowing people to know my true feelings.

Lilly said that Josh was supportive but did not say much. This is true; my husband is a man of few words as he is always methodically thinking. Lilly compared Josh's mind to a hamster running on a wheel. She reminded me about the conversation Josh and I had when we first found out I had tested positive for BRCA2. She said that Josh was more worried about me than he was indicating, and he did not want to be a single parent to our children. I had forgotten about the conversation until she brought it up. Lilly also confirmed that I did the right thing by not telling Mom the actual results of my test. She said Mom understood. Hearing this brought me tremendous peace and comfort.

During the reading, Lilly kept seeing Mom holding a little girl's hand. She could not figure out exactly what it meant, whether the girl was me when I was little or if she symbolized the daughter I longed for. She said something big was planned for me after my surgery, but because I still had my shield up, she could not tell what it was. This "big event" was something outside of my comfort zone. After the reading, I received an e-mail from Lilly stating that the baby chapter is definitely still alive in our lives. Time will tell whether this premonition proves to be true, but for now our three boys are keeping us very busy.

Lilly talked about a couple of things that happened in the days leading up to Mom's funeral, including our search for her earrings in the antique soap dish. Lilly saw some gold earrings an incident involving Scott. We explained that Scott had found the earrings, and Lilly said that was Scott's shining moment. Nothing he could say would make losing Mom easier on us, so finding her earrings was his contribution.

The next story really made us feel that Lilly was onto something. She described one of Mom's very close friends as being almost like a sister but not blood related. Dad, Rochelle, and I knew she was describing Mom's childhood friend, Kem. Lilly said that Kem had a private conversation with Mom's body the day before the funeral. She had been alone in the viewing room at the funeral home and leaned over and whispered to Mom, "I will do anything I can for your family. I am here for them."

At the time of the reading, we had no way to confirm the conversation Lilly described. On our way home from Gretna on Sunday, I called Kem to ask her about it. She did not know about our experience with the spiritual medium, and she told me about the private conversation she had during Mom's visitation. The details of the conversation were essentially what Lilly had described. This was yet another validating moment.

We went a half hour over our scheduled time with Lilly. When we were done, we called Josh, Scott, and Deanna to let them know they could come back to the house. They had been circling the subdivision. Unfortunately the kids all fell asleep so they did not have a fun night out like they planned. Instead, they drove around Omaha and Gretna for nearly three-and-a-half hours during a small snow storm. I went outside to help carry in the kiddos.

As soon as I saw Josh, I said, "Dad now knows about my genetic results." Josh smiled and said, "I figured." All the kids woke up when they were carried inside. We sat in the living room and described the awesome stories that came out during the reading. Deanna was crying as we talked. I was not sure if she was overwhelmed with the information or if something was wrong. She later told me she and Dad had been worried about my genetic testing. I have known Josh for eleven years and can count on one hand how many times I have seen him cry. He often sees both sides of arguments and typically plays the devil's advocate. He was very tearful during our discussion, as was Scott. They were both taken back by the amount and the accuracy of information that Lilly provided.

The experience with the spiritual medium was very therapeutic, and we felt whole again. We continued to miss Mom every day, but we were definitely at peace after the reading. We are so thankful our paths crossed with Lilly and that she has the gift of communicating with those who have gone before us.

At the beginning of the reading, Lilly said we would see the number three during our lives. In the spring of 2014, I started running in 5K races. I asked Josh to pick up my race packet the day before the race. When I got home from work, I opened the folder and saw my bib number: 333. I felt Mom's presence and was excited to run knowing she would be with me every step of the way.

One night, approximately one month after the reading, I could not sleep. I woke up at 3:00 a.m. I tossed and turned for what seemed like forever. When I looked at the clock it was 3:03 a.m. The next time I looked at the clock, it was 3:13 a.m. I smiled and thought about Mom. I finally went back to sleep and woke up again at 3:33 a.m. I am not sure about the significance of this event, but it definitely made me productive. I could not sleep so I sent an e-mail to Rochelle and Dad to tell them about the "night of the threes." Then I got ready for work and drove to the office.

# CHAPTER 28

# EMBRACE THE CHAOS

My consultation with the breast surgeon was on March 18, 2014. I was very nervous about the appointment because the reality of the surgery finally hit me. I had been thinking about it for approximately eighteen months, and I knew there was no other choice. I was excited to meet the surgeon and to get a surgery date on the calendar. Josh and I went to the appointment together so we would both have the opportunity to ask questions and to make sure we were both had confidence in the doctor. Within seconds of meeting Dr. Marilee McGinness, I knew she was the perfect surgeon for me. Her bedside manner is phenomenal, and I felt extremely comfortable with her. We talked about the different kinds of reconstruction and the timing of my surgery.

Dr. McGinness is a breast surgeon, and her objective is to remove as much breast tissue as possible. She explained that nothing is 100 percent, but by having this surgery, I would significantly reduce my chances of breast cancer. She is very meticulous and said she would take as long as she needed to be sure she removed as much breast tissue as was humanly possible.

She listened to what I wanted and suggested going with the skin-sparing prophylactic bilateral mastectomy with reconstruction. She explained that the breast tissue would be removed; however, the *skin* from my breasts would be saved for reconstruction purposes. Once the mastectomy was complete, the plastic surgeon would conduct his portion of the surgery.

There are other options for reconstruction, but I felt this method was best for me. After our discussion, the doctor referred me to a plastic surgeon.

I wanted a surgery date in April 2014, but that was not possible. I was only six months postpartum, and I had quit breastfeeding only two months earlier. Dr. McGinness explained that she likes her patients to be at least six months past breastfeeding because the diagnostic tests can show false positives due to the hormonal changes that take place during pregnancy and breastfeeding. I was adamant that I wanted to have surgery sooner rather than later due to my fear of developing breast cancer. My sister-in-law was getting married on June 13, 2014. Dr. McGinness suggested I wait until after the wedding; therefore we agreed on June 16, 2014, providing the date worked with the plastic surgeon she recommended.

Following my appointment with the doctor, I met with the scheduling department so we could keep moving forward. I was referred to a very talented plastic surgeon, Dr. Ponnuru. My consultation was scheduled for April Fool's Day. We all laughed a bit when this date was proposed. The date happened to work with Josh's schedule, so we booked it. I typically prefer female doctors, but I went into the appointment with an open mind. There are several plastic surgeons to choose from, and if the consultation did not go well I could always opt for another.

One requirement was a comprehensive diagnostic workup before the surgery. I told Dr. McGinness I was more nervous about the workup than I was about the surgery. Getting through the testing process and waiting for results would be very stressful for me. I had to have a mammogram and breast MRI before the doctor would agree to do surgery. Even though my surgery was for preventative purposes, they had to rule out any presence of cancer. It was surreal when I booked my mammogram and MRI because they also scheduled me for a biopsy should I need it. I appreciated how thorough they were, but it made me extremely anxious to see "biopsy" on the calendar containing my appointments. I left the clinic with mixed feelings. I was excited to be moving forward but I dreaded the diagnostic tests that were scheduled for May 9.

The morning of April 1 seemed to drag on. I hoped to connect with the plastic surgeon and was anxious to see whether he was available to do my surgery on June 16. Josh and I sat in the waiting room for almost an hour before my name was called. The nurse greeted us and took my history. Dr. Ponnuru walked in with a clear container.

He introduced himself and said, "I brought in my dessert tray."

He opened the container and inside were several saline and silicone implants. Josh and I laughed and agreed he was a good fit. I really liked his sense of humor and I felt comfortable talking about "everything boobs" with him.

Dr. Ponnuru explained he and the breast surgeon work together. Dr. McGinness performs the mastectomy, and Dr. Ponnuru reconstructs the area using tissue expanders. Once the breast tissue is removed, Dr. Ponnuru inserts tissue expanders into the skin. The expanders, which are made of cadaver skin, have ports so saline can be used to inflate them. Dr. Ponnuru explained he would fill the expanders during the surgery so I would not wake up completely flat. I would have a six-week lifting restriction and needed to take off at least four weeks of work. I would be unable to pick up my kids for at least six weeks, but they were my main motivation for getting the surgery in the first place.

He and Dr. McGinness had worked together several times in the past, and they seemed to have a lot of confidence in one another. At the end of the appointment Dr. Ponnuru confirmed his availability on June 16. In fact, when he opened his calendar, my surgery was already noted on the schedule, thanks to Dr. McGinness's office.

The breast MRI is very sensitive; therefore it usually is scheduled around a woman's monthly cycle. Due to my nervousness about the mammogram and MRI, my cycle did not come as planned. You have to be within a certain window before they will perform the MRI; otherwise the false positives can be rather high. I called the nurse early in the week leading up to my tests. She agreed that I was outside the preferred window; therefore my mammogram and MRI were rescheduled to May 13.

I took off from work on May 13 because I knew I would not be able to fully engage following my tests. My first appointment was for lab work. My doctor ordered a full panel so she could see where all of my numbers were. Once all five vials of blood were drawn, Josh and I made our way to the next appointment for my mammogram. I opted to have the 3-D ultrasound because the state-of-the-art technology allows the radiologist additional views, and it significantly reduces the callback rate.

They called three of us in the waiting room to the changing room. We were each given a gown and a key for a locker for our personal items. I had a hard time figuring out the gown. It appeared as if one of the ties on the inside were missing. I asked another woman for help, and she had the same problem. We did our best to cover up and entered the holding room.

In the past, the holding room was filled with quiet, nervous women. Generally, nobody talked to one another, and we waited anxiously for our names to be called. This time, a woman was talking and talking and talking. It was a nice change of pace. As soon as I sat down, a woman asked if I'd had problems with my gown. The wardrobe malfunctions seemed to be a great conversation starter and a decent distraction.

Typically I am the youngest woman by at least ten years. I always feel as if I have to explain why I am there, so the other women do not feel unnecessarily sorry for me. As I was telling my story, an older woman, approximately eighty years old, asked if I would like some water. I took her up on her offer. Unfortunately, she'd also received a gown with a missing tie. As she was walking back, the front of her gown opened, and there were her girls! As she handed me the water, her name was called. She told me she would pray for me, and I thanked her for the water and prayers. I was happy for the distraction; for a moment, I almost forgot why I was there.

The woman who had been talking when I entered the room continued to talk. She went on and on about everything under the sun. She had on the brightest colored purple sweatpants along with the lovely pink gown that matched the rest of ours. She got up to throw her cup away, and I noticed a long, aqua-colored string on the left side of her rear. I laughed out loud and then covered it up with a fake cough. I thought about Mom's sense of humor and immediately felt a sense of peace. I wanted to grab the string off the back of her pants and add it to my growing collection, but I did not. My experience in the holding room was out of the ordinary, and it was such a laidback experience compared to my prior appointments. Shortly thereafter, my name was called.

I was somewhat tearful during the mammogram because I was so nervous. I shared my story with the tech, and at the end she gave me a big hug and told me I was doing the right thing by opting to have preventative surgery. The techs are not able to say anything regarding what they see (or do not see) during the mammogram. In the past, I would go back to the holding room and wait for the nurse to tell me my test was clear and to schedule my next appointment in six months. Before the tech sent me on my way, I asked whether I would get the preliminary results that day as I had in the past or have to wait for the card in the mail. She told me I would not receive the results on that day but should get a call within the next twenty-four to forty-eight hours. I desperately tried to get her to budge and give me more information, but she would not. I left with a sick feeling in my stomach.

Once the mammogram was complete, Josh and I went to the MRI suite for my final appointment. I'd only had one MRI in the past, and I did not particularly enjoy it. The tech was a wonderful woman. I expressed my nervousness and shared my history and Mom's history with breast cancer. She comforted me by telling me she was a breast cancer survivor of ten years, and the small spot had been detected on her MRI. They caught the cancer in its earliest stage; she'd had a lumpectomy and radiation. To get through the MRI without having a nervous breakdown, I repeated songs in my head and tried to think happy thoughts.

During our drive home, I told Josh the mammogram tech had made me nervous with her comments. He said it did no good to worry about things out of our control, and I agreed. We hoped and prayed for good news so the surgery could go on as planned. I had high hopes of receiving clear results so I could really enjoy the three weeks leading up to June 16. That evening I sent an e-mail to Lilly to let her know about the aqua-colored string on the woman with purple pants. She replied that evening and reminded me that purple is a very significant color in my life.

I returned to work at my normal time the following day. I prayed so hard for a call that indicated all my tests were clean. I looked forward to getting home that evening so we could celebrate Holden's fourth birthday and my clean tests. Shortly after eleven in the morning, I received a call from the nurse at Dr. McGinness's office. As soon as I answered the phone, I could tell she did not have good news. She said the radiologist saw a suspicious spot on my left side, which was picked up on the mammogram. I was trying to comprehend the information, she said a suspicious spot was also detected on my right side during the MRI. I had a hard time catching my breath. I could not take in all of the information, because I was overwhelmed. The nurse told me she was calling the diagnostic department to find a date and time for my follow-up tests. I begged her to get me in as soon as possible so I did not have to play the waiting game.

As I waited for a call back from the nurse, I rang my boss and asked if he had time to visit. Usually, he is the one buzzing me, but this time the roles were reversed. Mike came to my office, and he could tell I was upset. I told him about the call I'd just received.

The nurse called me back; I had appointments on Thursday, May 15, at one in the afternoon for a follow-up mammogram for an ultrasound. She explained that if both tests came back negative, I still would have to have an MRI-guided biopsy. I was not excited about this but trusted the process. I was thankful for the quick turnaround time, but I wanted to go to the clinic that afternoon. It seemed like an eternity to wait twenty-six hours. The nurse did a great job explaining the results of both the mammogram and MRI. I put her on speaker so Mike could hear what she had to say. I was still in shock, so I was not fully listening and comprehending what she was saying. After the phone call, Mike said he could tell the nurse knew what she was talking about. His instincts were telling him I was okay, and they were just being thorough given Mom's history. I felt better once I calmed down. Mike told me to take the rest of the day off and to take as much time as I needed.

I took Mike up on his offer and went home for the day. I accessed my radiology reports online and read them over and over. I typically try not to research my medical concerns on the Internet, but I could not help myself. I researched every unknown medical term contained within my mammogram and MRI reports. I wanted to know the medical lingo so I could ask meaningful questions at my follow-up appointment.

I had a sense of peace, but I was nervous about my follow-ups. Josh went with me to my appointment the following day. I did my best to keep busy around the house until it was time to leave. As we were parking the car at the clinic, I showed Josh an e-mail that I received from Lilly on March 24, which would have been Mom and Dad's thirty-fifth wedding anniversary. We had not talked about their anniversary during the reading, so when I received her message on March 24, I was once again taken back.

Among other things, Lilly wrote, "Things will not go as you plan them. Things will be crazy, and the schedule will be constantly changing. Embrace the chaos, and know there is something great headed your way."

She said she had no idea what the "something great" was, but she kept seeing visions of a whole new chapter for me.

Josh was shocked by her e-mail. He and I talked about how things were not going as *I* had planned. My initial appointment was May 9, but it had been changed to May 13. I did not think I would get a call back or need the biopsy appointment but, unfortunately, I ended up having additional appointments. Josh agreed the e-mail was spot on, and once again he was awed by the accuracy of the information Lilly provided.

He and I walked into the office to check in for my repeat mammogram. One of the receptionists told me I looked familiar. I told her that I'd been there two days prior and got a call back. She had me fill out some forms and said my name would be called soon. When my name was called, I headed back to the dressing room, put on one of the pink robes, and entered the holding room. The room was rather full that day, so I sat in the only chair available. I was nervous, but I also knew I was in good hands. Just then I looked down, and on the side of the chair was a long white string. Finding the random string was exactly what I needed. As soon as I found it, all of my worries seemed to be put aside. I took it as a sign from Mom telling me everything would be just fine. It was almost as if I could feel her arms wrapped around me. That is just what I needed at that moment.

As I looked around the room, I noticed I was once again the youngest woman by several years. Rather than sitting there in silence, I burst out, "Have any of you ever gotten a call back?" Several women spoke up and confirmed they had gotten call backs in the past, and they ultimately got clear results. I then shared my story about choosing to have preventative surgery thanks to the knowledge I was given by genetic testing. Every woman in that room turned, and all eyes were on me. My palms got sweaty, and I also felt a strong desire to talk about Mom. One woman got up from her chair, walked over to me, put her hand on my shoulder, and asked the room to join her in prayer. It was truly a very moving experience. As soon as the prayer concluded with "amen," my name was called. I thanked the women and walked back with the tech.

As usual, I was a bit tearful during the mammogram. When I walked in the room, the area of concern was enlarged on the computer screen for me to see. The tech had a calming demeanor, and I felt completely comfortable. They repeated the mammogram only on the left side.

After the mammogram was over, I was sent back to the holding room. I desperately wanted the nurse to tell me they could not find the spot on the repeat exam. The nurse called my name and took me to the dressing room area to give me the report. She said the radiologist looked at my results, and he ordered follow-up ultrasounds on both the left and right side. I was sickened by the news. In my mind, it was clear there was something wrong.

I excused myself and went to the waiting room where Josh was. I was crying, and I told him, "I am convinced I have breast cancer!"

He reassured me and waited patiently. Once I got back to the holding room, there were some new faces. One woman had tears in her eyes; she told me she'd heard my story and would say some extra prayers for me.

My name was called a short time after for the bilateral ultrasound. I took my iPod with me so I could listen to music during the exam. When I had ultrasounds every six months for monitoring, the exams lasted approximately forty minutes. The ultrasound tech was very nice. She let me know the radiologist did not think there was anything to be concerned about on my left side, but he wanted to triple check with the ultrasound. When she was done with the exam, she said she did not see anything, but of course the radiologist had to read the images. She told me not to be paranoid if the doctor came back with her to discuss the results. She also said not to worry if the doctor decided to rescan the suspicious areas because in 99 percent of cases doctors rescan the area so they can see it for themselves. The tech left the room, and I sat on the exam table praying for good news.

The power of prayer is amazing! The doctor came in and said the suspicious spot on the left side was nothing. He also said the spot on the right that had showed up on the MRI was not on the ultrasound. I was so relieved, I cried. I usually do not cry until well after the fact, but I was so relieved I could not contain my emotions. The doctor told me it was great news that the spot on the right didn't show up on the mammogram or the ultrasound, but because it had been picked up on the MRI, protocol called for an MRI-guided biopsy. The spot on the right side was "microscopic," and the MRI has the highest false positive rate. He felt fairly confident the spot was hormonal, and he estimated there was a less than 10 percent chance it was cancer. He further said if it were cancer, it was so small, it would have no impact on my lifespan. Generally the treatment for stage 0 breast cancer is a lumpectomy, but with my upcoming surgery there would be no need for treatment should it turn out to be an early form of cancer. The MRI-guided biopsy was scheduled for May 22. I felt really good as we pulled away from the facility. We left with the best possible news and scenario. I was not excited about the biopsy, but once again I trusted the process and the doctors.

My dear friend Dena offered to take me to the biopsy appointment. She picked me up at work on Thursday, May 22. When I got in her car, she handed me a large bag filled with items. The first thing I pulled out was a beautiful purple running jacket. At first, she swore the jacket was dark blue but finally agreed it was purple. I told her the story about purple being significant to me and that her giving me a purple jacket was no coincidence. We joked and said our moms were probably high-fiving each other in heaven.

The biopsy was uneventful. I went in hoping the spot that was detected on the MRI on May 13 was hormonal and would not appear during the biopsy. The nurse told me she had experienced that scenario on more than one occasion, so I remained hopeful that would be my outcome. The first phase of the procedure was to locate the area so they could perform the biopsy. When the doctor entered the room, he said they'd found the spot, so they were going to move on with the procedure as planned. I was crushed but I told myself the biopsy was a character builder. I kept thinking about how Mom would have handled the situation. I was able to find a positive by thinking about other women I could help in the future by sharing my experiences with the biopsy.

The biopsy was not painful at all. The doctor did a great job of informing me about everything that would happen before he moved on to the next phase. As he was numbing the area, he told me it would hurt. I politely informed him that I'd had two C-sections so a little bee sting was nothing. He agreed, and I think he enjoyed my response. The biopsy was over before I knew it. I continued to lie facedown until they told me I could move. During the entire procedure, I could hear the doctor's voice. I imagined him being middle-aged, so I was surprised when I turned my head and looked at him; all I could think was Dr. McSteamy! He told me the suspicious area was linear, and he agreed it was small. The results would not be available until the following Tuesday due to the Memorial

Day weekend. The nurse told me they got clear margins, and the suspicious area was completely removed during the biopsy. I was told to expect a call from the MRI department the following day to see how I was doing.

I returned to work on Friday, May 23. Around two in the afternoon, the University of Kansas showed up on my caller ID. I did not have the nervous pit in the bottom of my stomach, because I assumed it was the nurse from the MRI department following up. The woman on the other end of the line was a nurse but not the nurse from the MRI department. She was Dr. McGinness's nurse, Mary Jo, who had excitement in her voice.

The first thing she said was, "Great news! The biopsy results are in, and it is benign!" Mary Jo had been watching my case all day because she knew I did not want to wait the long holiday weekend wondering what the results were. As soon as the results were posted, she dialed my number. I was very appreciative.

I heard the song "You Won't Let Go" by Michael W. Smith for the first time in the days leading up to my biopsy. I was captivated by the message, the lyrics, and the overall sound. It is an upbeat song that reminds us God will never abandon us. I downloaded the song to my iPod and listened to it during a portion of my ultrasound on May 15. I was not permitted to take my iPod into the MRI, so I replayed the following lyrics in my head:

> You are the anchor for my soul.
> You won't let go.
> No matter what may come, I know.
> You won't let go.

I was able to relax during the procedure by trusting the Lord and having faith he would see me through the situation according to His will.

I believe our series of unfortunate events happened for a reason, and I am on a mission to spread the word about being proactive. Shortly before my presurgical workup I spoke on the phone with a client's mother named Leslee. One thing led to another, and we started talking about our families. Leslee's teenage daughter is a Hodgkin's lymphoma survivor, and her mother passed away from breast cancer at a young age. I immediately told her Rochelle was Hodgkin's lymphoma survivor and about Mom's battle with breast cancer. There were many parallels, and I felt a connection with her. Her name is spelled slightly different but Dad's name is also Leslie. I told her about my upcoming surgery, and she was really intrigued. She asked me several questions, and I gave her the information to the breast cancer prevention center.

A few weeks later I called Leslee to obtain some documents for written discovery requests involving her daughter's case. I could tell she was not engaged in our conversation about the documents, and she wanted to pick up where we'd left off during our prior conversation. She said our conversation had an impact on her, and she had scheduled a mammogram. Something in my voice grabbed her attention, and she believed our paths had crossed for a reason. Unfortunately, a spot was detected on her right breast. It was an area of concern and had to be monitored every six months. She was in tears as she told me her story. Leslee said I was on her mind constantly, and she was praying for me. I feel really blessed and fortunate to be able to take our experiences and make other people aware of the importance on being proactive.

CHAPTER **29**

# KNOWLEDGE IS POWER

Once I received the benign results of the biopsy, I felt as if the weight of the world had been lifted from my shoulders. I looked forward to spending the days leading up to my surgery as stress free as possible. I wanted to get as much done around the house and at work, because I was not sure what to expect following the surgery. The plastic surgeon emphasized the importance of adhering to the six-week lifting restriction and to taking time to recover. We were getting ready to celebrate the marriage of my sister-in-law Betsy to her wonderful fiancé, Justin on Friday, June 13. I am so thankful I was able to help Betsy and her bridal party with the decorating and really enjoy time with family and friends at the wedding.

After the wedding, we returned home on Saturday. As I was in Holden's room hanging up clothes, I noticed a AA battery at my feet. I was not sure where it came from, but I immediately picked it up off the floor so I did not have to worry about Layton choking on it. At that moment, I felt an overwhelming urge to check on Layton. He is a very busy boy, and he gets around the house rather quickly. I went to our room and found him getting ready to put a battery in his mouth. In the short time I was in Holden's room, Layton had found the remote and unfortunately the back of the remote fell off, allowing him to access the batteries. In the four years Holden has been in his room, not once have I found a battery in there. I firmly believe Mom is our personal guardian angel, and she was there in that moment protecting Layton from harm's way. The battery scenario brought back memories of Holden falling in the four-and-a-half-foot window well, when he'd miraculously walked away without any injuries. When I shared this story with my family, they agreed Mom was working overtime to protect her grandchildren. I could hear her say, "You guys! Seriously? Do not let anything happen to my grandchildren!"

I could not wait to have my surgery. I had the date circled, starred, and highlighted on my calendars at work and at home. I was not afraid of the pain, because I knew it would be temporary. I was really excited to rid myself of the fear of breast cancer and to really start living. I was only ten years old when Mom was diagnosed the first time, so the thought of reducing my lifetime risk of developing breast cancer was the most liberating feeling. I'd promised Mom I would be proactive, and I knew she would be watching over me during the surgery and recovery.

Sunday, June 15 was Father's Day. We celebrated all the wonderful men in our lives by hosting a barbecue at our house. It was a lot of fun to relax and hang out in the hours leading up to my surgery. I slept really well the night before. I embraced sleeping on my stomach because I was not sure how long it would be before I would be able to comfortably do so after the surgery. I was at peace as my head hit the pillow. Rochelle, Scott, and the girls would stay at our house to take care of the boys. Dad and Deanna made a special trip so they could be at the hospital. My mother-in-law Linda and my friend Dena made plans to be at the hospital as well.

I had to check in at five thirty in the morning, as the surgery was scheduled for eight o'clock. I could not believe how relaxed I was. I figured the nerves would set in, but honestly they never did. I was so thankful to have the opportunity to have preventative surgery rather than waiting for cancer to strike.

Josh, Dad, Deanna, and I left the house as planned and headed to the hospital. I checked in, and we were directed to the waiting room, where we waited with several other patients and their families. As we were waiting, I gave paper copies of the first few chapters of my book to Dad, Deanna and Josh. At that time, I'd typed only twelve chapters. Initially I'd set a goal to complete a majority of the book so my family could be distracted during my surgery, but being a mom, wife, and full-time employee did not allow that to happen. I hoped to spend most of my recovery time working on the remaining chapters.

I got called back to the pre-op room and was prepped for surgery. I still was not nervous. The nurse who was assigned to me was incredible. We connected right away, and we shared stories about our families. She had tears as she described losing her daughter only a few years prior. She said she would look for me in recovery because she felt a strong connection with me. I lost count of the number of doctors, residents, research assistants, administrators and nurses who came in and out of my pre-op room. I continued to remain relaxed and embrace the chaos as Lilly had suggested in her e-mail. Once I was settled in, Josh came back to hang out before surgery. I asked him how my father was doing, and he said Dad did not make it through the first page of my book without crying. I felt bad because the goal had been to distract my family, not make them cry! I kept replaying a line from another e-mail from Lilly, about the big event that was planned for me. Often you hear stories about people having near-death experiences and getting a tour of heaven. I was *not* hoping for a near-death experience but I thought Mom might come to me in a dream while I was having surgery. Unfortunately, that did not happen, but thankfully the surgery was uneventful and went as planned.

The last thing I remember is the anesthesiologist putting the mask over my face and telling me to have a nice nap. It seemed like I'd been out for only a short time when I was awakened by the sound of a man moaning. It took me a few moments to figure out where I was. I asked the nurse to get my husband. A few minutes later, Josh was at my side, and I started coming out of the anesthesia. The nurse said I had been in surgery for approximately seven hours. I immediately thought about how anxious Dad must have been. Josh said the staff did a great job of giving him periodic updates throughout the surgery. I do not have a good track record with anesthesia, so they took extra precautions and time with me in recovery. Whatever they did worked wonders because not once did I feel nauseous. I did feel incredibly sore. My chest hurt something fierce, but I kept reminding myself the pain was worth the mental relief I was already experiencing.

I continued to hear moaning in the recovery room. A gentleman to my right was moaning, and just as he let up, the gentleman to my left would start. It is almost as if they were feeding off of each other. I laughed and told the nurse I did not expect her to respond to my comment. She smiled and asked what I had to say. I said, "Men!" She laughed hysterically. She desperately wanted to respond but knew she couldn't.

After about an hour in the recovery room, I was stable enough to be moved to my assigned room. The nurse told me to hit the button on my pain pump one more time before they wheeled me out of the recovery room. As I was being transferred to my room, we stopped by the waiting room to pick up Dad and Deanna. Linda and Dena left the hospital once they found out I was doing well. I absolutely dreaded being moved from the gurney to the bed. I was in a lot of pain and questioned how they would successfully get me from one bed to the other without creating more pain. I started panicking a bit and just then I felt like I was in a hammock and was being swung into my bed. That was the first time I found myself in tears following surgery. It was the most excruciating pain I have ever experienced. I was put in a Tropicana room for recovery purposes. When Dr. McGinness told me she'd ordered a Tropicana room, she assured me there were no palm trees or piña coladas. The room was set to eighty degrees to promote active blood flow. I was physically uncomfortable but I tried to keep the big picture in mind as I fought the pain. I was so thankful the surgery was behind me, and I felt more empowered and liberated than ever.

My two-day hospital stay went really well. When people called and asked how I was doing, I told them it was definitely more painful than I'd anticipated, but it was worth it. It was nice to be home with the boys and have our family under one roof. Rochelle and Scott stayed an extra day to help out. The boys had a great time, and they enjoyed being with their aunt, uncle, and cousins. It was comforting to have a nurse in the house; I turned to Rochelle for help with the drains and questions about my medications.

Josh assumed the caregiver role with ease. He did not hesitate to jump in and take care of me during my recovery phase. We organized all of my medications similar to way Dad handled Mom's. We kept a piece of paper by all of the bottles and a detailed schedule of what time I was to take each one. I could not believe how many medications I'd been prescribed. Generally, I only take a few Tylenol per year, so it was a bit intimidating to be prescribed six medications at once. I was definitely on some heavy-duty pills during the first few weeks of my recovery. I spent most of my day resting and occasionally working on the book. I also caught up on the boys' scrapbooks. My personality does not allow me to sit around and do nothing. I wanted to keep my mind busy so the transition back to work would not be difficult. The most challenging part of recovery was not being able to be as involved with the boys. I could not pick up Layton, and I could not spend much time with the boys during the day.

Before my surgery, Josh, Bryson, and Holden had signed up for family camp weekend with the cub scouts. They planned to leave on Friday, June 20, and would return on Sunday. Josh's mom, Linda, came over to help out with Layton and keep me company. We had a nice visit, and I greatly appreciated the help. I was happy the boys were able to go camping with Josh. Mom's theme of normalcy definitely rubbed off on me. I did not want the boys to feel like we could not do normal family things because of my surgery. I wanted them to be busy being kids rather than to sit around the house worrying about me. Being the patient and a mom rather than the caregiver made me reflect on Mom's experiences. I wanted my boys to be happy and carefree. I had Mom to thank for her ability to emphasize normalcy during her multiple illnesses.

Our family, neighbors, coworkers, and friends took great care of Josh, the boys, and me in the days and weeks following my surgery. My friend Gloria and the wonderful women at her church set up a meal train. We were provided with delicious home-cooked meals. People also gave us groceries and other acts of kindness.

I had an appointment with Dr. McGinness one week after surgery. It felt really good when she reported the pathology came back clean following the surgery. I did not anticipate the pathology to come back positive, but you just never know. Throughout Mom's and Rochelle's experiences, I had learned to expect the worst and hope and pray for the best.

My recovery was fairly uneventful; however, I had minor problems with the left surgical drain. The right one was draining properly, but the left one was not following suit. It was not putting out as much as it should, and the color was a lot darker than it was on the right side. I had planned to follow up with my plastic surgeon no earlier than two weeks after the surgery, but instead I had several unscheduled visits due to the potential infection.

Early one morning I was reading through my e-mail and was excited to see a new message from Lilly. She was responding to a message I'd sent after I found out the results of the biopsy. She said she was happy for me and that God is good! Then she wrote, "I do have to say, I feel that you may have another baby in the future, which could have been why there was such indifferent energy when we first met." Her e-mail brought a smile to my face. I shared the message with Josh, and he just smiled and playfully shook his head in disbelief.

During the reading Lilly kept having visions of Mom walking with a little girl. I thought about this a lot and talked to some friends about it. One friend thought it could have been an image of the daughter I'd longed for, and another suggested it was a symbol of me living a worry-free life as I did when I was little. We were happy with our three boys and believed our family was complete. We learned through Rochelle's situation that if a baby is meant to be then it will happen, whether or not we plan on it but I also like to tease Josh by reminding him he never liked to argue with Mom.

On June 24, I called the nurse at my plastic surgeon's office because the left drain was still not draining properly. She told me to come in at nine o'clock. We had very little time to get ready and arrange for a babysitter, so we took the boys with us. Josh stayed with the boys in the waiting room as I was being examined by the doctor. The doctor was glad I'd called but assured me the drain was not problematic. He encouraged me to continue to keep a watchful eye on it.

As we walking out of the plastic surgeon's office, a maintenance worker turned off his vacuum and said, "You have three boys?"

I said, "Yes, and I am the queen bee of our house!"

The man pointed to the sky with his right finger and said, "You need to have one more baby. It will be a girl."

Josh and I were speechless, and we looked at each other and smiled. We try to not read too much into things but this chain of events made us wonder whether a daughter was in our future. We joked and said if we were to try, we would probably have twin boys. We know it is in God's hands and we are at peace with whatever happens.

About three weeks after my surgery, my drains were removed. The drains were not as bothersome as I had anticipated, but I was glad to get rid of them. It was nice to check that item off the list and move forward

225

with the next step—the expansion process. I received my first fill on Tuesday, July 8. I arrived at the plastic surgeon's office expecting to have an ultrasound on the left side because fluid had been building up under my skin rather than draining. When I showed up, he looked at the area and decided there was no need for an ultrasound because the fluid had reabsorbed into my body. I was ready to get my first fill out of the way because I planned to return to work on Wednesday, July 16.

Before the nurse came in to do the fill, I asked the doctor if there was any way I could have my replacement surgery on October 13. At first he said he thought that would push it, but he also said it was not impossible. He required the last fill to take place two months before the replacement surgery. He said I would have to get to my desired size in a short period of time to allow for the two-month waiting period. I emphasized how much it would mean to have my replacement surgery on the two-year anniversary of Mom's passing. It would be very symbolic to start a whole new chapter in my life on that date, but I also wanted to complete the process when my body was ready rather than rush to achieve a self-imposed deadline. He looked at his calendar to see if October 13 was available on his calendar, and he had only one other surgery scheduled on that day. We agreed to revisit the issue in a few weeks.

I made each appointment on Friday afternoons at 3:40 p.m. so I would not have to miss work and would have the weekend to recover. The filling process was a lot more painful than I'd anticipated. I started questioning my pain tolerance. I read about other women who said they had no problems or pain through the process, while other women compared it to childbirth. I assumed I would fall right in the middle of the spectrum, but I was closer to the childbirth scenario rather than the pain-free scenario.

The plastic surgeon filled me to 350 cc during the surgery. He said it is a delicate balance to have the woman wake up feeling whole again rather than have her be in pain. The more saline he puts in during surgery, the more pain the woman will be in when she wakes up. It felt as if an elephant was sitting on my chest after surgery and in the weeks that followed. I was just starting to feel somewhat normal when my first fill took place. He suggested starting with 25 cc on each side then working up to 50 cc. I wanted to have a little more volume when I went to work, so I asked if he would allow 50 cc on the first fill, and he agreed. I was a little nervous, but

I was also excited to get it out of the way so I would know what to expect in the upcoming weeks. The nurse used a handheld device to locate the magnetic ports in the expanders. Once she located the ports, she marked them with a purple pen and inserted a large needle into a port. Once the needle was in place, she filled the expander with saline. I no longer had feeling there, so the procedure was not painful. As she filled the expanders, I told her I felt like "the Rock." My chest felt tight, and my upper back started to spasm.

I really struggled with the first fill. That evening I told Josh I might stop at 400 cc rather than reaching my goal of 800 cc. I was in so much pain, and the medications did not seem to do much. Every time I stood up, gravity worked against me. After about four days, I started feeling better. I dreaded the next fill because I didn't look forward to feeling bad for several days. The nurse put in 60 cc during the next appointment, and it was more uncomfortable than the first round. I was miserable for five days. At the following appointment I expressed my difficulties during the last couple of weeks, and she agreed there was no need to rush the process. We backed off to 40 cc on each side, and I was prescribed a different muscle relaxer. The combination of less fluid and a different medication did the trick. I felt much better, and I found a new sense of determination and energy to get through the next appointments.

After approximately one month, the nurse suggested I meet with the plastic surgeon so he could evaluate me and make sure I was proportionate. When I met with him, we decided it would be rushing to schedule the replacement surgery. We decided to continue with the fill process, and he discussed the next step. He explained the surgery was an outpatient procedure, and I would not have drains. He also noted that there would be another six-week lifting restriction and I could not lift more than ten pounds.

I believed Mom was by my side guiding me through this process. I knew she was smiling down from heaven, watching me go through this journey. Mom had felt guilty about being a carrier of the BRCA2 mutation. She prayed hard that neither Rochelle nor I would have to ever experience breast cancer. I am so thankful she insisted that we get tested and be proactive with our health. I highly doubt I would have gotten genetically tested had Mom not pressed the issue. I used to put my head in the sand and maintain that ignorance is bliss, but I was able to take charge of my life and have the preventative surgery thanks to modern medicine and Mom's persistence. Mom saved Rochelle's life and my life. I now see that her early death was purposeful, and it was part of God's plan. During Mom's illness I wanted to know why everything was happening the way it was. It was hard to understand why such a young, vibrant woman was being denied the chance to live and see her grandchildren and great-grandchildren grow up. We still do not have all the answers to our questions, but our faith is stronger than ever, and I have developed a relationship with God that I never knew was possible. Thanks to our faith and modern medicine, Rochelle and I were given the chance to be mothers to our children. Who knows how long Rochelle would have gone on before discovering her cancer if she had not fulfilled her promise to Mom. Who knows if I would have been diagnosed with breast cancer at a young age as Mom was. The doctor at the Breast Cancer Prevention Center told me, "More times than not, daughters follow in their mother's footsteps."

I found the last string on June 2, two weeks before my surgery. The timing was perfect each and every time. I felt a sense of peace and comfort when I found them. I honestly believe the strings were sent from above, and they were the physical signs I needed to get through a stressful time. Since my surgery, I have had a whole new outlook on life. I no longer dread and fear breast cancer. Instead I am excited to see what each new day is going to bring and I want to help empower other women to be proactive about their health. Mom's light continues to shine, and I want her legacy to live on. Her life and death were purposeful, and even though she is not physically here, her spirit is present in my and my family's lives every day.

On August 10, we walked in the Komen Race for the Cure. My boss made a very generous donation to support our team, Hakuna Ma-TA-TAs. Our team raised $10,800 for the fight against breast cancer. Mike was always incredibly supportive of me during Mom's illness and my preventative surgery. Despite rain on the morning of the race, we had a great time walking three miles in downtown Kansas City along with approximately twenty thousand other participants.

Matt Brooker, and Mike Matteuzzi, sponsors
of our team Hakuna-Ma-TA-TAs.

In Memory of
Nancy Marie Schmidt
(02/21/56-10/13/12)
Our hero, our guardian
angel!

Kirby with her remembrance tulip following the walk for the cure.

October 13, 2014, marked two years since Mom's death. While Josh was at work, the boys and I watched her tribute video on the evening of October 12. I am glad the boys watched it with me because their innocent comments definitely lightened the mood. As pictures of Mom appeared on the video, Holden would say, "There's Ro!" and "There's you, Mom. I never realized how much Rochelle and I resemble Mom, and was comforting that my kids can see their nana in us. I told the boys that the pictures were of Nana when she was younger. This was a hard concept for them. Holden did not recognize Dad in any of the older pictures. Once we got to more recent pictures, he said, "There's the normal Papa!" I have yet to make it through the tribute video without crying. Bryson could tell I was upset, so he demanded I stop crying or he would turn off the video and we would go to bed! I love their innocence and their ability to distract me.

As I drove to work on the morning of October 13, I couldn't help but mentally go back in time two years. I imagined us sitting around Mom in the living room, watching her fade away. All of a sudden a song on the radio caught my attention. I turned it up and was immediately hooked. It felt as if that song was meant for me that very moment. The song was "Today Is Beautiful" by David Dunn. It encourages listeners to look at situations in a positive manner. It reminded me that it is okay to be sad about not having Mom on earth, but at the same time, "today is beautiful." Rather than mourning her loss, we are celebrating her life. Our family has become even stronger, and we have all developed an even closer relationship with God. Had these life-changing events not occurred, each day would be just another day. We will continue to celebrate Mom's life and be grateful for all of the memories we made with her.

On November 2, my thirty-first birthday, I ran in the Overland Park Overrun to help support research for ovarian cancer. Thanks to Dena, I started participating in several 5K races in 2014 to be healthier and support great causes. As the 1,200 participants were lining up, a woman with bib number 333 stood directly in front of me. The instructions had been to wear the bibs on the front, but because it was bitterly cold out, most people's numbers were covered by layers of coats and sweatshirts. I smiled when I saw the threes in front of me. I felt it was Mom's way of wishing me happy birthday. I love how we continue to receive subtle signs.

# CHAPTER 30

# STEPMOM

I have so many wonderful memories of my childhood. I will forever cherish our family traditions, such as frozen cranberry dessert at Thanksgiving and eggnog on Christmas morning. I am so thankful for the memories we made during our annual ski trips to Keystone, Colorado, and visits to Georgetown, Colorado. We took many mini summer vacations as we followed Rochelle through USA Track and Field. We also spent a lot of quality time on the farm during the summer, irrigating and pulling weeds in the fields. When I think about my past, I am so grateful I grew up in small-town Nebraska and had a simple and seemingly carefree life.

As a child, I often thought about what the future would be like and how I would instill tradition in my family. I envisioned growing up and having a family of my own, and Mom and Dad were always part of my thoughts and plans. I couldn't visualize what any of us would look like as we aged, but I always saw us spending time together and having fun with all of our adventures. I could see Mom and Dad growing old together and enjoying the next phase of their lives as grandparents and maybe even great-grandparents.

When it came time to graduate from college and move out of Nebraska, I was excited to see what the future would bring, however, a part of my heart was in Indianola. It was difficult to be several hours away from my immediate family, but my parents encouraged my sister and me to seek other opportunities. I longed to have Mom and Dad live closer to my sister and me so we could spend more time together and not have to plan well in advance to see one another for a short weekend. As my sister and I started having kids, I enjoyed watching Mom and Dad become grandparents. The grandkids had Nana and Papa wrapped around their tiny fingers (and toes). They were so excited when they found out they were going to be grandparents for the first, second, third, and fourth times. Mom would have been equally excited to find out she was going to be a nana for the fifth and sixth time.

As a child and young adult, the thought of one of my parents not being in my life never crossed my mind. As with life, I knew the day would come when we would lose our parents, but I assumed that day would be years down the road, not when I was twenty-eight years old. When it became apparent that Mom was losing her battle with breast cancer, I still had a hard time accepting the fact she would soon be a memory. I couldn't stand the thought of Dad coping with losing the love of his life and being alone for the rest of his life. During her terminal illness, Mom gave Dad her blessing to move on and find love and happiness once again. In that moment, Dad could not imagine loving anybody the way he loved Mom, and he was deeply saddened at the thought of letting Mom go. Dad is such a loving, kind, and loyal soul, and his heart was with Mom throughout their thirty-four years of marriage. Since her passing, he prays for her soul daily, and he will forever cherish the beautiful life they had together.

Rochelle and I were delighted when we found out Dad found happiness in August 2013. The road was long after Mom's passing. He kept himself busy and maintained a positive attitude, but his heart was broken. Once he met Deanna, the twinkle in his eyes returned, and the smile on his face said it all. It was wonderful to see that Dad could be happy again and that he found somebody as kind and caring as Deanna.

Deanna and Dad became inseparable shortly after they met. It was clear they had chemistry, and the love they had for one another was genuine. Dad told Rochelle and me several times that he would always love Mom, and he is very happy with Deanna. He also told us he has only loved one other person the way he loves Deanna. It is such a blessing to know Dad's life is once again filled with love and happiness. Mom was so worried that he would spend the rest of his life alone, and we all know she is smiling down from heaven. We truly feel Deanna was handpicked especially for Dad.

The movie *Stepmom* with Julia Roberts holds special place in my heart. The storyline is about a biological mom who is dying from breast cancer, and shortly after her diagnosis, her ex-husband meets another woman. The biological mom dislikes the new woman in her ex-husband's and her children's lives. The two women begin to get along, and they create a bond centered around the kids. At one point, the biological mom tells the stepmom, "I had their past. You can have their future."

Our life story differs from the movie, but I can rest assured that Mom approves of Deanna and her presence in our lives. I know Mom would be grateful to Deanna for bringing joy back to us. Our hearts were broken the day Mom left the earth, but pieces of our hearts have been mended by the love Deanna brings to our family.

There has not been a day I have not woken up and gone to bed thinking about Mom. She is always on my mind. She had such an impact on my life during the twenty-eight years in which I was privileged to know her and call her Mom. My heart still aches for her, but I know she would be proud of our family and how we have fulfilled our promise to live and be happy. I am not sure if the thought of Mom will ever diminish, but right now, I find peace and comfort knowing she is with me every minute of the day. Throughout the last couple of years, I have learned to cherish the past, embrace the present, and not fear the future.

Dad and Deanna got engaged on February 14, 2014. They chose November 15, 2014 as their wedding date. The engagement seemed to go relatively fast. The summer months flew by, and next thing we knew, it was time to spend four days in Indianola for the wedding. I started feeling rundown the week of the wedding. I woke up with a terrible sore throat on Tuesday, November 11. I am not one to go to the doctor, so I opted for hot beverages, Tylenol, and throat lozenges. I hoped I would turn around soon so I could enjoy the weekend. It became evident on Tuesday that I had more than a cold. I had a fever and was chilled all day. I went home from work early and took a short nap to try and sleep it off. Josh came home early and took over the evening shift so I could get some rest. I woke up Wednesday morning after twelve hours of sleep feeling somewhat better. I powered through work but felt quite fatigued by the end of the day. I tried to see the doctor, but I could not be seen until the following morning. I eventually was diagnosed with strep throat and was prescribed antibiotics.

We picked up the boys from school and started the seven-hour trip west. Just as we were getting on I-70, the sensor on the dashboard indicated we had low tire pressure. We turned around in Lawrence, Kansas, and headed to a gas station to check the tires. As Josh got out of the vehicle, he could hear air leaking from the right rear tire. He filled up the tire, and we went to a tire store. Unfortunately there was a two-hour wait, so we opted to go to Jiffy Lube. It took some time to unpack the back of the vehicle so they could access the spare tire, but they eventually got it done. The workers were very accommodating, and they put our spare tire on free of charge. We tipped them as we pulled out of the garage, and we got back on the road. We stopped in Junction City, Kansas, for a restroom break. We decided to fill up with gas before we continued down the road in the middle of nowhere Kansas. The pump shut off at fifty dollars, but unfortunately it takes more than fifty dollars to fill our tank. He went inside to pay for more gas and was told they were unable to sell gas for the next twenty minutes, because they were lowering the price, and it would take some time to reprogram everything. We had to laugh at the minor inconveniences we were experiencing along the way. Thankfully, the rest of the trip was uneventful. We arrived around eight thirty at night, and Rochelle's family arrived just before midnight.

The following morning, the guys watched the kids so the women could decorate the reception hall. We had a great group of workers, and we were able to get all of the decorating done by half past noon. We wanted to go to Mac's Drive-In for lunch, but we figured it would be too busy during the noon hour. Rochelle suggested we go have margaritas to help pass the time, so that is just what we did. We enjoyed our cocktails followed by the always-delicious meal at Mac's. We had to run a few other errands before returning to the farm. Once we got back to the house, we visited for a short while before we got ready for the rehearsal. It went really well, and we celebrated at Loop's in McCook. It was fun to spend time with friends and family we do not see very often. It was also nice to meet Deanna's son, Cory, and her brother and family.

The day of the wedding finally arrived. When we woke up, there was a light dusting of snow, and the kids were excited to see the first snow of the season. Dad and Deanna were relieved we did not receive the predicted snowfall amount. Deanna left for her hair appointment at a quarter to eight, and Rochelle and I planned to leave by 8:10 a.m. so we could get Anisten's and Kardyn's hair done. Dad called a meeting in the living room. He delivered a very heartfelt message to our family, and he shared a nice message from Deanna. She acknowledged that the wedding day would be emotional for Rochelle and me, and she wanted us to have time with Dad that morning. Deanna is so selfless and kind. We expressed our happiness for Dad and his upcoming marriage. Shortly thereafter, we and the girls left for McCook. As usual, Scott and Josh did a wonderful job taking care of the other kids. They assume the role of "Mr. Mom" without hesitation.

We arrived at the salon just as Deanna was leaving. She looked beautiful, and she was anxious to get to the church to finish getting ready. Pictures had been scheduled for ten o'clock. Her maid of honor, Vickey, was at the salon getting her hair done as well. Anisten and Kardyn had a great time getting pampered. Rochelle and I went to the church to get the girls dressed and get ready for pictures. As we entered the dressing area, our beautiful Deanna emerged. She looked absolutely stunning, breathtaking really. We hugged her and told her how beautiful she was and reiterated how much we love her.

Deanna's father, Larry, had been having health problems. We all prayed he would be well enough to attend the wedding. Shortly before ten o'clock, Deanna talked to Cory and was told her father would not make it. She was sad, and we all felt for her. The day would have been perfect had her father been there, but we knew he would have attended if he'd been able. Larry was definitely there in spirit.

Around a quarter after ten, the wedding coordinator told Deanna the photographer was ready for the first view in the sanctuary. The pictures of brides and grooms seeing each other for the first time on their wedding day is priceless. Deanna told us later that when she walked up to Dad for the first time, she noticed a long black string on the leg of his gray suit. They both teared up and hugged one another. The string symbolized that Mom was present and had accepted the union.

We had fun during picture taking, and the photographer was able to capture some great images. The kids were excited to get the wedding started so they could participate in the big day. Deanna had shirts made for the girls that said "Princess of the Petals" and the boys' shirts said, "Ring Security." The kids wore the shirts to the rehearsal, and they took their roles very seriously. We were not sure how long the kids, ages two to six, would stand at the front during the ceremony. With kids, anything is possible.

After pictures, we gathered in the basement for a quick lunch. Holden was acting like he did not feel well, so he took a short nap; we woke him around one thirty. The wedding was scheduled to start at two o'clock. At 1:59 p.m. (and thirty seconds), Holden got a panicked look on his face and said he needed to go to the restroom. At the same time, the wedding coordinator told us it was time to start.

I said, "He has to poop!"

Holden and I ran to the restroom in order to avoid an accident. I rushed Holden through the process; once he was done, he said he felt better and was ready to go. We went back into the room, and the wedding started. Dad ushered Deanna's mother, Karen, to her seat, and Rochelle and I were escorted by the ushers to our seats. We had our arsenal of cheerios, juice, and entertainment for Layton. He'd discovered his independence a few days before, so we were not sure how long he would sit during the ceremony.

The maid of honor and best man came in next, followed by the flower girls and ring bearers. The kids did a wonderful job. They remembered what they had been told to do during the rehearsal the night before. Finally, it was Deanna's shining moment. She entered the doorway, and Cory escorted her down the aisle. All eyes were on her, and her eyes were on Dad. It was a wonderful moment.

Mr. and Mrs. Les Schmidt

The wedding was beautiful. Dad and Deanna were so happy, and they embraced their special day. After the wedding we told them about the activity on the altar from the youngest ring bearer and the youngest flower girl. Kardyn decided to sit down and dump her petals out of her basket. She was so precious as she counted, "one … two … three." In the meantime, Holden had a look of panic on his face. My gut told me he needed to go to the restroom again. I debated whether or not to get him, but finally I went to the front to ask him what the problem was. He reported his feet hurt from standing "all day." I had to laugh but was relieved he did not have to go to the restroom. Layton lasted a whole two minutes before he started screeching. Josh and Layton joined Scott and Kardyn in the back of the church during the ceremony. Dad and Deanna were oblivious to the activity as they were absorbed in each other. We all had a good laugh after the wedding.

A cake and punch reception followed in the church basement. Although it was opening day for hunting, the weather was cold, and there was a husker football game, approximately two hundred people came to the wedding to support Dad and Deanna. It was nice to visit with the guests during the reception.

Once we cleaned up after the reception and ceremony, Dad and Deanna went to Larry and Karen's house so her dad could see her in her dress. We told the newlyweds to spend as much time there as they wanted. We headed out to the house to set out the food for supper and unload the totes. Dad and Deanna arrived at the house, and we had a light supper. Shortly afterward, Deanna's son, brother, and other family members arrived at the house so we could visit and get to know them. It was a nice, relaxing evening, and we all thoroughly enjoyed it.

As a child, I never thought we would have a blended family. I did not entertain the idea of having a stepparent because according to *my* plans, Mom and Dad would live to be a ripe old age. God obviously had other plans for our family, and Rochelle and I are so blessed to call Deanna our stepmom. She brought life and happiness back to Dad and our family, and we wish them many years together.

## CHAPTER 31

# LUCKY (OR UNLUCKY) THIRTEEN

Mom had an incredibly positive outlook on life despite her struggles with her health. She had the profound ability to see the glass as half full rather than half empty. Many people relied on her to get them through trying times, however, she was by no means superhuman. She would get angry, sad, and scared, but she quickly bounced back and search for the positive in nearly every situation. Positivity radiated from her, and you couldn't help but feel better after talking to her.

Mom was our rock, and we turned to her for comfort in uncertain situations. At times, when I am sad, I still have the urge to pick up the phone and dial Mom's cell, longing to hear her reassuring voice say, "Everything is going to be fine." Now that she is gone, we have had to learn to be strong for one another and to make the best of out the situations we've been dealt. We have definitely gotten in our fair share of practice of supporting one another during the last couple of years. I am sure Mom would be proud, knowing her legacy is being carried on.

Mom's favorite number was thirteen, and she always referred to it as her lucky number. I scratched my head, trying to figure out why thirteen was such a great number when it is associated with many negative and unsettling times in our lives. Her explanation never made a whole lot of sense to me, but I figured it was her prerogative. The only positive thing I associated thirteen with was Rochelle's high school and college volleyball number.

People have superstitions when it comes to this number; there is Friday the thirteenth, and some hotels and large buildings skip the number thirteen and go straight to the fourteenth floor from the twelfth. Triskaidekaphobia means the fear of thirteen. I would not put myself in that category, but the number definitely catches my attention. I am not superstitious, but thirteen has certainly made its appearance throughout our lives. As you read the rest of this chapter, you may wonder why Mom didn't refer to it as her *unlucky* number. I wondered this for many years as well. It wasn't until recently that I finally appreciated her fondness for the number thirteen.

Mom received her first diagnosis of breast cancer on December 13, 1993. After her mastectomy and lymph-node removal, pathology showed thirteen of the seventeen lymph nodes had tested positive for cancer. In February 2011, Mom underwent a mastectomy on her right side, and it was found that four of the thirteen lymph nodes were cancerous. In September 2012 following her terminal diagnosis, thirteen rounds of full brain radiation were ordered to minimize the symptoms.

On its surface, the number thirteen appears to be a curse. I really disliked the number, because it seemed to rear its ugly head in ways that had a negative impact on Mom. Given all of our run-ins with the number, I became quite leery of it. I tried to understand why Mom considered December 13 to be lucky. Of course, she experienced all of the terrifying emotions of being diagnosed with stage 3 breast cancer in her 30s', but once she regrouped, she saw past the negative. She explained her cancer was both aggressive and advanced and had much more time passed, it could have spread to her organs and bones. She said how grateful she was that no more than thirteen lymph nodes were positive for cancer. I heard what she was saying but fixated on the fact she had so many positive nodes. In my mind, one positive node was one too many. Mom found it ironic that the doctor decided to take thirteen lymph nodes during her surgery in February 2011. She was thankful only four came back positive and that she could receive radiation to knock out the cancer cells one final time. When her oncologist ordered full brain radiation, Mom knew it was not a cure; however, she was grateful something could be done to relieve her dizziness and nausea.

Mom passed away on October 13, 2012, shortly after one o'clock or 1300 hours. Knowing how much Mom liked thirteen gave us peace. Dad said, "What was the chance of Mom passing away on the thirteenth?"

In the days after her passing, one of Mom's coworkers, a dear friend, told us about Our Lady of Fatima. She provided us with a paperback that told the story, and we learned that the Blessed Virgin Mary appeared six times to three shepherd children between May 13 and October 13, 1917, so they could warn the world of the upcoming trials and tribulations.

Mary visited the little village of Fatima in Portugal, which had remained faithful to the Catholic Church despite recent persecutions by the government. On May 13, 1917, the three children took their flocks out to pasture; two bright flashes in the clear sky startled them. One of the girls described "a lady, clothed in white, brighter than the sun, radiating a light more clear and intense than a crystal cup filled with sparkling water, lit by burning sunlight."

The lady smiled and said, "Do not be afraid, I will not harm you. I come from heaven. I have come to ask you to come here on the thirteenth day of each month, at this same hour. Later I shall say who I am and what I desire."

As promised, she appeared to the girls on June 13, July 13, August 13, and September 13, and each time she delivered messages to them.

The children were told that God would perform a miracle so that people would believe in the apparitions. On October 13, 1917, nearly seventy thousand people arrived, and they witnessed a miracle in the sky above Fatima. Everyone was able to stare at the sun without blinking or even harming their eyes. As they watched the sun, it rotated, got large and small, drew close to the people, and went far away from them. People who were present testified to seeing the phenomenon; even nonbelievers immediately dropped to their knees and begged for forgiveness.

The people of southwest Nebraska are blessed to have an Our Lady of Fatima Shrine at the Catholic Church in Arapahoe. Since Mom's passing, Dad visits the shine on the thirteenth of every month, and he prays the rosary. In addition, on the thirteenth of each month, the mass at Saint Catherine's in Indianola is offered to Mom.

My presurgical appointments were supposed to be on May 9, 2014, but they were delayed until May 13. I smiled when the nurse informed me about the new date.

Dad is a numbers person. He used to create silly number sentences to remember dates. He would get carried away, and Mom finally told him to stop with the number game. He eventually stopped, but occasionally, he could not help himself. After Rochelle and Scott announced Grady's arrival, Dad sent me a text to see if I noticed anything about the time when Grady was born. Grady had been born at 8:41 a.m., but because I am not a math person I did not notice anything unique. Dad pointed out $8 + 4 + 1 = 13$. My first thought was Mom would tell Dad to stop with the numbers game, but I also found it to be neat. All babies are miracles, but Grady is something very special. According to science, he was never meant to be. God is good all of the time, and with God, *anything* is possible!

What does all of this mean? The number has clearly shown up in our lives on numerous occasions. I recently realized the number thirteen is nothing more than a tool to help me recognize that, no matter how bad the situation seems, good things can come out of it. As a child, it was difficult to understand and appreciate just how incredibly strong and positive Mom was. She taught us always to be faithful and thankful and to see the good in the situation at hand. It has taken a lot of trials and time, but I now see life in a whole different light. I try my best to find the positive in every situation. I also try to help others through their difficult situations. I am still a work-in-progress because at times I revert to a pessimist, but overall, I am a much more positive person.

Now that we only have photographs and memories to rely upon, I see more clearly and have a much deeper understanding what Mom stood for and how much of a warrior she really was. Despite her fears and the burdens she carried, her unwavering faith made her the person she was. She knew this earthly life was temporary, and there were far greater things waiting for her in eternal life. She coped with her earthly fears by finding the positives.

I am sure she was frightened when she received her diagnosis in 1993, and the thought of a bone marrow transplant was terrifying. I cannot even imagine being told at the age of thirty-seven that survival was unlikely. The fear of leaving behind her young family had to have been heartbreaking.

I am sure she had a nervous feeling in the bottom of her stomach when December 13 came around in the few years following her initial diagnosis. I cannot imagine the fear and sadness she felt when her doctor told her thirteen lymph nodes were positive for cancer. Who knows, she may have had a bit of triskaidekaphobia, but she refused to let negativity get her down. She powered through situations by praying and believing.

Death is part of the circle of life, and we are all on borrowed time. Mom did not view death as a scary thing. She wanted to be free from earthly problems and the pain she was experiencing due to the disease. Mom would have loved to have more time on earth so she could see her grandchildren grow and do what she did best—live life to its fullest! God called Mom home at the age of fifty-five, and she gladly accepted the invitation. She told us during her terminal illness that if "this is all that is left for me on this earth, I don't want it." She told Rochelle she was not afraid to die. Two days before she passed away, we believe she told God she was ready to go to heaven. Mom was a woman of faith, and there is no doubt in my mind she was welcomed into heaven with open arms.

# CHAPTER 32

# BLACK PEARL

As I sit back and think about my life, my heart is filled with happiness and joy. I often am reminded about all of the good times we shared and the experiences we had as a family. We have all heard the saying "time heals all," and we have all probably used that line to help others find comfort in a time of sorrow. I do believe that the passage of time helps the body and soul heal. The nightmares surrounding Mom's illness and the difficult memories of Mom's final days are starting to fade, and her witty demeanor and the precious moments we had together are now my prominent memories. A piece of my heart will always be broken, but I know Mom is watching over our family, and that brings me tremendous peace.

It is hard to believe we have celebrated several holidays without Mom. She loved the holiday season, and she did not want to ruin future holidays because the family was reminded about the sadness of her diagnosis. Mom was always thinking about other people, putting her feelings aside and focusing on others. Christmas is a wonderful reason to celebrate, and I find comfort in remembering our past Christmases and our family traditions.

In December 2014, we got together with Rochelle's family to celebrate Anisten's sixth birthday, Grady's baptism, and Christmas. Christmas music played in the background for most of the weekend. Rochelle and I talked in the kitchen about how we could hear Mom whistling and singing along with the tunes. She loved preparing holiday meals for our family and being surrounded by those she loved. We continue to cherish past memories and make new ones with our friends and family.

Dad and Deanna spent a week in Hawaii for their honeymoon. They chose a great week to enjoy the tropical paradise as the rest of us in the Midwest fought through the tundra. We periodically received text messages saying it was eighty degrees, and my typical response was "It is a balmy fifteen degrees here!" They had a week filled with activities and site seeing.

One of their adventures took them to a jewelry shop where they could chose an oyster. Deanna was on the hunt for a pearl necklace, so they thought this would be the perfect opportunity. They were told the ugliest oysters typically produced the prettiest pearls. Deanna took her time choosing the perfect oyster, and much to her surprise there were two black pearls inside. The attendant at the store said it was uncommon for there to be two pearls in an oyster, but when it does happen, the pearls are usually white. Deanna and Dad got busy looking for a setting for the pearls. Once they were done, they decided to pick out another oyster. The search was on for another ugly, cracked oyster. Deanna and Dad picked out the second oyster, and once again they found two black pearls! This definitely caught the attention of the workers, who repeated "This never happens." Deanna thought a matching pair of earrings would look nice with her new necklace. She looking at settings when all of a sudden she and Dad looked at one another. Deanna said, "I think these pearls are meant for the girls." They started looking for settings for necklaces for Rochelle and me.

They were taken back by their experience and were enjoying sharing their story with other customers. They had watched other customers purchase pearls, but not once did another black pearl surface. The lady that had been helping them insisted that they open one more oyster. At first they resisted because they were satisfied with their purchases, not to mention their two-for-one deal. The worker insisted they pick one more oyster free of charge. After little debate, they agreed. Lo and behold, the third oyster contained two more black pearls! They all were baffled at this, as were the other customers who watched this unfold. Deanna picked out a setting for some earrings to match her necklace.

Approximately an hour or so later, they were ready to pay and leave the store. The total amount caught their attention, and that is when the emotions set in. The final amount was $1,313.04. Dad said he grabbed the invoice from the lady to see the amount with his own eyes. They called us from Hawaii and said they had a story to share with us, but we had to wait until we got together for Christmas. They wanted Rochelle and me to be together to hear the awesome story. We gathered together and opened the beautiful pearl necklaces, and they told us the story.

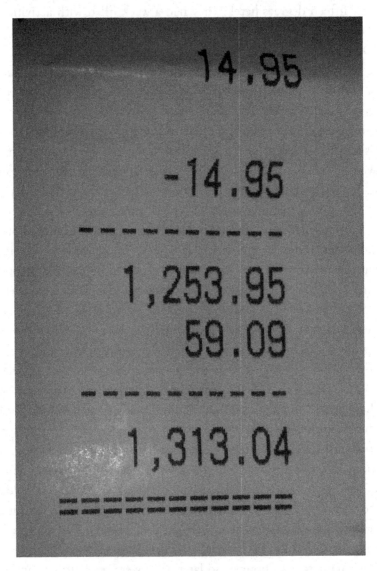

Receipt from the pearl adventure

A few days after Dad and Deanna's wedding, we heard that one of our family friends had been involved in an accident involving a train. Many prayers, from near and far, were said for Jared and his family. This news was difficult to comprehend because we had all been together a few days earlier, and we had a lot to celebrate and be thankful for. Jared's dad, Doug, was Dad's best man in the wedding. Jared's mom, Deb, had just celebrated her sixtieth birthday, and Doug and Deb were getting ready to celebrate their wedding anniversary. It is amazing how quickly life can change. When I heard about the accident, it seemed impossible. I remembered talking to Jared at the wedding reception and seeing his beautiful children and wife.

Once they returned from their honeymoon, Dad and Deanna went to visit Jared and his family. They spent time at the hospital and were very happy to hear about the remarkable progress Jared was making in his recovery. It is natural to say somebody is lucky when he or she beats the odds by surviving in unlikely circumstances, but we know this is all part of God's plan. It is human nature to want to know "why this happened," but clearly it was not Jared's time, and God has big plans for him. As Dad and Deanna were leaving the hospital, they talked about how blessed Jared is and how fortunate he was to walk away from the accident. A few minutes later, a car passed them, and the license plate was "13 13 58" (5 + 8 = 13). The number thirteen appeared three times, and Dad and Deanna took this as a sign. We continue to pray for continued healing and strength for Jared and his family.

Josh and I planned on hosting Thanksgiving at our home in 2014. Josh wanted to experiment with the turkey by frying it. I was supportive of his ambition, but I also wanted to stay close to tradition by roasting the turkey. I purchased two turkeys so we could have a cook-off. We were looking forward to getting together to kick off the holiday season. Deanna's father, Larry, struggled with health issues, and his health continued to decline during November. Dad and Deanna needed to stay around McCook to help Larry and Karen. Rochelle's kids were sick during the week, so we decided it was best to postpone our get-together. By this time the two turkeys had been thawing, so Josh and I decided to continue with our plans. We had a turkey cook-off and enjoyed our Thanksgiving dinner at home.

Deanna's parents hosted Thanksgiving at their home in McCook. Their son, David, and his family made it home from Colorado, knowing it would likely be Larry's last Thanksgiving. Right after Thanksgiving, his health took a turn for the worse. He continued to decline at a steady pace, and on December 2, 2014, he was called home.

Rochelle and I received some heartfelt messages from Deanna during the course of her father's illness. She told us that Dad was her rock and that she and her family were so grateful for all of the emotional support he had provided. We truly feel Deanna came into our lives at the right time and that Dad entered her life at the right time too. We are so thankful that they both were given the opportunity to love and to be loved unconditionally at this phase of their lives. Larry's celebration of life was on Monday, December 8.

Phase two of my reconstruction was set for December 8. Josh and I made arrangements for the boys, and we set out for the hospital that morning. I was scheduled to check in at eight, and the surgery was at ten. I was not nervous about the surgery, but I was anxious about getting stuck in traffic. I do not like being late, and it tends to stress me out when I am not on time. Traffic was very heavy that morning, and several accidents made us question whether we would get to the hospital in time. After a very stressful drive, we arrived at the hospital at a quarter after eight. Josh parked the car, and I checked in at admissions. Thankfully my name was called right away, and I was able to get through the process rather quickly. We made our way to the surgical waiting room on the second floor.

This was only the second time I had been in this waiting room, but once again I was surprised by the number of people waiting for surgery. When I was in the hospital in June, I asked the nurse how many operating rooms there were at the hospital, and she said there were sixty-four on that floor and approximately ten more divided between the cardiac floor and the maternity ward.

We checked in at the front desk. Each patient is identified by a number to protect their privacy. Family members are given a sticker with a number so during the surgery they can receive updates about their loved ones. I was assigned number thirty-three. I felt an overwhelming sense of peace, and I immediately texted Dad to let him know about my assigned number. I was more than ready to take on the surgery.

I was called into the presurgical suite and was greeted by a wonderful nurse. Protocol requires a pregnancy test before the surgery can move forward. The anesthesiologist and I were talking about that, and I told her I was confident I was not pregnant. She told me a couple of stories about past patients who were certain they were not pregnant, but the test proved otherwise. I told her Rochelle's remarkable story, and we had a good laugh. A short time later, Josh came back to be with me.

The anesthesiologist peeked behind the curtain and said, "Congratulations!" I could not imagine why she was congratulating us. She then said, "You are *not* pregnant!" I loved her sense of humor and her ability to make me feel very comfortable.

Just before ten o'clock, we made our way to the operating room. I was wheeled down the hall and situated on the table. The anesthesiologist put the mask over my face and told me to take a nap. Nowadays, I will find any excuse to take a few minutes to lie down and take a nap. I welcomed the invitation, and off to sleep I went.

During surgery I had a very vivid dream about Mom. She and I were standing together. The background was black, but a bright light was shining on top of us. I could see her, hear her, and feel her. It was so amazing, and I did not want to let go. Right before I woke up, I hugged Mom and held her hand. Then we both turned and started walking in opposite directions. We were holding each other's hand, and it was all we could do to not let go. Once we were far enough apart from one another, we let go, and I woke up crying. Tears were streaming down my face, and I could not get it together. The nurse asked what was wrong, and I told her I'd had the most amazing dream about my mom. She comforted me, and Josh came in, so I immediately told him about my experience. It truly was a very special moment and one I will never forget.

I spent the remainder of the week recovering at home. The surgery was very successful, and I managed the pain with Tylenol for a couple of days. Josh and I spent some much-needed time together. We got our Christmas shopping done and went out to dinner for our eighth anniversary. We also went to the theater and enjoyed dinner and a movie. He has been so supportive during this journey as well as a great caregiver and Mr. Mom, just to name just a few of his roles. I could not have gone through this journey without the support of Josh, my family, my friends, and my boss. The year 2014 has been a year of change and personal growth. I am excited to see what the future holds for our family.

## CHAPTER 33

# WRITE YOUR STORY

I hope our family's story has provided you with happiness, peace, hope, and even some laughter. The last couple of years our family has definitely been challenged, but through it all, we never lost faith. We accepted God's will, and we embraced the situations we were in. We learned a lot about ourselves and each other during the darkest of our days. We came through life's storms as stronger individuals and as a stronger family unit. Our perspectives on life have changed, and we are prepared for the unknown challenges that will come along the way. I have learned not to take things for granted or to take things so seriously. Life is too short to get caught up in the things that ultimately do not matter. We continue to cherish our past, and we look forward to the future. Every day is a gift, and we strive to identify the positives in the situations in which we find ourselves.

I have enjoyed sharing our family story. It has been both fulfilling and therapeutic. I laughed and cried as I typed each chapter because all of the feelings and emotions of our past came flooding back as I remembered each event. We truly believe God has blessed our family and that He wants us to share all of the unexplained events and miracles we have experienced. We have so many things to be thankful for, and we are truly blessed. When I started thinking about documenting our life events, my goal was to provide our children with a timeline of happenings so they could better understand everything our family went through before they were born and when they were little. My hope is that through our documented story, our children will feel a connection with their nana.

It truly has been my pleasure to share our events, and I am so thankful I accepted the challenge to tell the "untold 'God thing' stories" in our lives. I really believe God wanted our family to share our experiences with others to provide them with faith and hope during desperate times. The article that was placed on my chair on May 5, 2014, gave me the courage to spread God's Word by telling our story.

I challenge you to tell the "untold 'God thing' stories" in your life. Do not be afraid to write your story and share the wonderful things God is doing in your life. God is the author of all of our lives, but we have the opportunity to make a mark in this world by sharing His constant love with others. We have to have faith in God and trust Him. While the timing of events may not make sense to us, it is all part of the miraculous plan God has for us. Nobody knows what the future will bring, but I am more prepared than ever to live and love with everything I have. May God's blessings continue to shine in your life as you face each day and the challenges that arise.

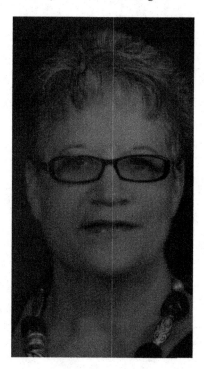

Our guardian angel